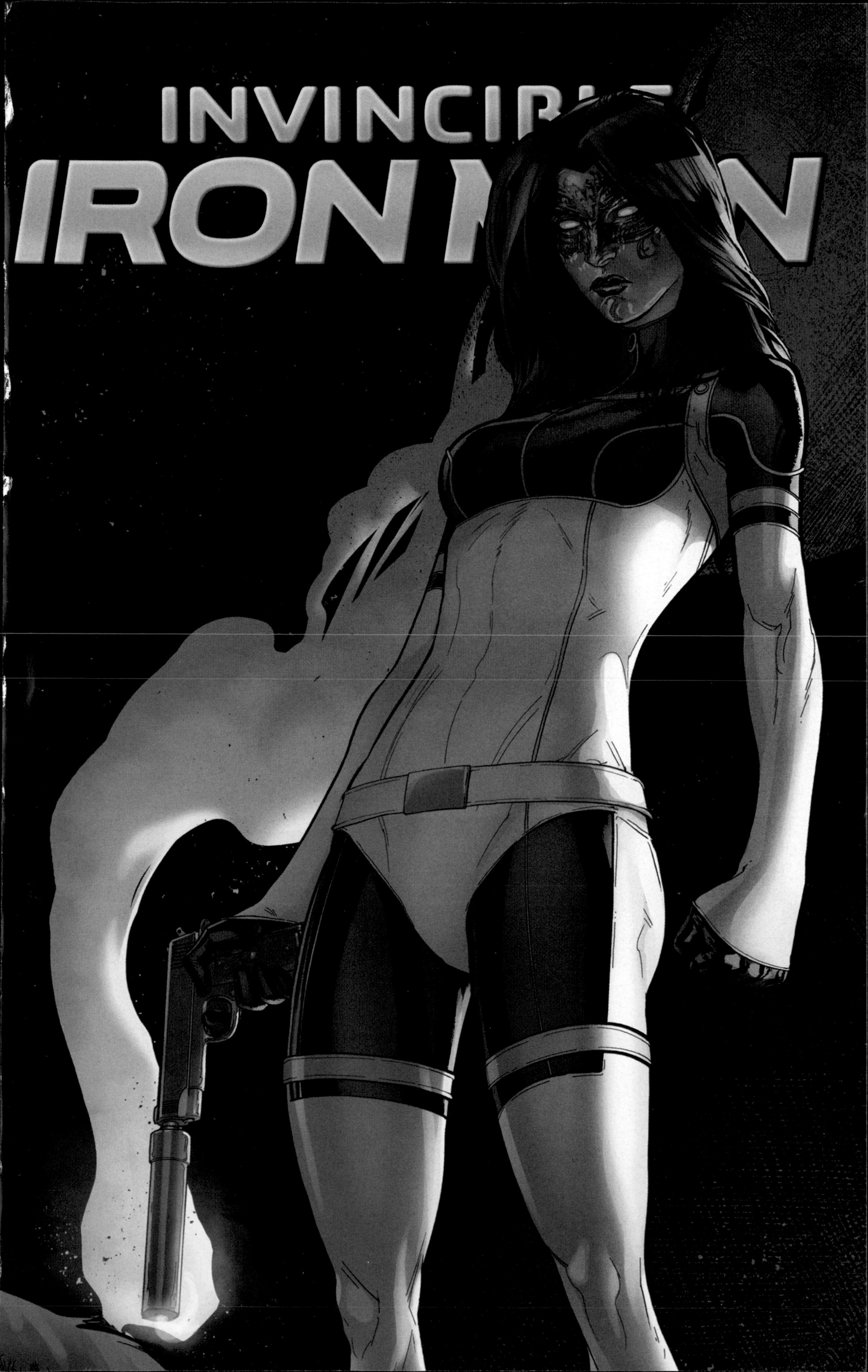
INVINCIBLE
IRON MAN

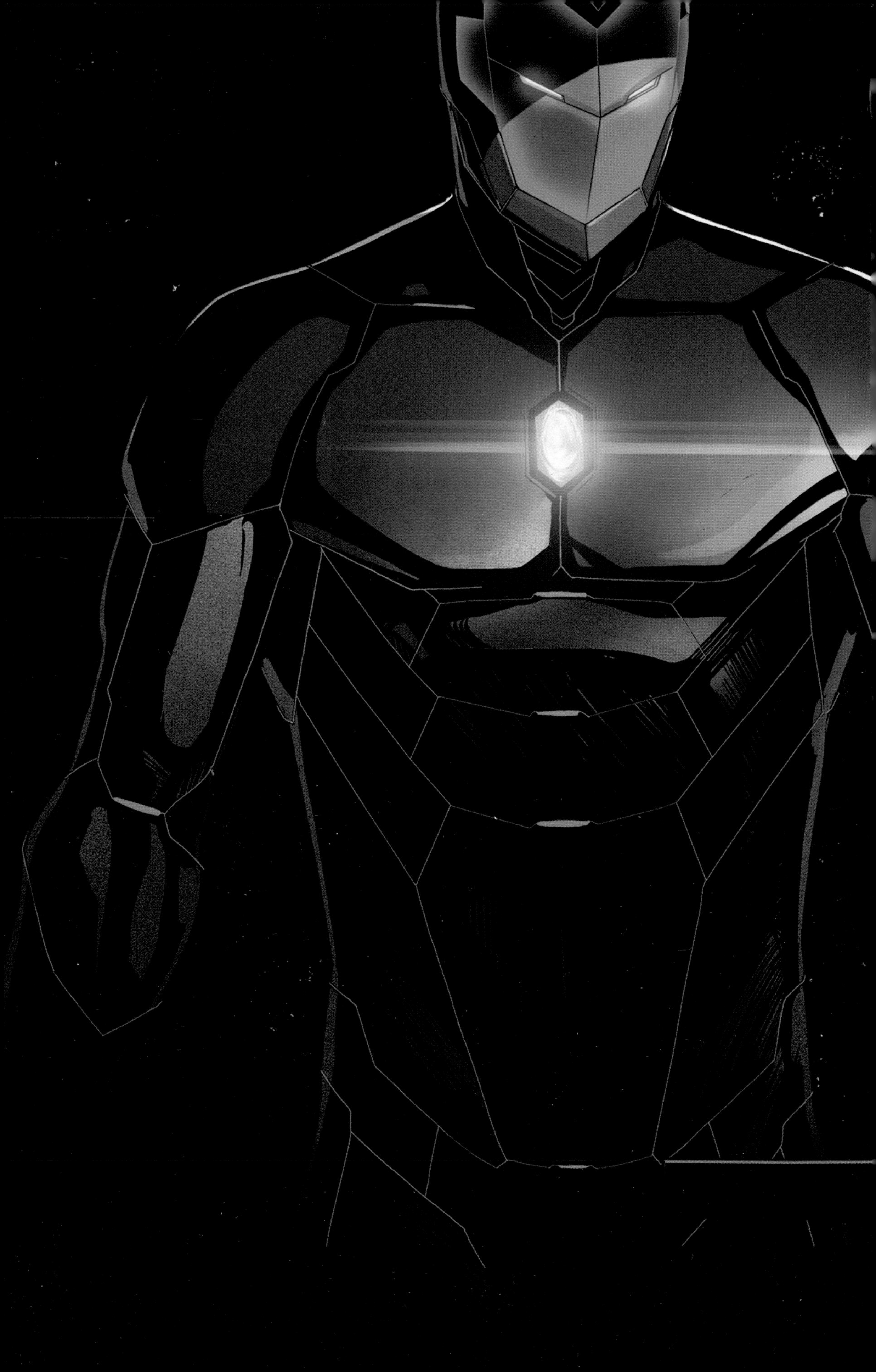

INVINCIBLE IRON MAN

REBOOT

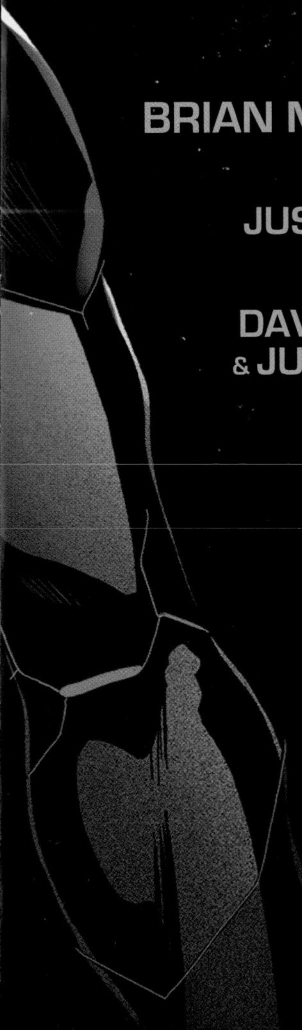

BRIAN MICHAEL BENDIS
WRITER

DAVID MARQUEZ
ARTIST

JUSTIN PONSOR
COLOR ARTIST

VC'S CLAYTON COWLES
LETTERER

DAVID MARQUEZ & JUSTIN PONSOR
COVER ART

ALANNA SMITH
ASSISTANT EDITOR

TOM BREVOORT WITH KATIE KUBERT
EDITORS

IRON MAN CREATED BY STAN LEE, LARRY LIEBER, DON HECK & JACK KIRBY

COLLECTION EDITOR: **JENNIFER GRÜNWALD**
ASSOCIATE EDITOR: **SARAH BRUNSTAD**
ASSOCIATE MANAGING EDITOR: **ALEX STARBUCK**
EDITOR, SPECIAL PROJECTS: **MARK D. BEAZLEY**
VP, PRODUCTION & SPECIAL PROJECTS: **JEFF YOUNGQUIST**
SVP PRINT, SALES & MARKETING: **DAVID GABRIEL**
BOOK DESIGNER: **JAY BOWEN**

EDITOR IN CHIEF: **AXEL ALONSO**
CHIEF CREATIVE OFFICER: **JOE QUESADA**
PUBLISHER: **DAN BUCKLEY**
EXECUTIVE PRODUCER: **ALAN FINE**

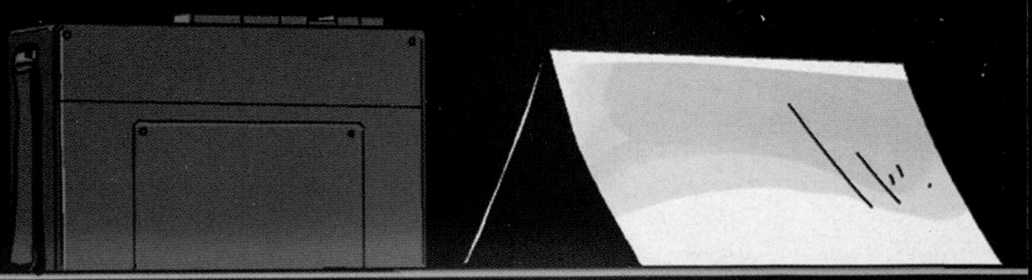

INVINCIBLE IRON MAN VOL. 1: REBOOT. Contains material originally published in magazine form as INVINCIBLE IRON MAN #1-5. First printing 2016. ISBN# 978-0-7851-9520-7. Published by MARVEL WORLDWIDE, INC., a subsidiary of MARVEL ENTERTAINMENT, LLC. OFFICE OF PUBLICATION: 135 West 50th Street, New York, NY 10020. Copyright © 2016 MARVEL No similarity between any of the names, characters, persons, and/or institutions in this magazine with those of any living or dead person or institution is intended, and any such similarity which may exist is purely coincidental. **Printed in the U.S.A.** ALAN FINE, President, Marvel Entertainment; DAN BUCKLEY, President, TV, Publishing & Brand Management; JOE QUESADA, Chief Creative Officer; TOM BREVOORT, SVP of Publishing; DAVID BOGART, SVP of Business Affairs & Operations, Publishing & Partnership; C.B. CEBULSKI, VP of Brand Management & Development, Asia; DAVID GABRIEL, SVP of Sales & Marketing, Publishing; JEFF YOUNGQUIST, VP of Production & Special Projects; DAN CARR, Executive Director of Publishing Technology; ALEX MORALES, Director of Publishing Operations; SUSAN CRESPI, Production Manager; STAN LEE, Chairman Emeritus. For information regarding advertising in Marvel Comics or on Marvel.com, please contact Vit DeBellis, Integrated Sales Manager, at vdebellis@marvel.com. For Marvel subscription inquiries, please call 888-511-5480. **Manufactured between 2/5/2016 and 3/21/2016 by R.R. DONNELLEY, INC., SALEM, VA, USA.**

10 9 8 7 6 5 4 3 2 1

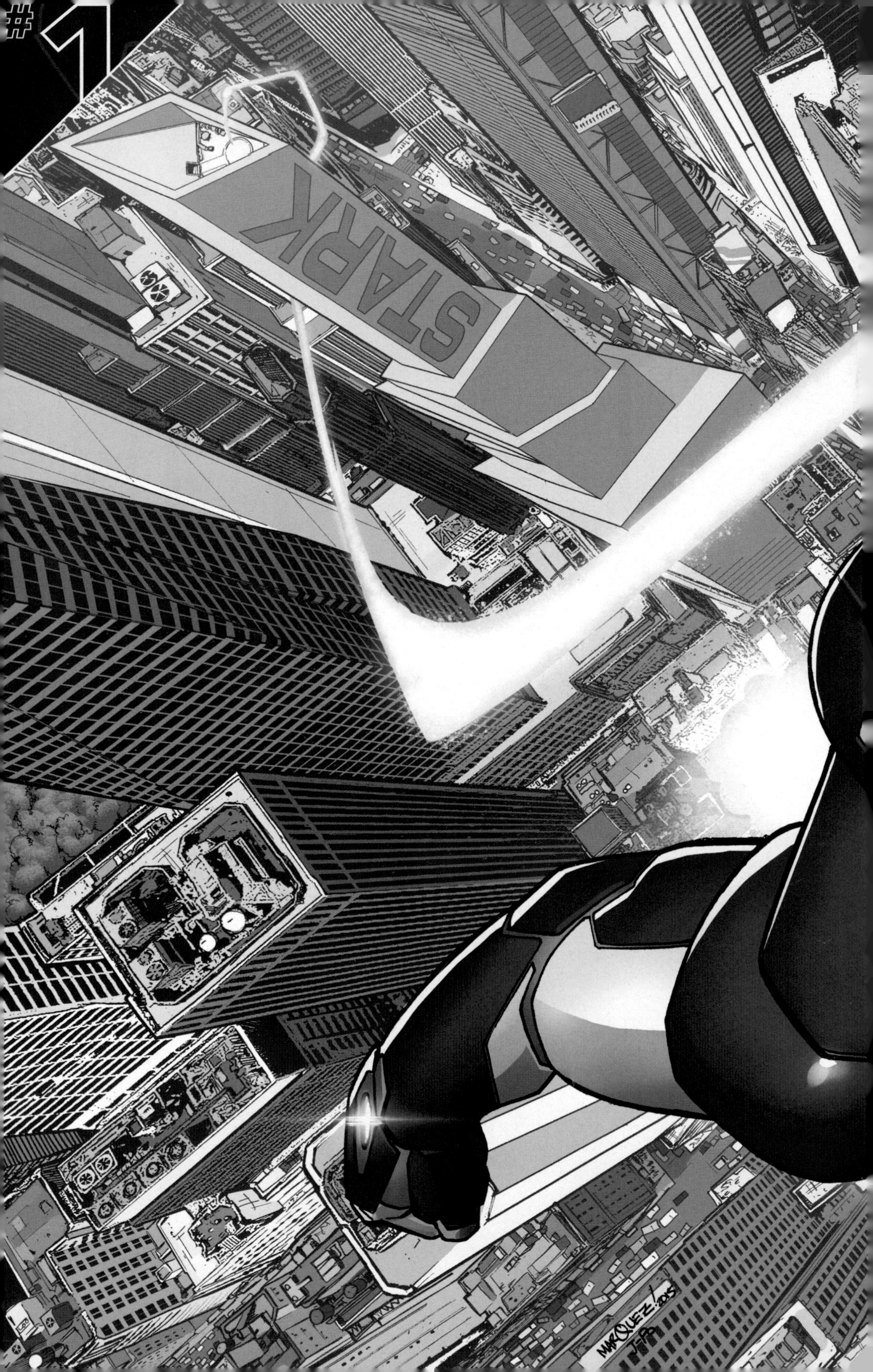
#1
STARK
MARQUEZ/2015

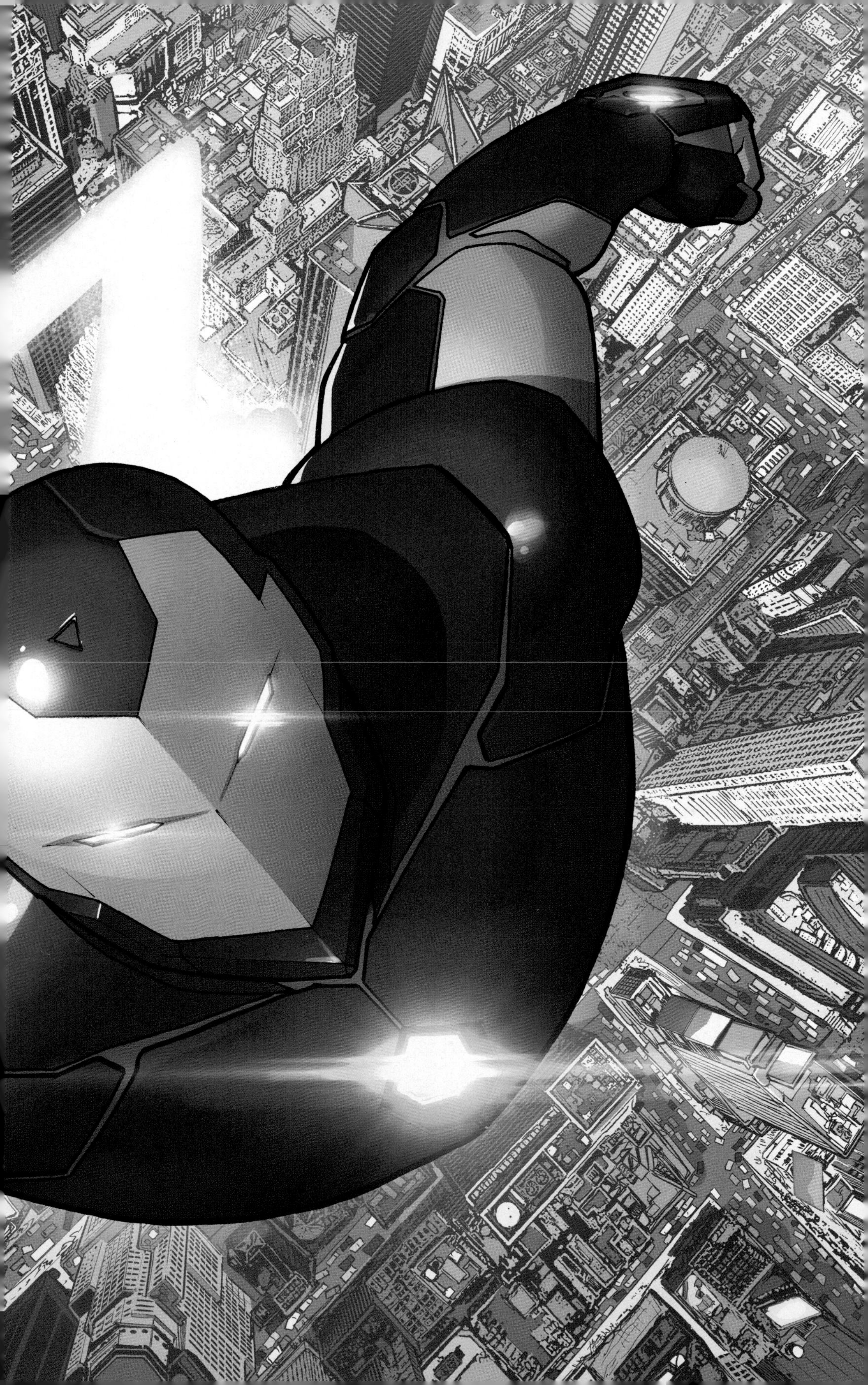

INVINCIBLE IRON MAN

ANOTHER STARK INNOVATION

Billionaire playboy and genius industrialist Tony Stark was kidnapped during a routine weapons test. His captors attempted to force him to build a weapon of mass destruction. Instead he created a powered suit of armor that saved his life. From that day on, he used the suit to protect the world as the invincible Avenger IRON MAN.

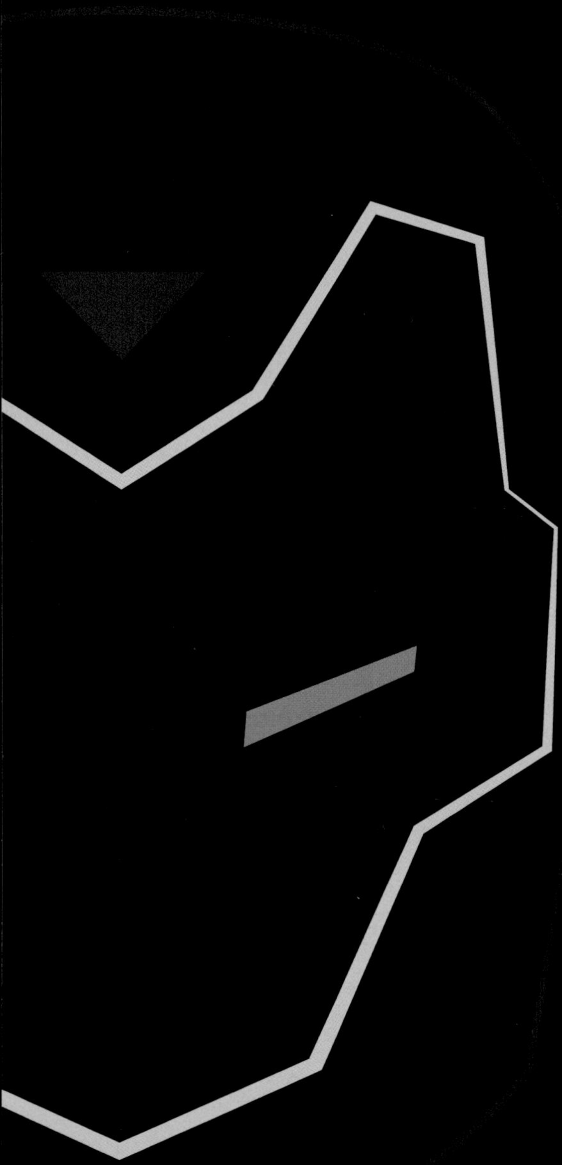

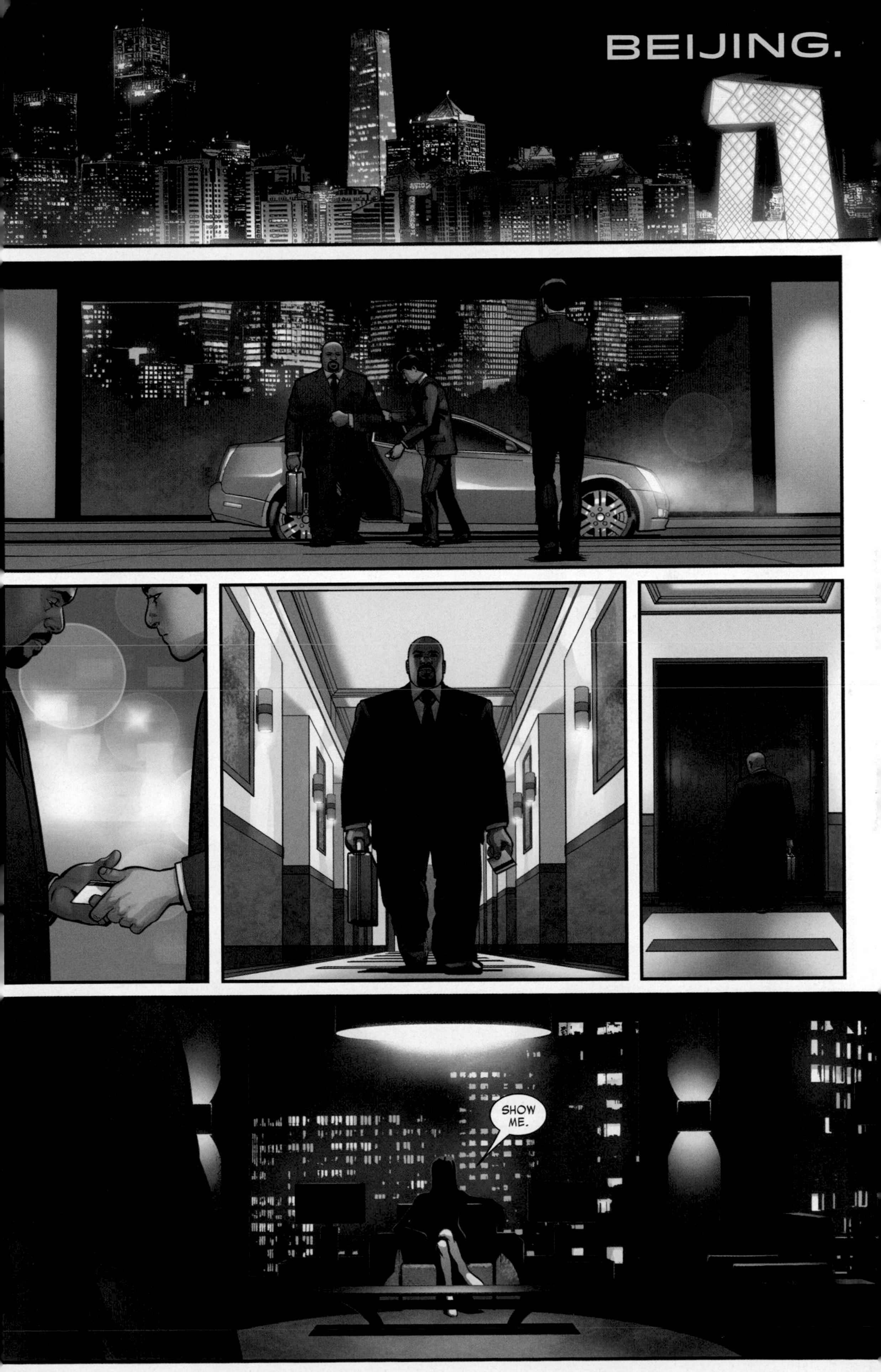
BEIJING.
SHOW ME.

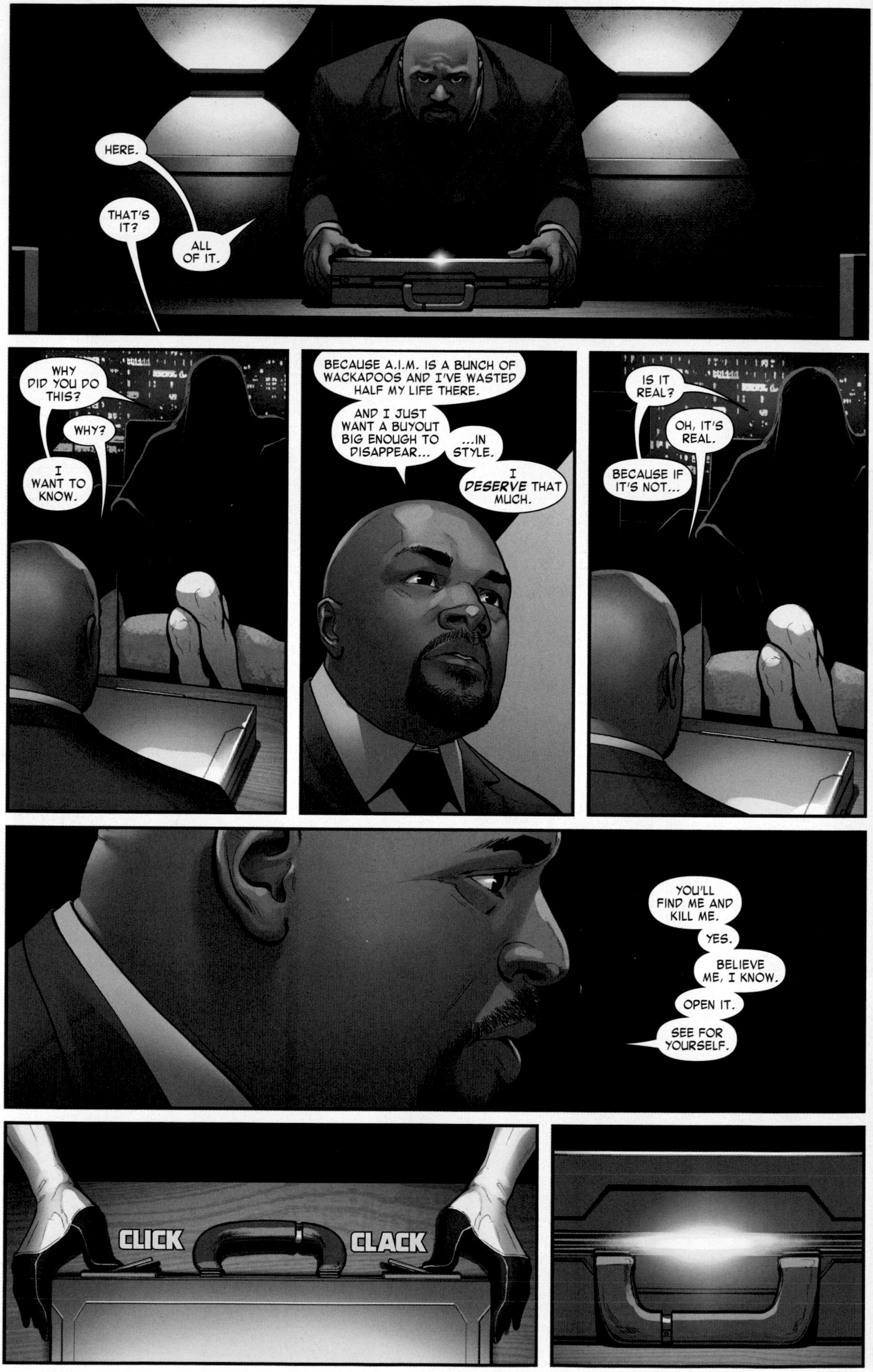
HERE.
ALL OF IT.
THAT'S IT?
WHY DID YOU DO THIS?
WHY?
I WANT TO KNOW.
BECAUSE A.I.M. IS A BUNCH OF WACKADOOS AND I'VE WASTED HALF MY LIFE THERE.
AND I JUST WANT A BUYOUT BIG ENOUGH TO DISAPPEAR...
...IN STYLE.
I DESERVE THAT MUCH.
IS IT REAL?
OH, IT'S REAL.
BECAUSE IF IT'S NOT...
YOU'LL FIND ME AND KILL ME.
YES.
BELIEVE ME, I KNOW.
OPEN IT.
SEE FOR YOURSELF.
CLICK
CLACK

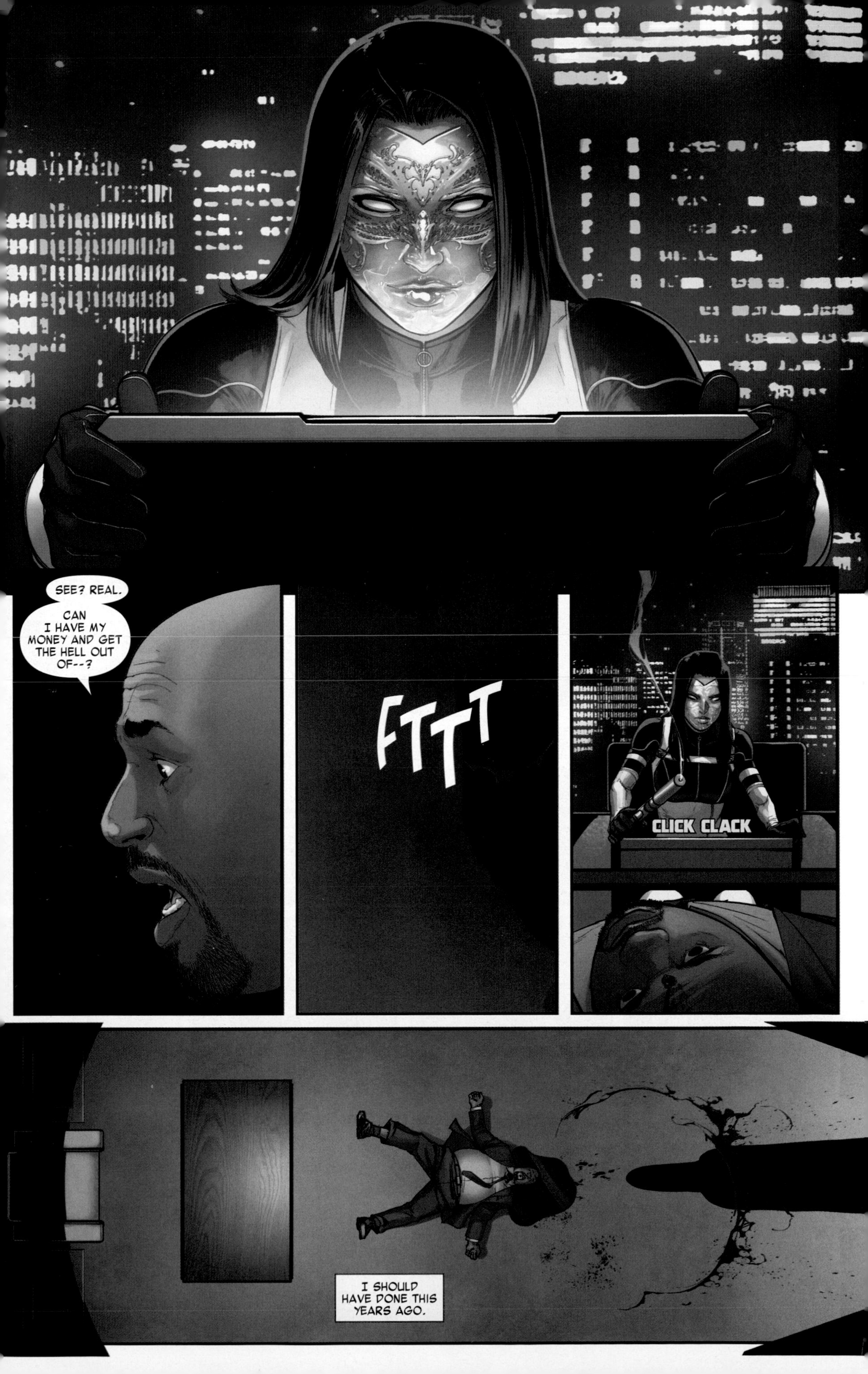

SEE? REAL.
CAN I HAVE MY MONEY AND GET THE HELL OUT OF--?
FTTT
CLICK CLACK
I SHOULD HAVE DONE THIS YEARS AGO.

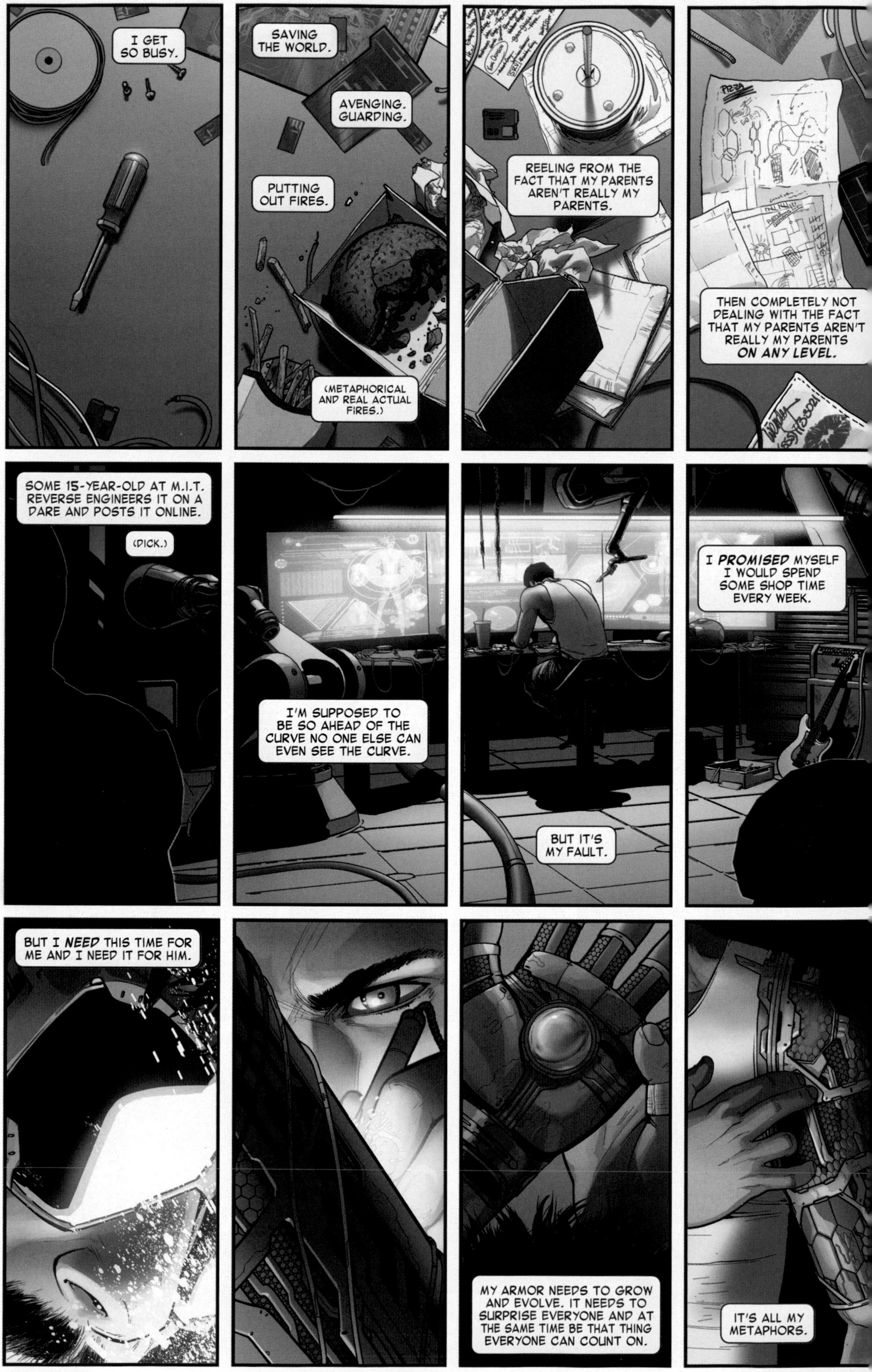
I GET SO BUSY.
SAVING THE WORLD.
AVENGING. GUARDING.
PUTTING OUT FIRES.
(METAPHORICAL AND REAL ACTUAL FIRES.)
REELING FROM THE FACT THAT MY PARENTS AREN'T REALLY MY PARENTS.
THEN COMPLETELY NOT DEALING WITH THE FACT THAT MY PARENTS AREN'T REALLY MY PARENTS ON ANY LEVEL.
SOME 15-YEAR-OLD AT M.I.T. REVERSE ENGINEERS IT ON A DARE AND POSTS IT ONLINE.
(DICK.)
I'M SUPPOSED TO BE SO AHEAD OF THE CURVE NO ONE ELSE CAN EVEN SEE THE CURVE.
BUT IT'S MY FAULT.
I PROMISED MYSELF I WOULD SPEND SOME SHOP TIME EVERY WEEK.
BUT I NEED THIS TIME FOR ME AND I NEED IT FOR HIM.
MY ARMOR NEEDS TO GROW AND EVOLVE. IT NEEDS TO SURPRISE EVERYONE AND AT THE SAME TIME BE THAT THING EVERYONE CAN COUNT ON.
IT'S ALL MY METAPHORS.

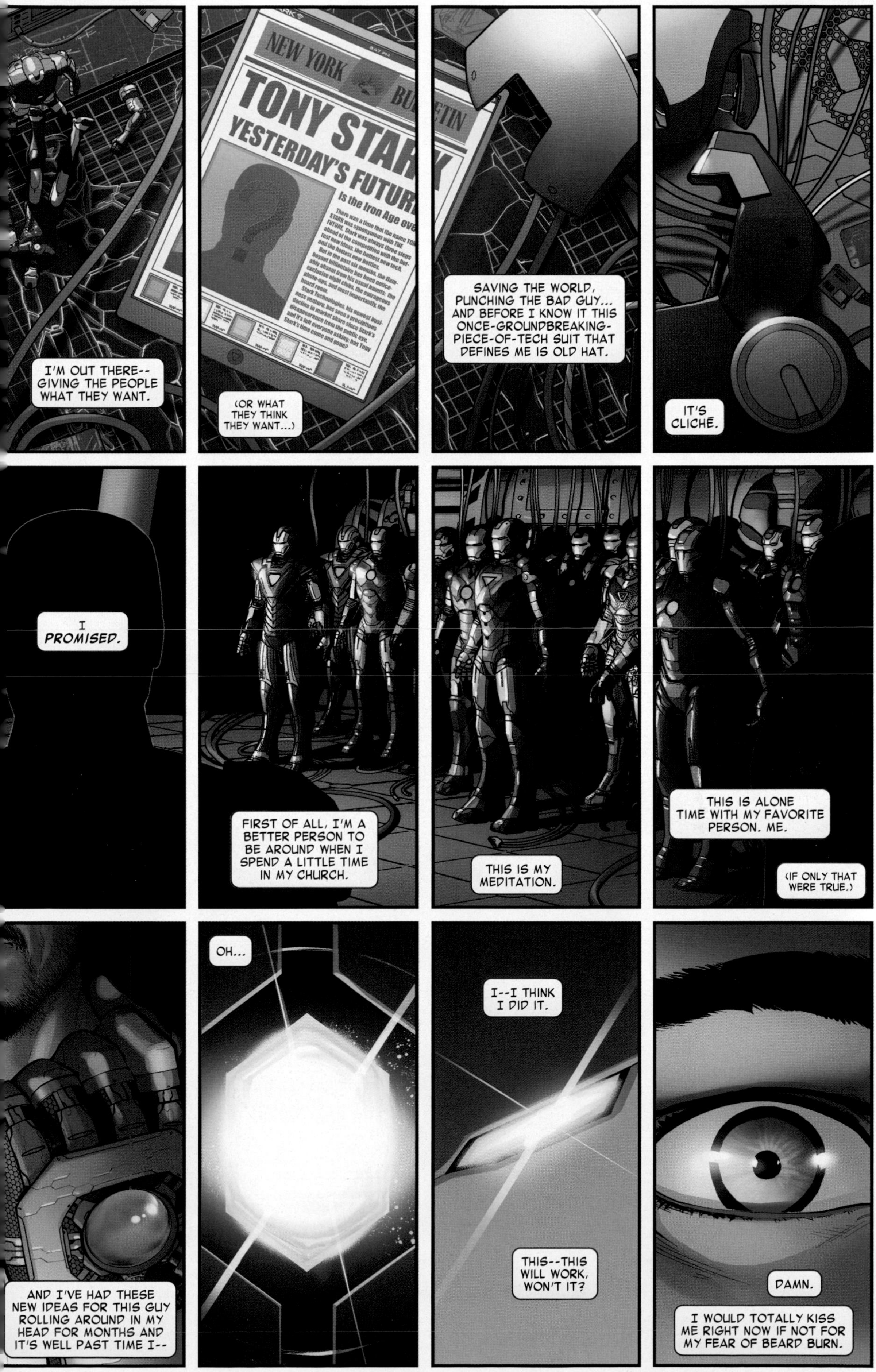
I'M OUT THERE--
GIVING THE PEOPLE
WHAT THEY WANT.
(OR WHAT THEY THINK THEY WANT...)
SAVING THE WORLD, PUNCHING THE BAD GUY... AND BEFORE I KNOW IT THIS ONCE-GROUNDBREAKING-PIECE-OF-TECH SUIT THAT DEFINES ME IS OLD HAT.
IT'S CLICHÉ.
I PROMISED.
FIRST OF ALL, I'M A BETTER PERSON TO BE AROUND WHEN I SPEND A LITTLE TIME IN MY CHURCH.
THIS IS MY MEDITATION.
THIS IS ALONE TIME WITH MY FAVORITE PERSON. ME.
(IF ONLY THAT WERE TRUE.)
AND I'VE HAD THESE NEW IDEAS FOR THIS GUY ROLLING AROUND IN MY HEAD FOR MONTHS AND IT'S WELL PAST TIME I--
OH...
I--I THINK I DID IT.
THIS--THIS WILL WORK, WON'T IT?
DAMN.
I WOULD TOTALLY KISS ME RIGHT NOW IF NOT FOR MY FEAR OF BEARD BURN.

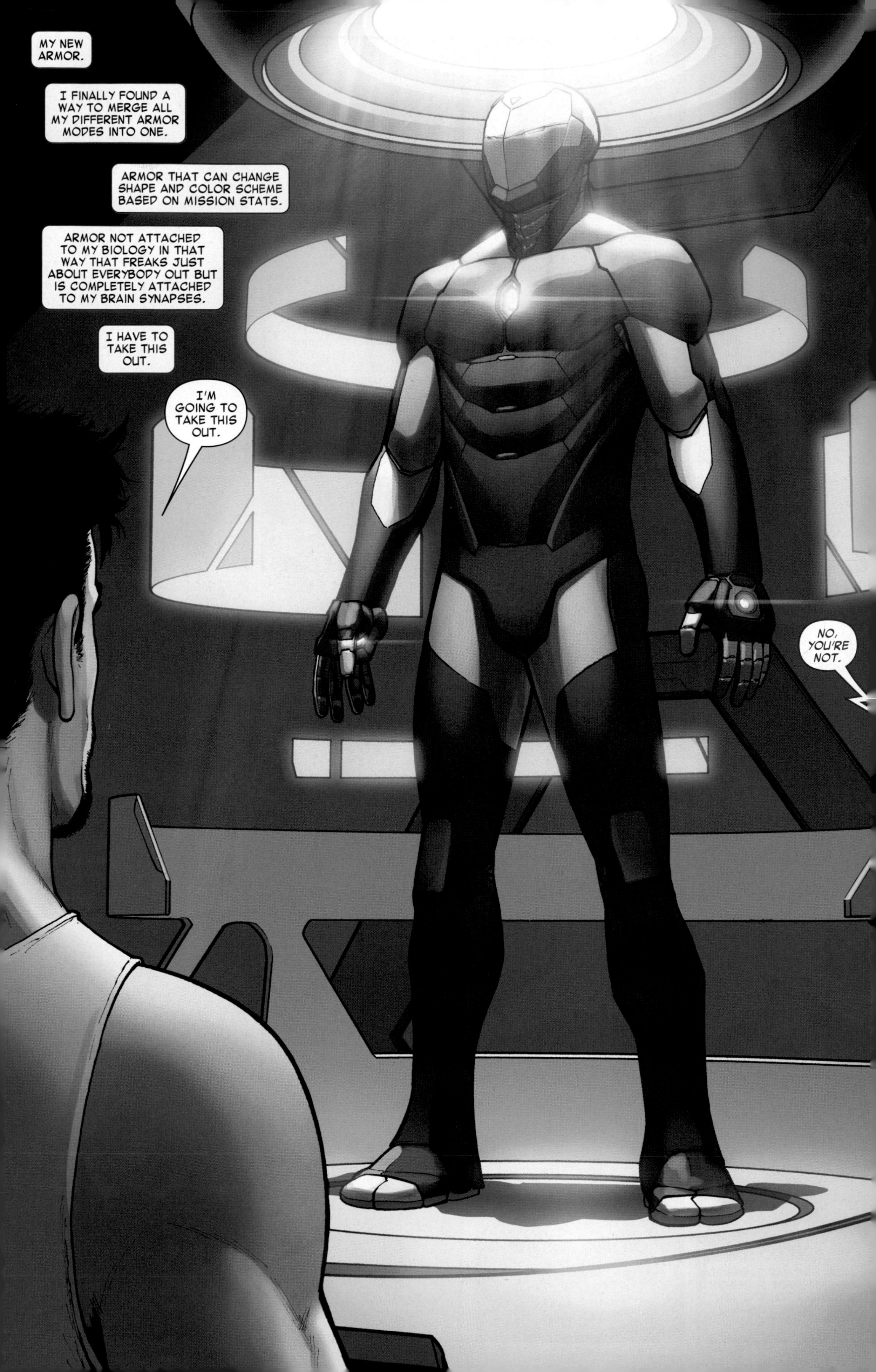
MY NEW ARMOR.
I FINALLY FOUND A WAY TO MERGE ALL MY DIFFERENT ARMOR MODES INTO ONE.
ARMOR THAT CAN CHANGE SHAPE AND COLOR SCHEME BASED ON MISSION STATS.
ARMOR NOT ATTACHED TO MY BIOLOGY IN THAT WAY THAT FREAKS JUST ABOUT EVERYBODY OUT BUT IS COMPLETELY ATTACHED TO MY BRAIN SYNAPSES.
I HAVE TO TAKE THIS OUT.
I'M GOING TO TAKE THIS OUT.
NO, YOU'RE NOT.

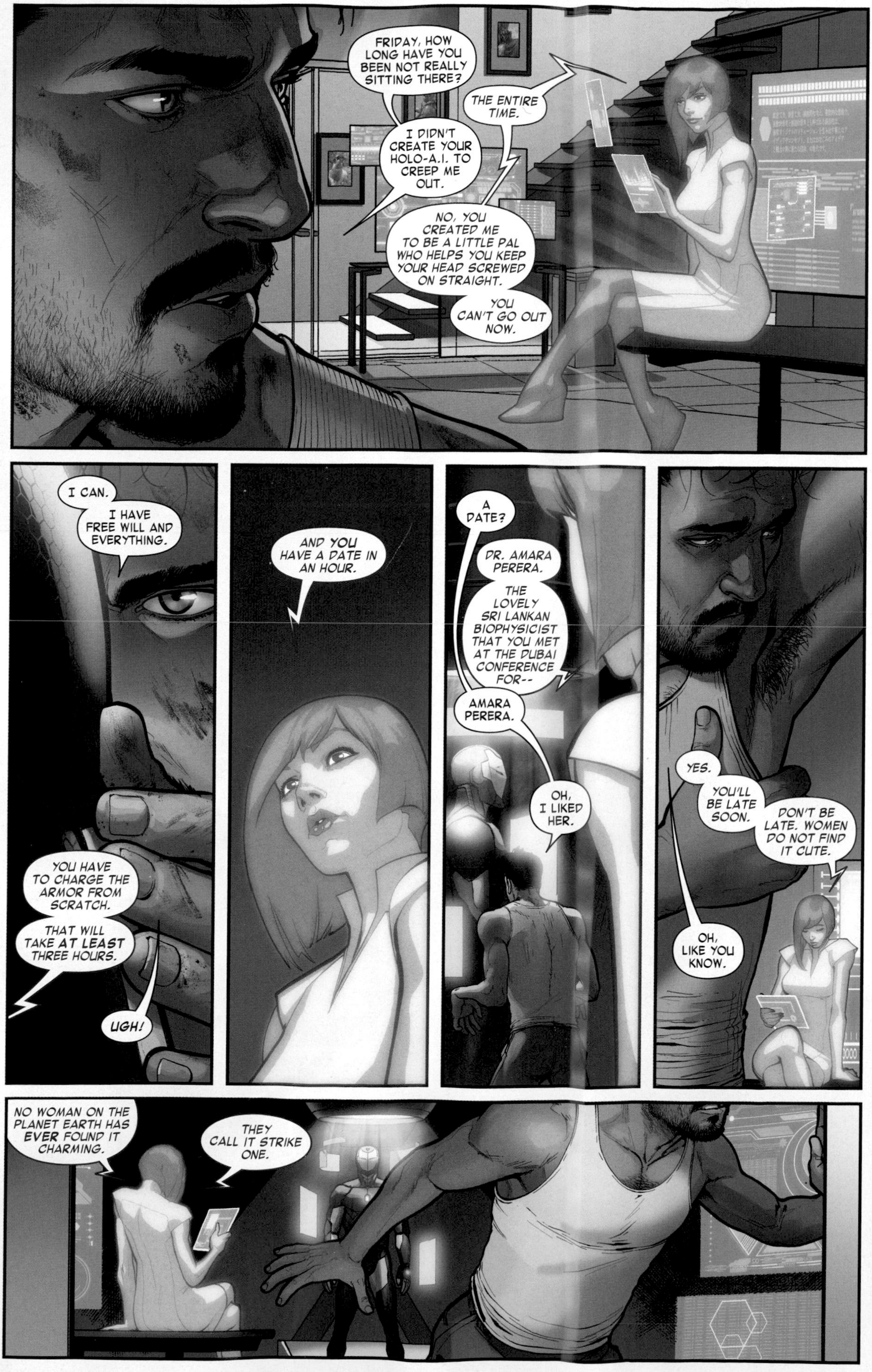
FRIDAY, HOW LONG HAVE YOU BEEN NOT REALLY SITTING THERE?
THE ENTIRE TIME.
I DIDN'T CREATE YOUR HOLO-A.I. TO CREEP ME OUT.
NO, YOU CREATED ME TO BE A LITTLE PAL WHO HELPS YOU KEEP YOUR HEAD SCREWED ON STRAIGHT.
YOU CAN'T GO OUT NOW.
I CAN.
I HAVE FREE WILL AND EVERYTHING.
YOU HAVE TO CHARGE THE ARMOR FROM SCRATCH.
THAT WILL TAKE AT LEAST THREE HOURS.
UGH!
AND YOU HAVE A DATE IN AN HOUR.
A DATE?
DR. AMARA PERERA.
THE LOVELY SRI LANKAN BIOPHYSICIST THAT YOU MET AT THE DUBAI CONFERENCE FOR--
AMARA PERERA.
OH, I LIKED HER.
YES.
YOU'LL BE LATE SOON.
DON'T BE LATE. WOMEN DO NOT FIND IT CUTE.
OH, LIKE YOU KNOW.
NO WOMAN ON THE PLANET EARTH HAS EVER FOUND IT CHARMING.
THEY CALL IT STRIKE ONE.

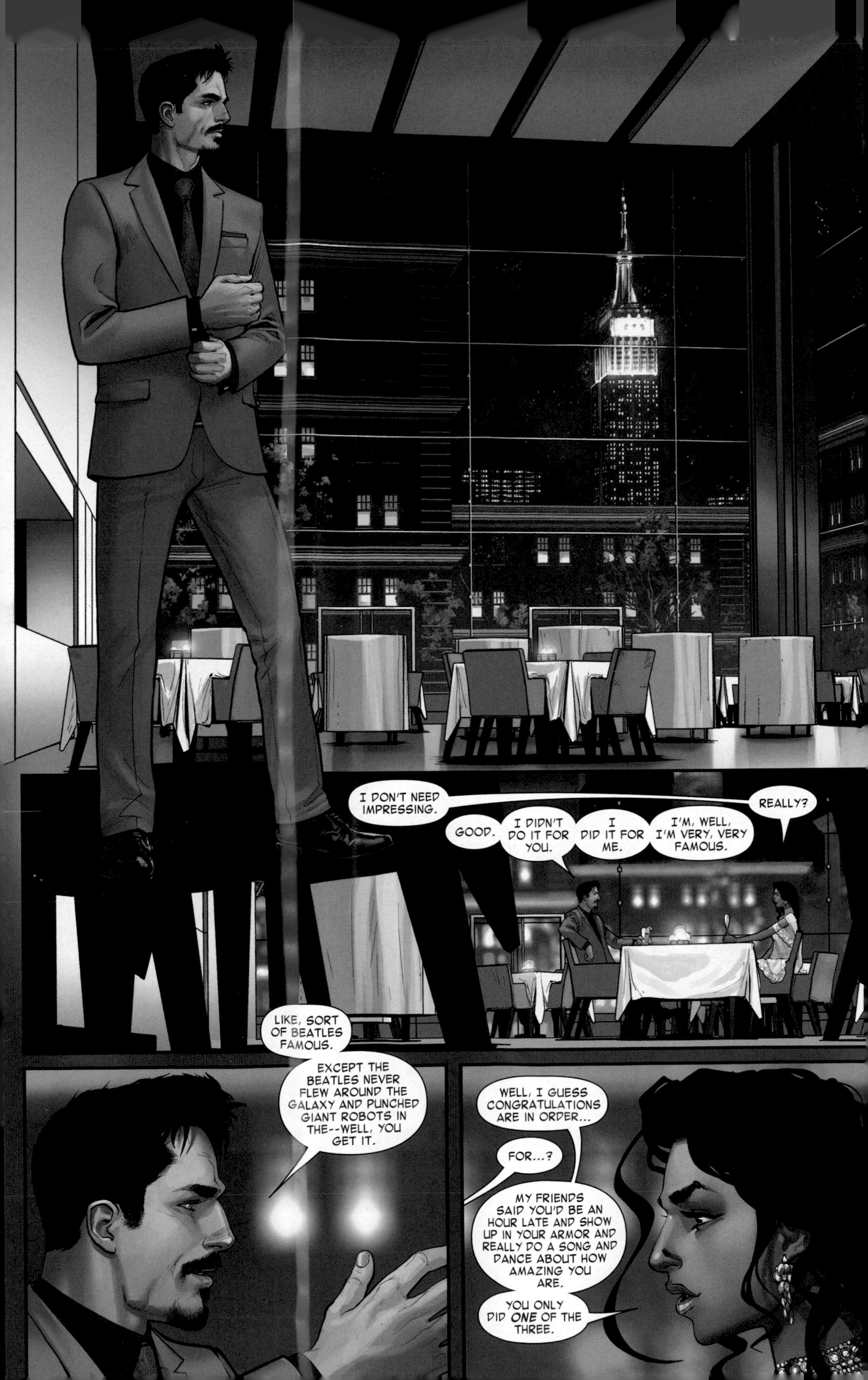
I DON'T NEED IMPRESSING.
REALLY?
GOOD.
I DIDN'T DO IT FOR YOU.
I DID IT FOR ME.
I'M, WELL, I'M VERY, VERY FAMOUS.
LIKE, SORT OF BEATLES FAMOUS.
EXCEPT THE BEATLES NEVER FLEW AROUND THE GALAXY AND PUNCHED GIANT ROBOTS IN THE--WELL, YOU GET IT.
WELL, I GUESS CONGRATULATIONS ARE IN ORDER...
FOR...?
MY FRIENDS SAID YOU'D BE AN HOUR LATE AND SHOW UP IN YOUR ARMOR AND REALLY DO A SONG AND DANCE ABOUT HOW AMAZING YOU ARE.
YOU ONLY DID ONE OF THE THREE.

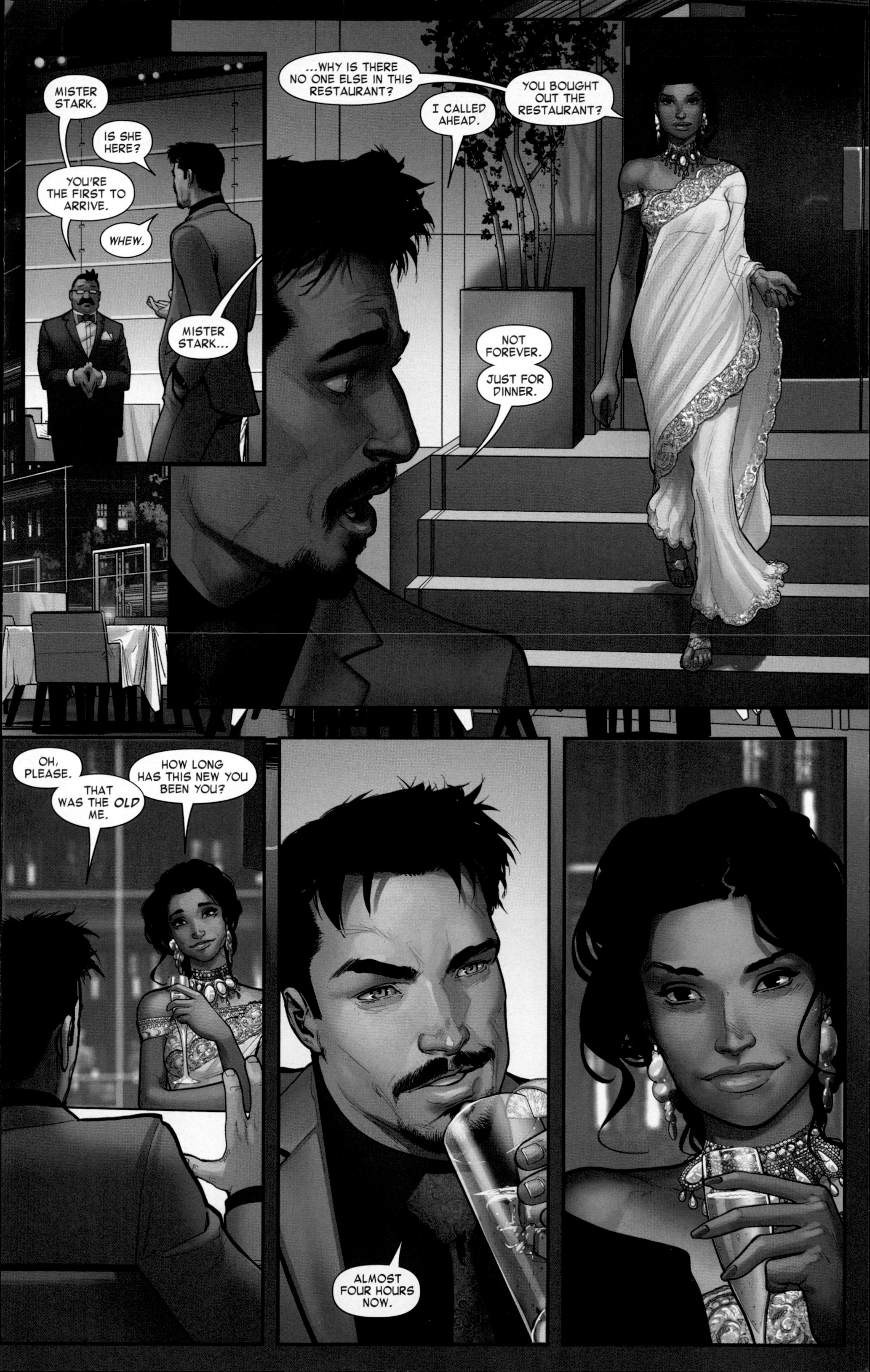
MISTER STARK.
IS SHE HERE?
YOU'RE THE FIRST TO ARRIVE.
WHEW.
MISTER STARK...
...WHY IS THERE NO ONE ELSE IN THIS RESTAURANT?
I CALLED AHEAD.
YOU BOUGHT OUT THE RESTAURANT?
NOT FOREVER.
JUST FOR DINNER.
OH, PLEASE.
THAT WAS THE OLD ME.
HOW LONG HAS THIS NEW YOU BEEN YOU?
ALMOST FOUR HOURS NOW.

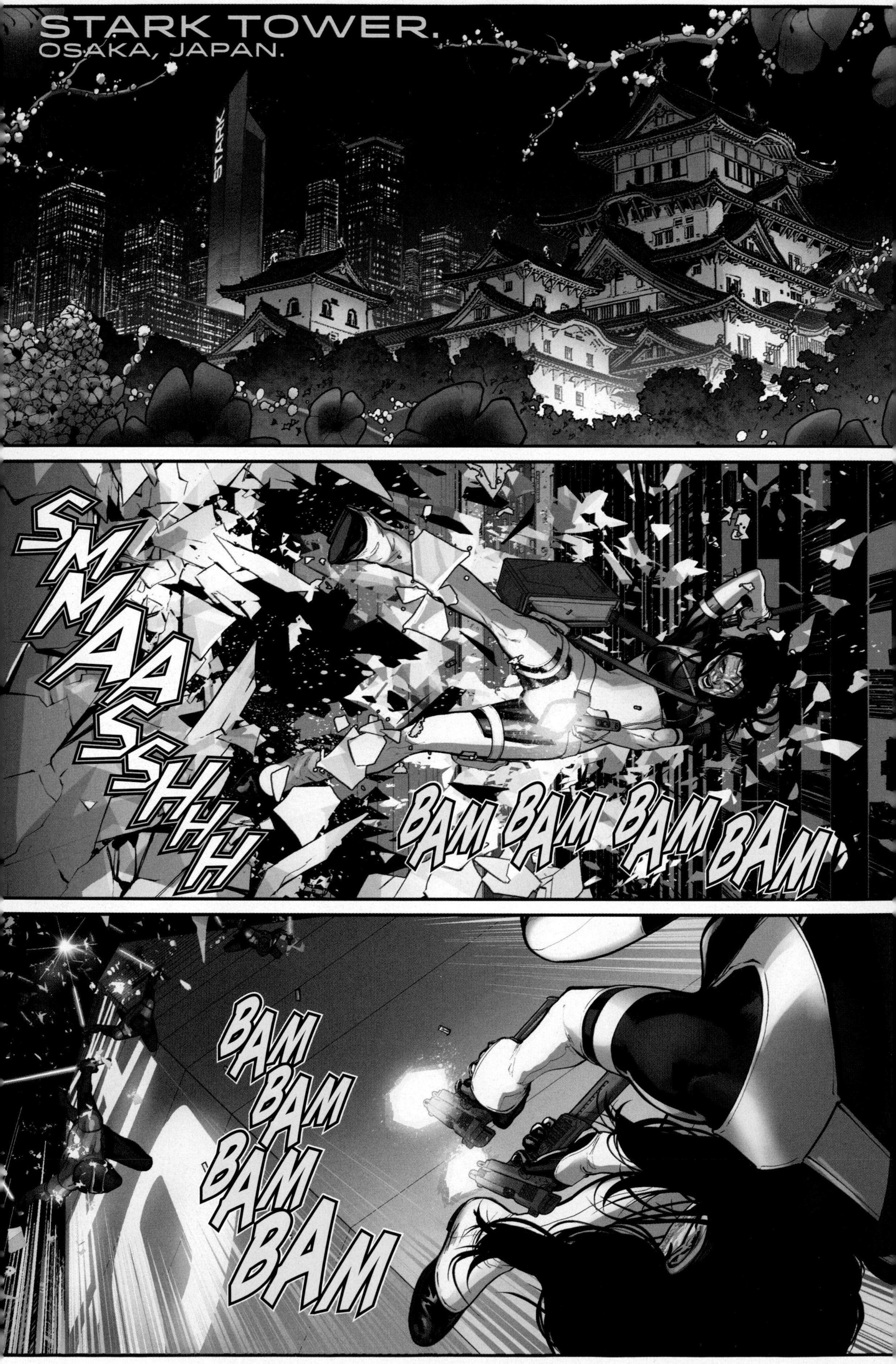
STARK TOWER.
OSAKA, JAPAN.
STARK
SMMAASSHHH
BAM BAM BAM BAM
BAM BAM BAM BAM

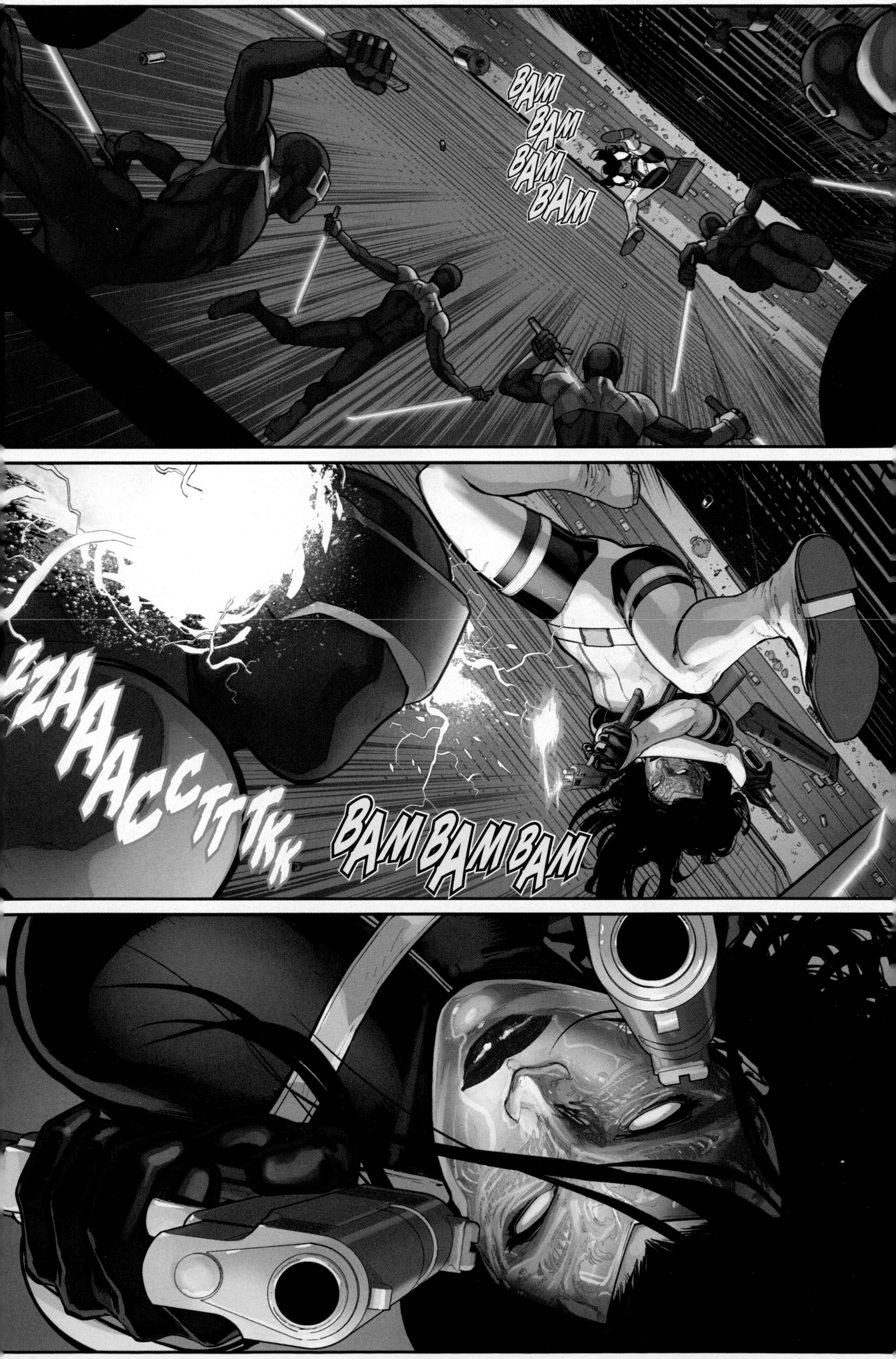
BAM BAM BAM BAM
ZZAAAACCTTTKK
BAM BAM BAM

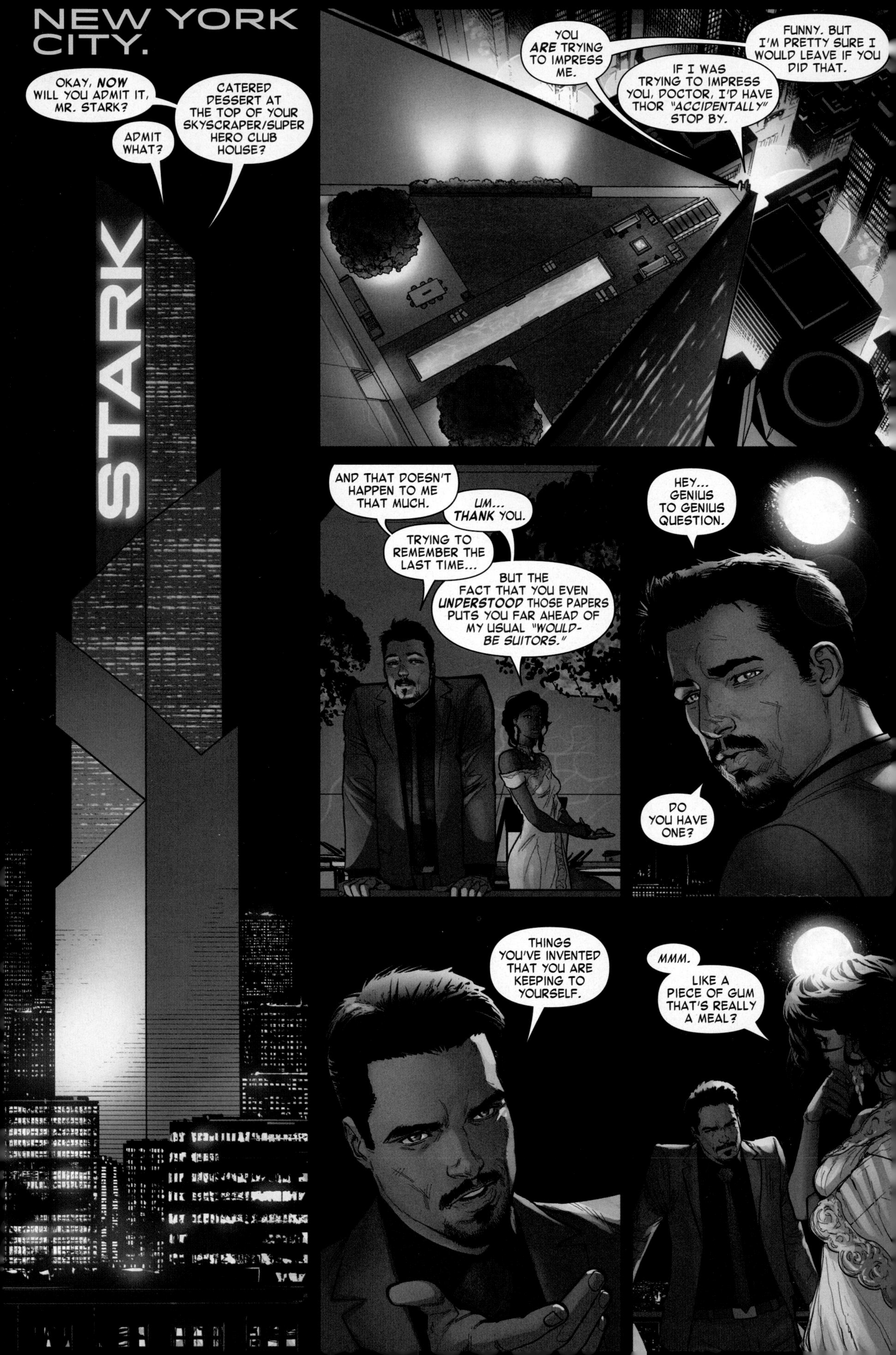
NEW YORK CITY.
OKAY, NOW WILL YOU ADMIT IT, MR. STARK?
ADMIT WHAT?
CATERED DESSERT AT THE TOP OF YOUR SKYSCRAPER/SUPER HERO CLUB HOUSE?
STARK
YOU ARE TRYING TO IMPRESS ME.
FUNNY. BUT I'M PRETTY SURE I WOULD LEAVE IF YOU DID THAT.
IF I WAS TRYING TO IMPRESS YOU, DOCTOR, I'D HAVE THOR "ACCIDENTALLY" STOP BY.
AND THAT DOESN'T HAPPEN TO ME THAT MUCH.
UM... THANK YOU.
TRYING TO REMEMBER THE LAST TIME...
BUT THE FACT THAT YOU EVEN UNDERSTOOD THOSE PAPERS PUTS YOU FAR AHEAD OF MY USUAL "WOULD-BE SUITORS."
HEY... GENIUS TO GENIUS QUESTION.
DO YOU HAVE ONE?
THINGS YOU'VE INVENTED THAT YOU ARE KEEPING TO YOURSELF.
MMM.
LIKE A PIECE OF GUM THAT'S REALLY A MEAL?

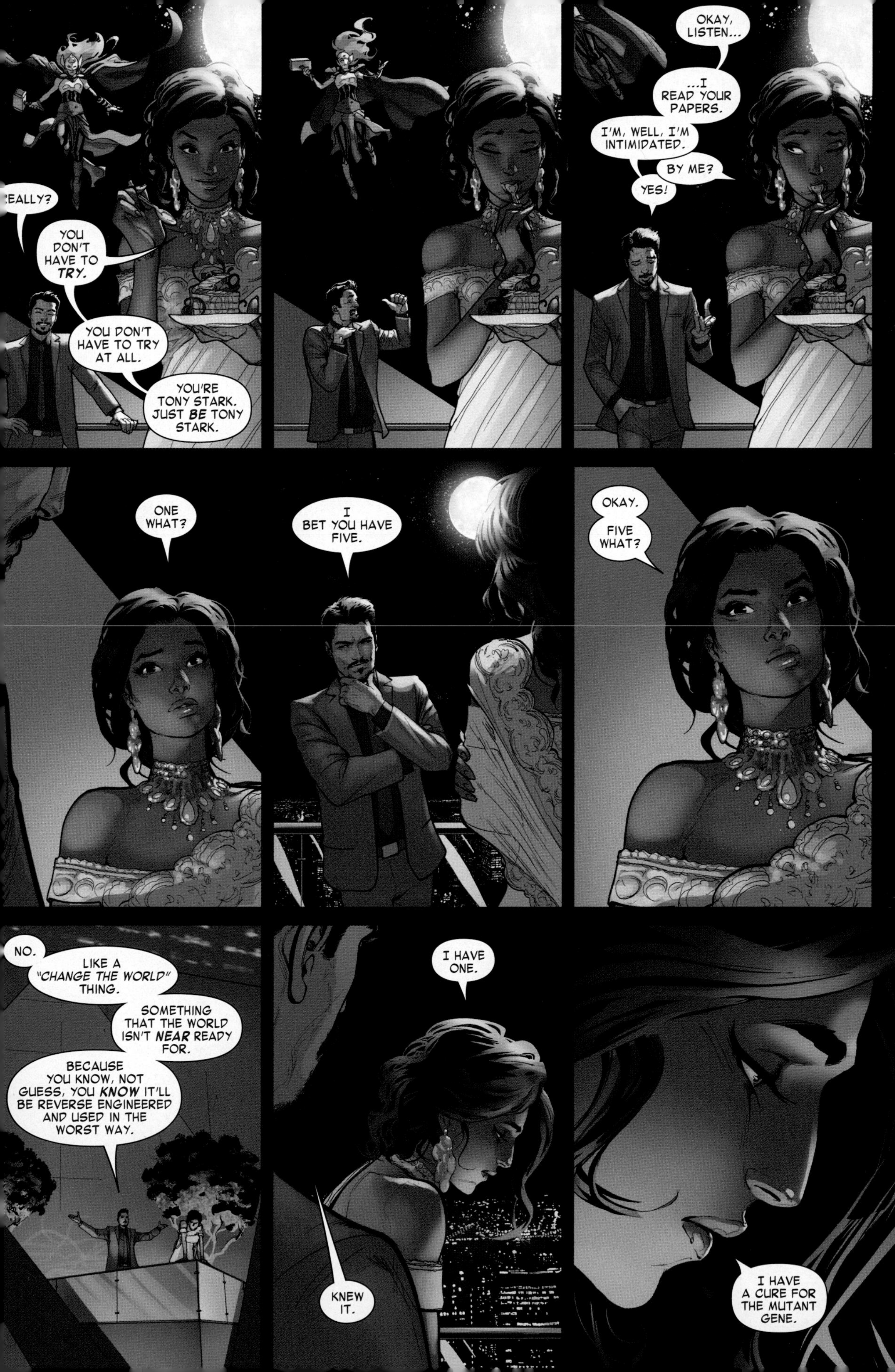
EALLY?
YOU DON'T HAVE TO TRY.
YOU DON'T HAVE TO TRY AT ALL.
YOU'RE TONY STARK. JUST BE TONY STARK.
OKAY, LISTEN...
...I READ YOUR PAPERS.
I'M, WELL, I'M INTIMIDATED.
BY ME?
YES!
ONE WHAT?
I BET YOU HAVE FIVE.
OKAY.
FIVE WHAT?
NO.
LIKE A "CHANGE THE WORLD" THING.
SOMETHING THAT THE WORLD ISN'T NEAR READY FOR.
BECAUSE YOU KNOW, NOT GUESS, YOU KNOW IT'LL BE REVERSE ENGINEERED AND USED IN THE WORST WAY.
I HAVE ONE.
KNEW IT.
I HAVE A CURE FOR THE MUTANT GENE.

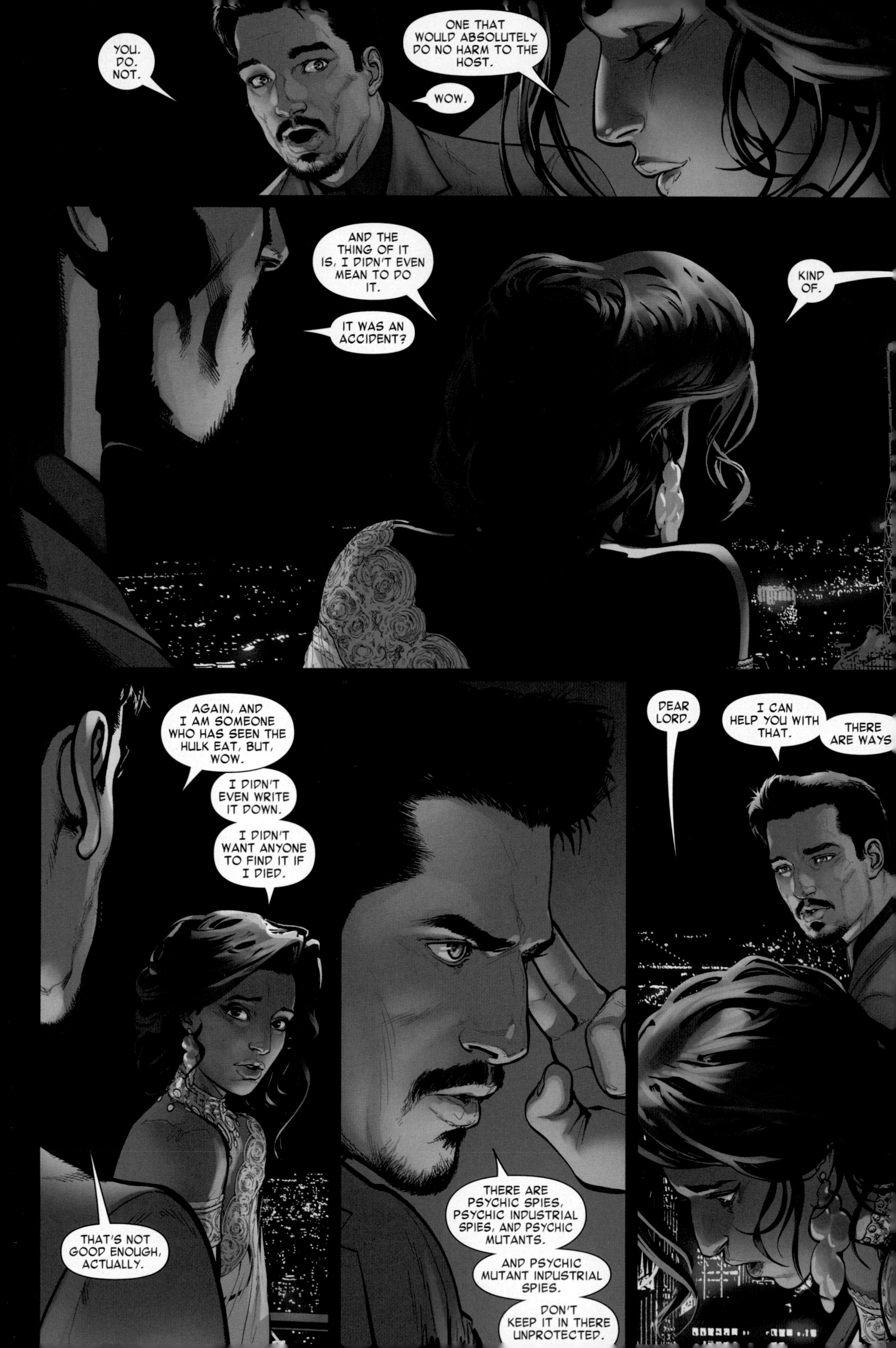
YOU. DO. NOT.
ONE THAT WOULD ABSOLUTELY DO NO HARM TO THE HOST.
WOW.
AND THE THING OF IT IS, I DIDN'T EVEN MEAN TO DO IT.
IT WAS AN ACCIDENT?
KIND OF.
AGAIN, AND I AM SOMEONE WHO HAS SEEN THE HULK EAT, BUT, WOW.
I DIDN'T EVEN WRITE IT DOWN.
I DIDN'T WANT ANYONE TO FIND IT IF I DIED.
THAT'S NOT GOOD ENOUGH, ACTUALLY.
THERE ARE PSYCHIC SPIES, PSYCHIC INDUSTRIAL SPIES, AND PSYCHIC MUTANTS.
AND PSYCHIC MUTANT INDUSTRIAL SPIES.
DON'T KEEP IT IN THERE UNPROTECTED.
DEAR LORD.
I CAN HELP YOU WITH THAT.
THERE ARE WAYS

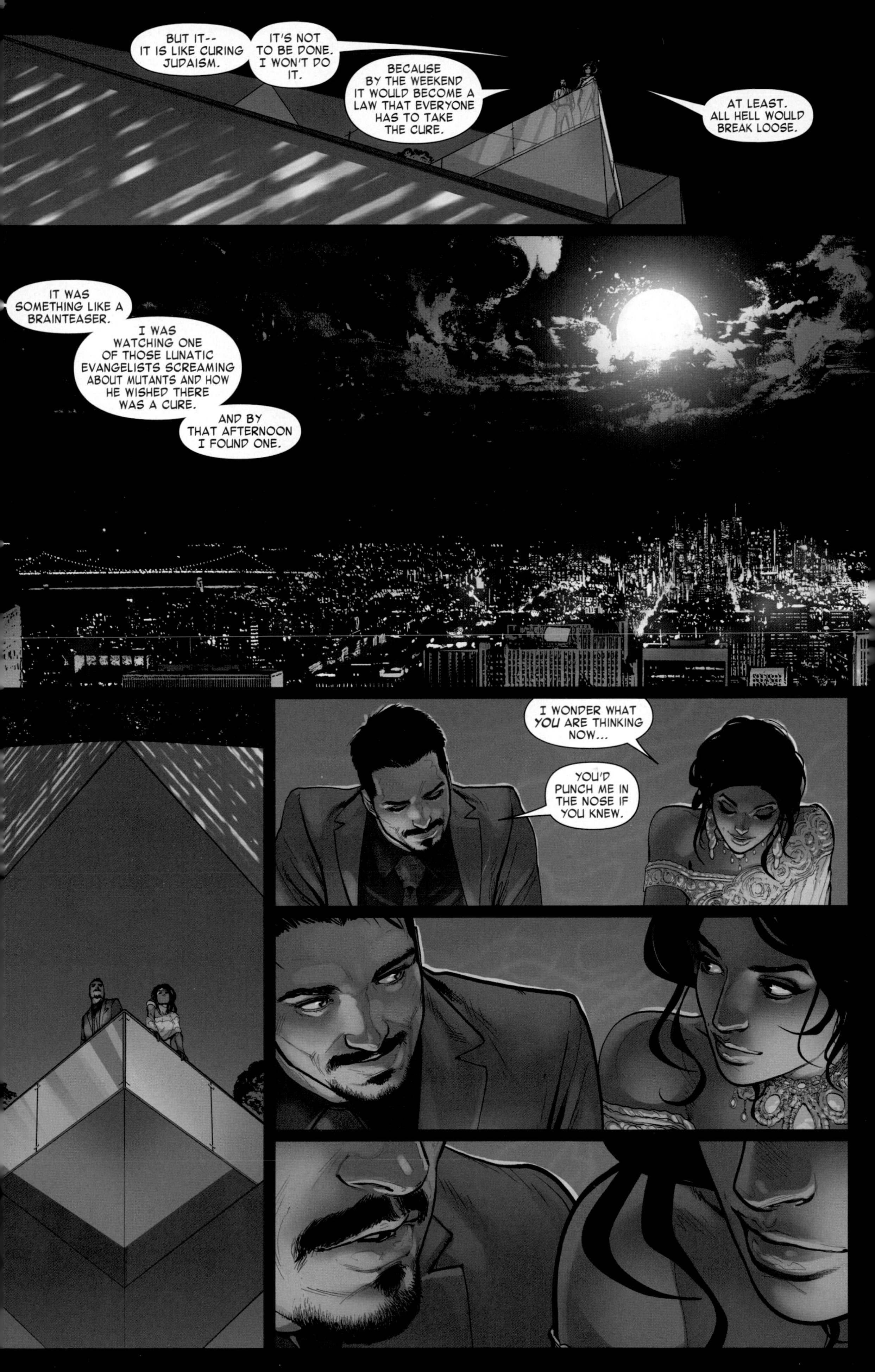
BUT IT-- IT IS LIKE CURING JUDAISM.
IT'S NOT TO BE DONE. I WON'T DO IT.
BECAUSE BY THE WEEKEND IT WOULD BECOME A LAW THAT EVERYONE HAS TO TAKE THE CURE.
AT LEAST. ALL HELL WOULD BREAK LOOSE.
IT WAS SOMETHING LIKE A BRAINTEASER.
I WAS WATCHING ONE OF THOSE LUNATIC EVANGELISTS SCREAMING ABOUT MUTANTS AND HOW HE WISHED THERE WAS A CURE.
AND BY THAT AFTERNOON I FOUND ONE.
I WONDER WHAT YOU ARE THINKING NOW...
YOU'D PUNCH ME IN THE NOSE IF YOU KNEW.

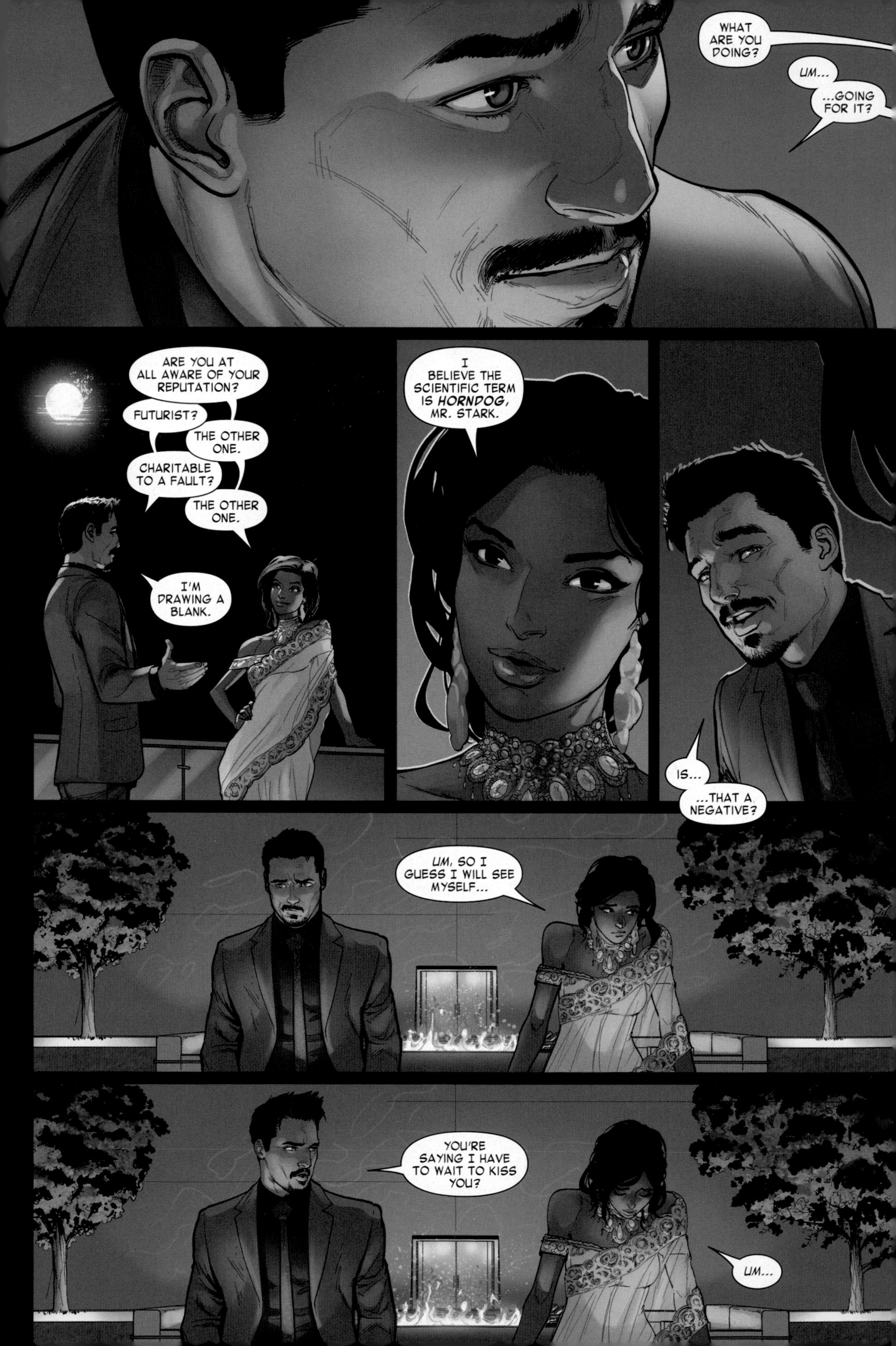
WHAT ARE YOU DOING?
UM...
...GOING FOR IT?
ARE YOU AT ALL AWARE OF YOUR REPUTATION?
FUTURIST?
THE OTHER ONE.
CHARITABLE TO A FAULT?
THE OTHER ONE.
I'M DRAWING A BLANK.
I BELIEVE THE SCIENTIFIC TERM IS HORNDOG, MR. STARK.
IS...
...THAT A NEGATIVE?
UM, SO I GUESS I WILL SEE MYSELF...
YOU'RE SAYING I HAVE TO WAIT TO KISS YOU?
UM...

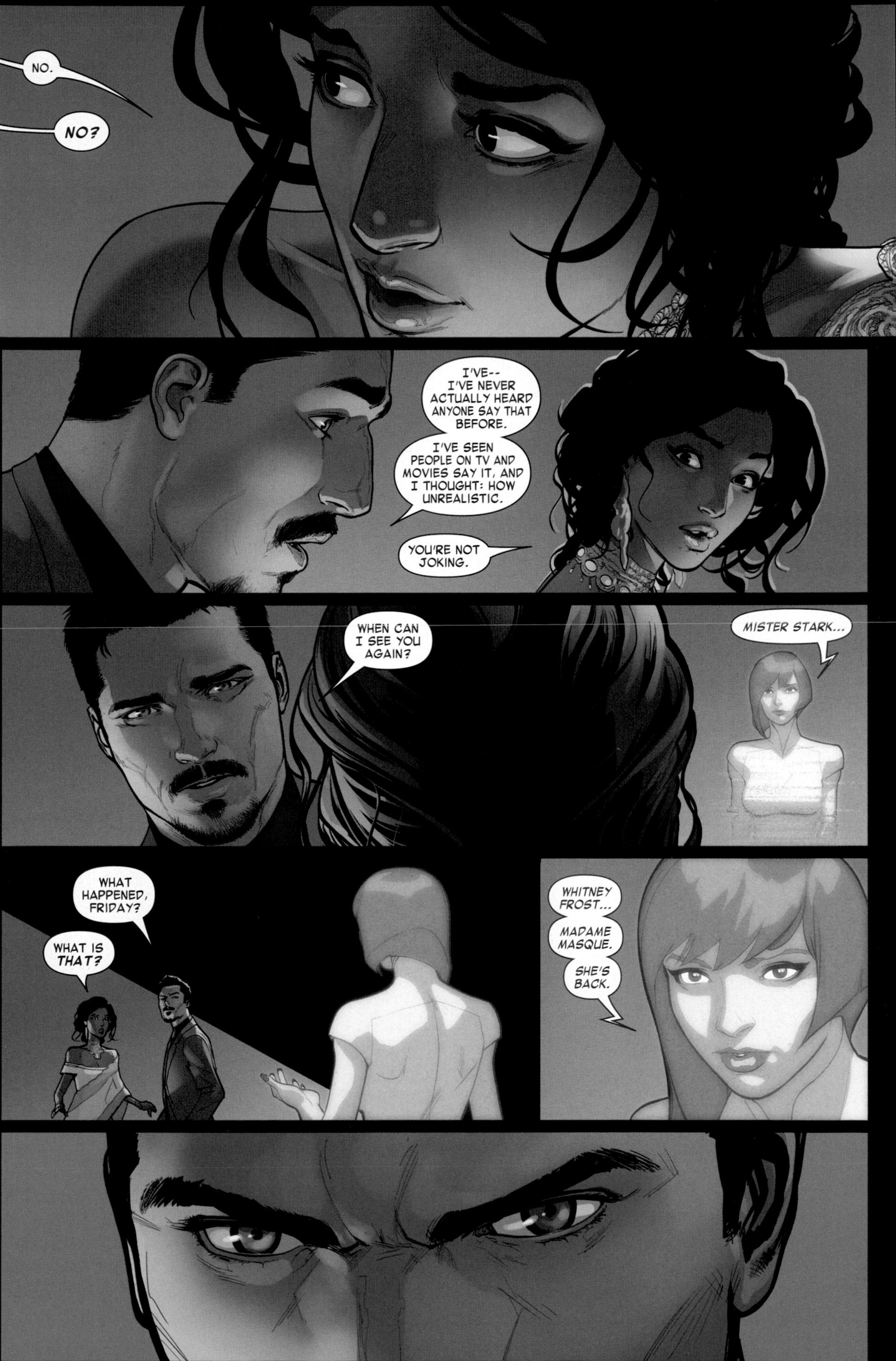
NO.
NO?
I'VE-- I'VE NEVER ACTUALLY HEARD ANYONE SAY THAT BEFORE.
I'VE SEEN PEOPLE ON TV AND MOVIES SAY IT, AND I THOUGHT: HOW UNREALISTIC.
YOU'RE NOT JOKING.
WHEN CAN I SEE YOU AGAIN?
MISTER STARK...
WHAT HAPPENED, FRIDAY?
WHAT IS *THAT*?
WHITNEY FROST...
MADAME MASQUE.
SHE'S BACK.

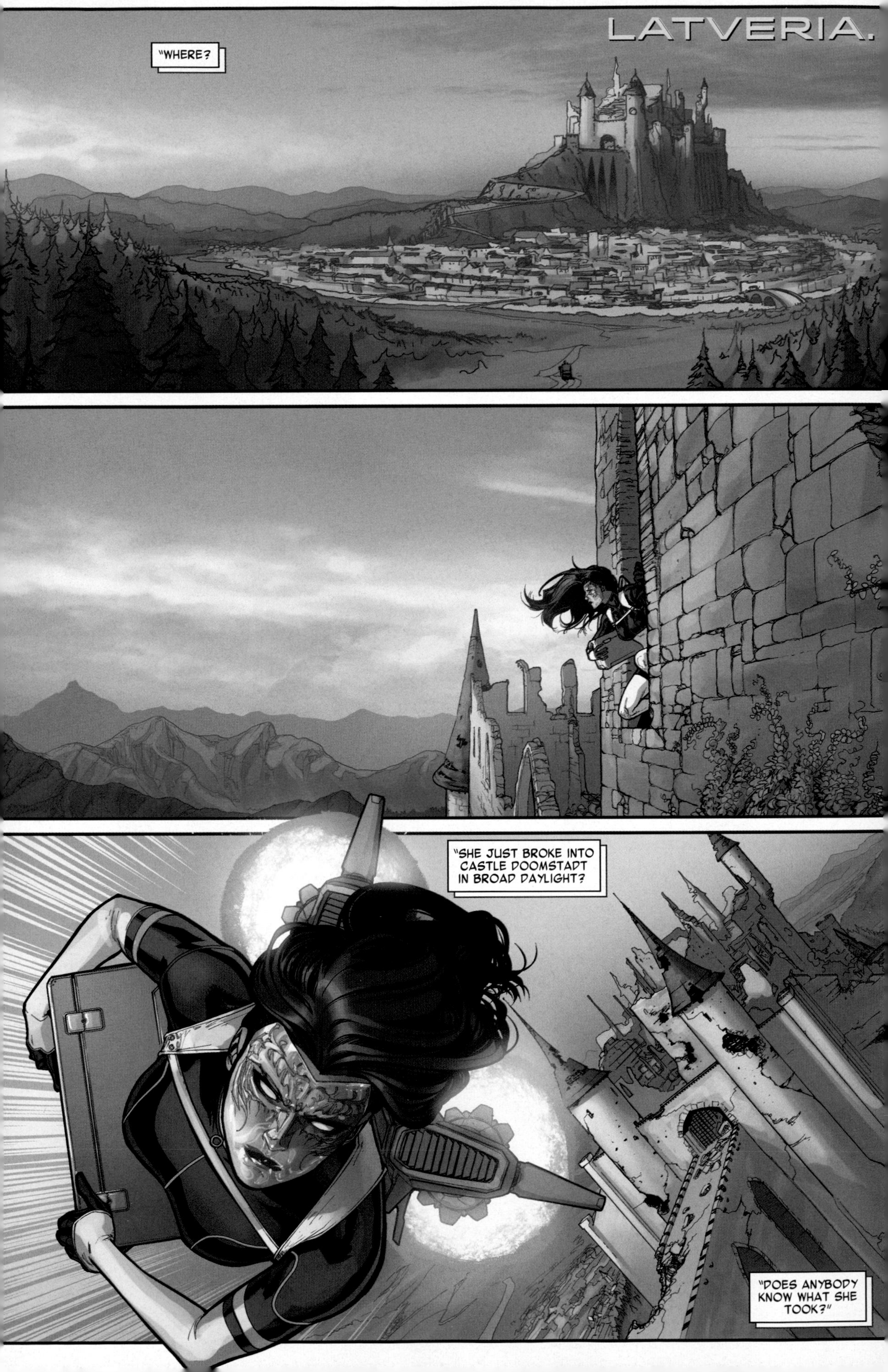
LATVERIA.
"WHERE?
"SHE JUST BROKE INTO CASTLE DOOMSTADT IN BROAD DAYLIGHT?
"DOES ANYBODY KNOW WHAT SHE TOOK?"

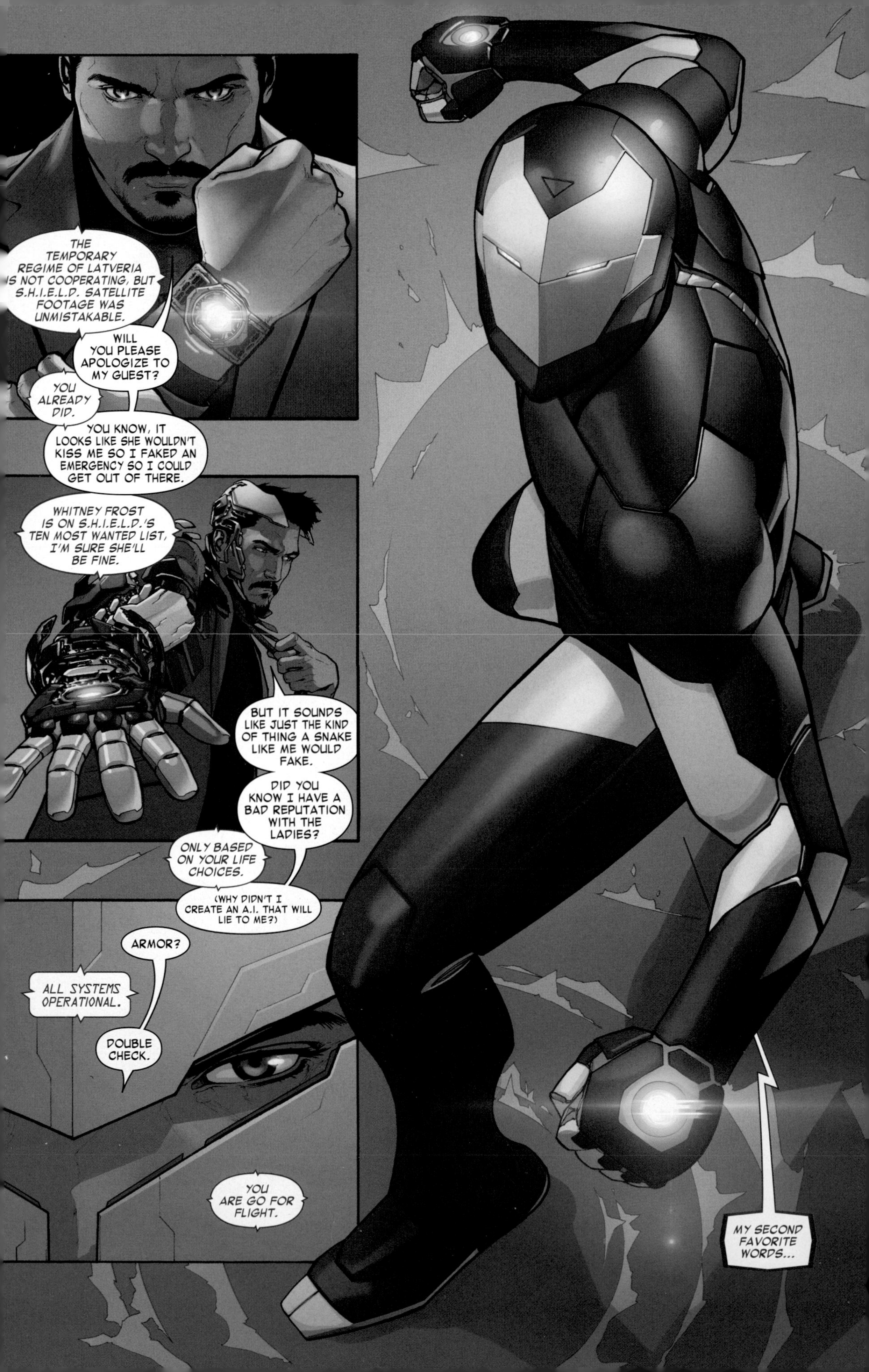
THE TEMPORARY REGIME OF LATVERIA IS NOT COOPERATING, BUT S.H.I.E.L.D. SATELLITE FOOTAGE WAS UNMISTAKABLE.
WILL YOU PLEASE APOLOGIZE TO MY GUEST?
YOU ALREADY DID.
YOU KNOW, IT LOOKS LIKE SHE WOULDN'T KISS ME SO I FAKED AN EMERGENCY SO I COULD GET OUT OF THERE.
WHITNEY FROST IS ON S.H.I.E.L.D.'S TEN MOST WANTED LIST, I'M SURE SHE'LL BE FINE.
BUT IT SOUNDS LIKE JUST THE KIND OF THING A SNAKE LIKE ME WOULD FAKE.
DID YOU KNOW I HAVE A BAD REPUTATION WITH THE LADIES?
ONLY BASED ON YOUR LIFE CHOICES.
(WHY DIDN'T I CREATE AN A.I. THAT WILL LIE TO ME?)
ARMOR?
ALL SYSTEMS OPERATIONAL.
DOUBLE CHECK.
YOU ARE GO FOR FLIGHT.
MY SECOND FAVORITE WORDS...

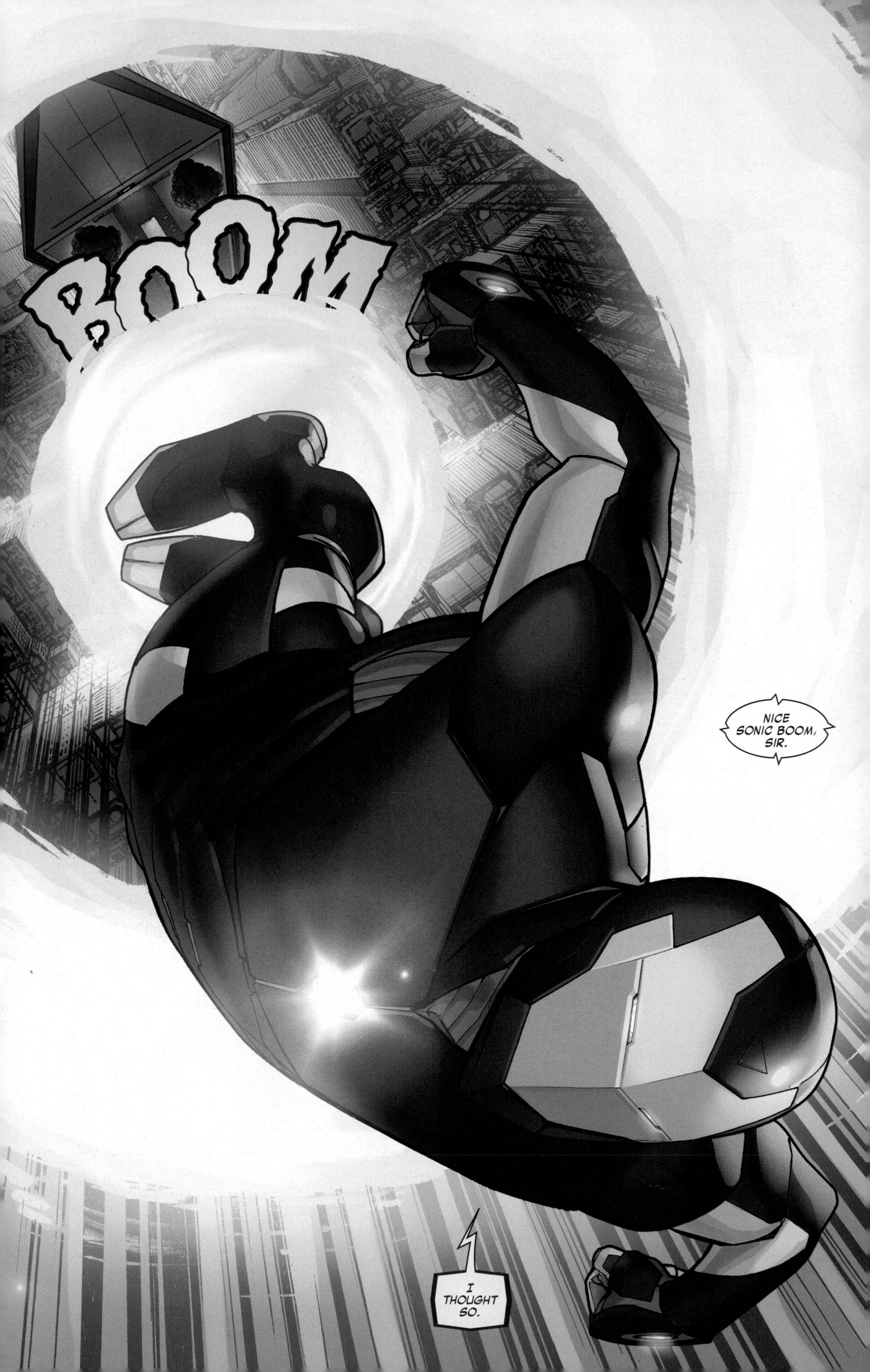
BOOM
NICE SONIC BOOM, SIR.
I THOUGHT SO.

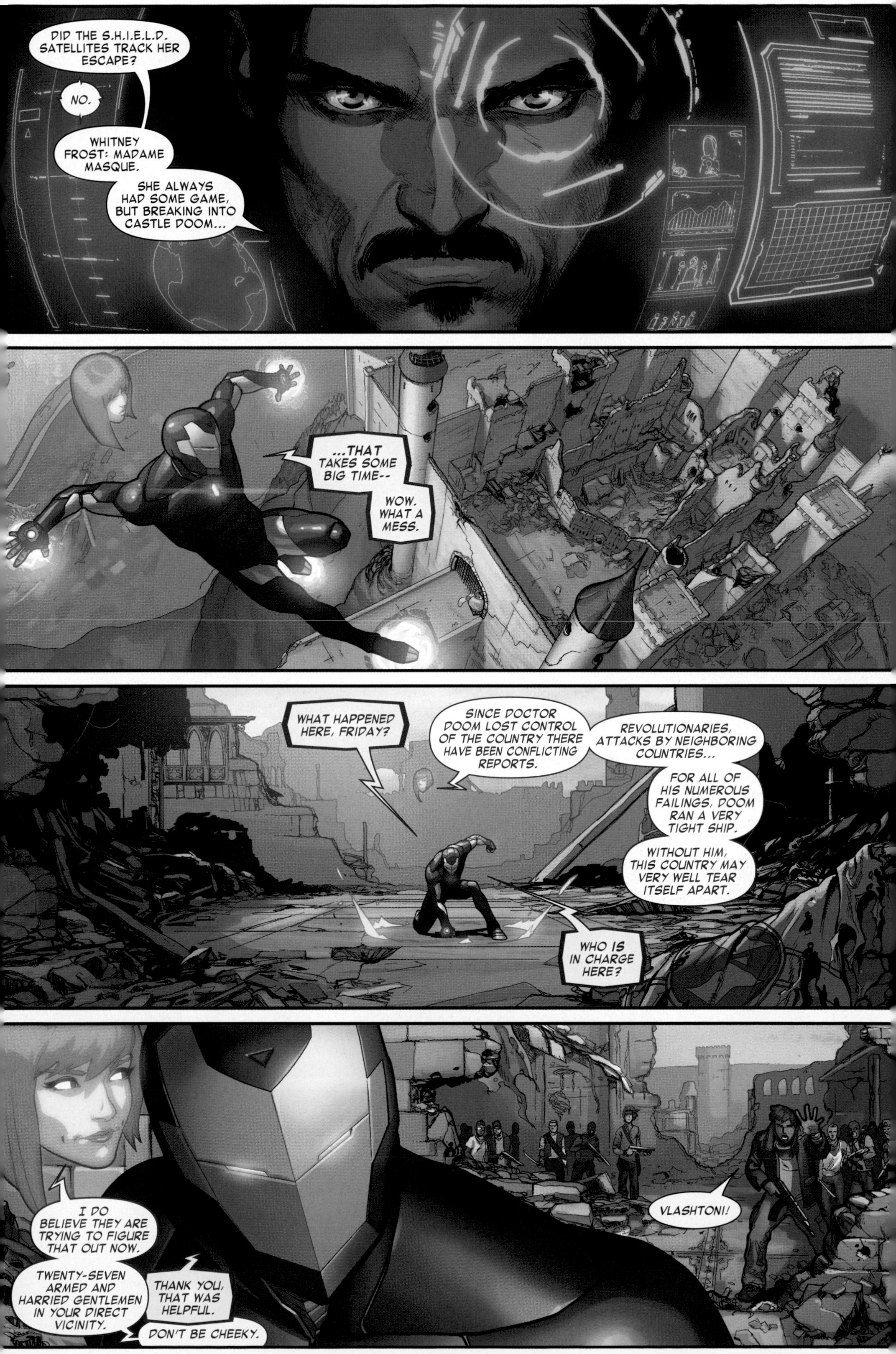
DID THE S.H.I.E.L.D. SATELLITES TRACK HER ESCAPE?
NO.
WHITNEY FROST: MADAME MASQUE.
SHE ALWAYS HAD SOME GAME, BUT BREAKING INTO CASTLE DOOM...
...THAT TAKES SOME BIG TIME--
WOW. WHAT A MESS.
WHAT HAPPENED HERE, FRIDAY?
SINCE DOCTOR DOOM LOST CONTROL OF THE COUNTRY THERE HAVE BEEN CONFLICTING REPORTS.
REVOLUTIONARIES, ATTACKS BY NEIGHBORING COUNTRIES...
FOR ALL OF HIS NUMEROUS FAILINGS, DOOM RAN A VERY TIGHT SHIP.
WITHOUT HIM, THIS COUNTRY MAY VERY WELL TEAR ITSELF APART.
WHO IS IN CHARGE HERE?
I DO BELIEVE THEY ARE TRYING TO FIGURE THAT OUT NOW.
TWENTY-SEVEN ARMED AND HARRIED GENTLEMEN IN YOUR DIRECT VICINITY.
THANK YOU, THAT WAS HELPFUL.
DON'T BE CHEEKY.
VLASHTONI!

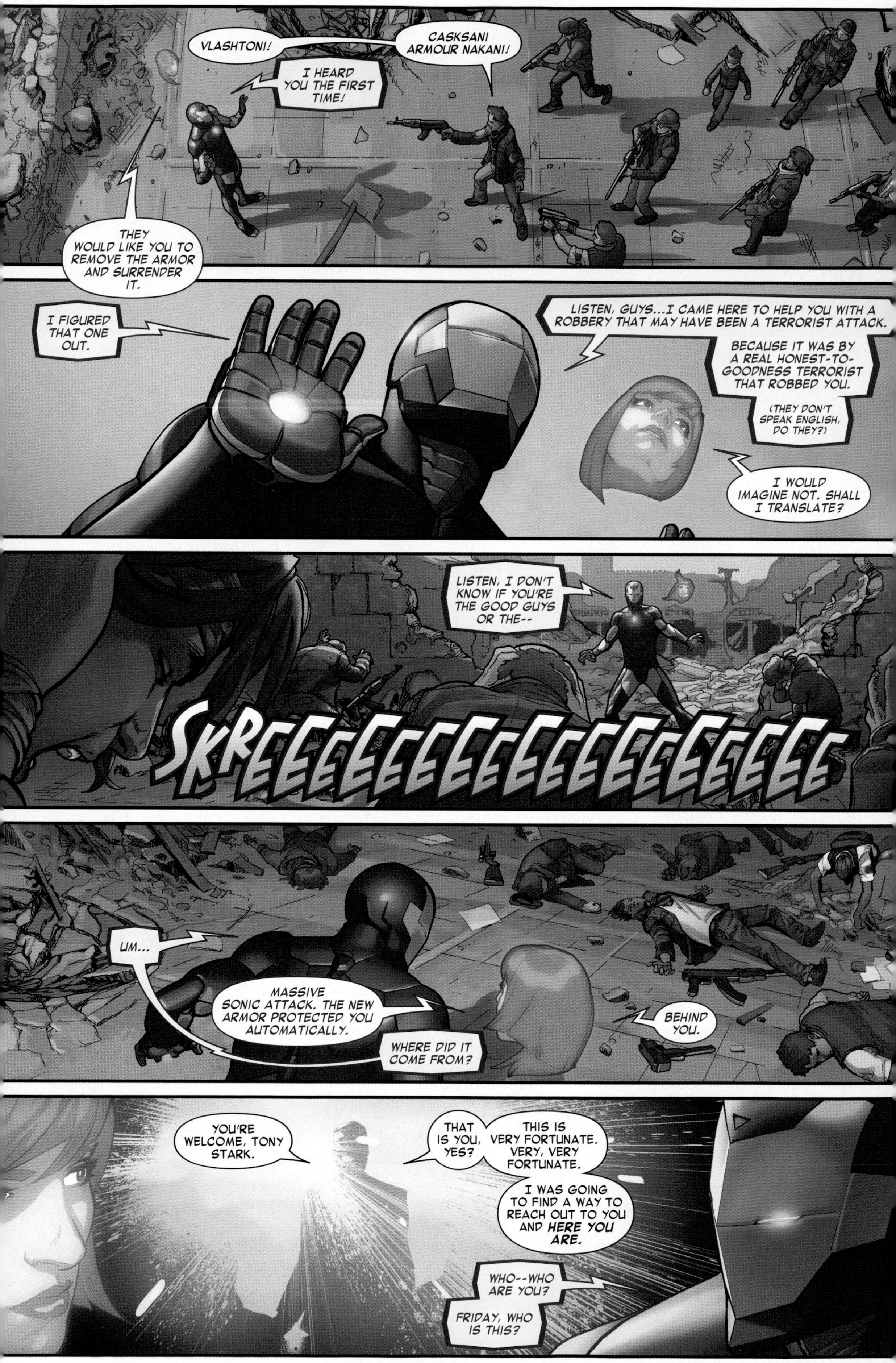
VLASHTONI!
CASKSANI ARMOUR NAKANI!
I HEARD YOU THE FIRST TIME!
THEY WOULD LIKE YOU TO REMOVE THE ARMOR AND SURRENDER IT.
I FIGURED THAT ONE OUT.
LISTEN, GUYS...I CAME HERE TO HELP YOU WITH A ROBBERY THAT MAY HAVE BEEN A TERRORIST ATTACK.
BECAUSE IT WAS BY A REAL HONEST-TO-GOODNESS TERRORIST THAT ROBBED YOU.
(THEY DON'T SPEAK ENGLISH, DO THEY?)
I WOULD IMAGINE NOT. SHALL I TRANSLATE?
LISTEN, I DON'T KNOW IF YOU'RE THE GOOD GUYS OR THE--
SKREEEEEEEEEEEEEEEEEEEEEEE
UM...
MASSIVE SONIC ATTACK. THE NEW ARMOR PROTECTED YOU AUTOMATICALLY.
WHERE DID IT COME FROM?
BEHIND YOU.
YOU'RE WELCOME, TONY STARK.
THAT IS YOU, YES?
THIS IS VERY FORTUNATE. VERY, VERY FORTUNATE.
I WAS GOING TO FIND A WAY TO REACH OUT TO YOU AND HERE YOU ARE.
WHO--WHO ARE YOU?
FRIDAY, WHO IS THIS?

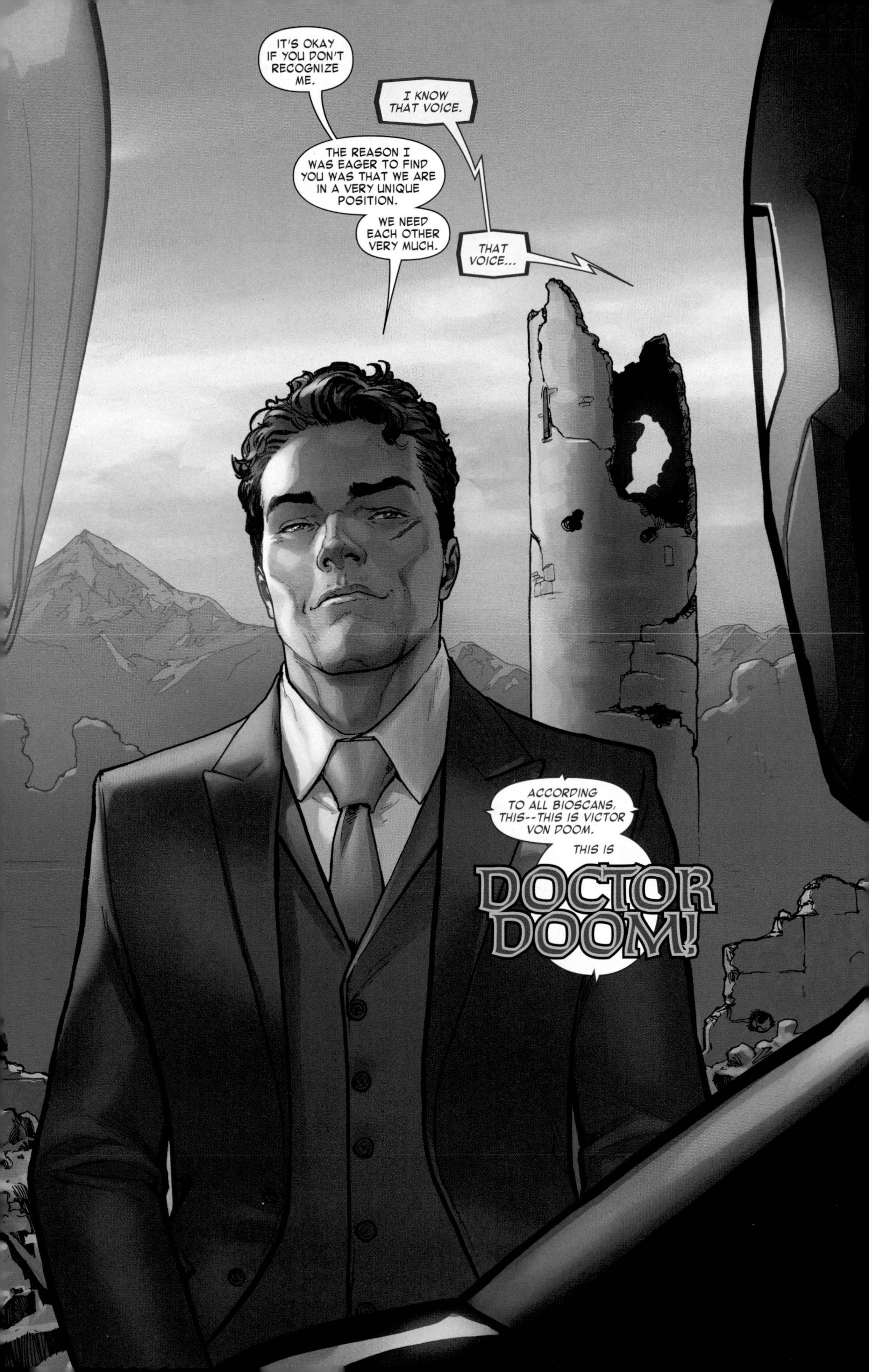
IT'S OKAY IF YOU DON'T RECOGNIZE ME.
I KNOW THAT VOICE.
THE REASON I WAS EAGER TO FIND YOU WAS THAT WE ARE IN A VERY UNIQUE POSITION.
WE NEED EACH OTHER VERY MUCH.
THAT VOICE...
ACCORDING TO ALL BIOSCANS, THIS--THIS IS VICTOR VON DOOM.
THIS IS DOCTOR DOOM!

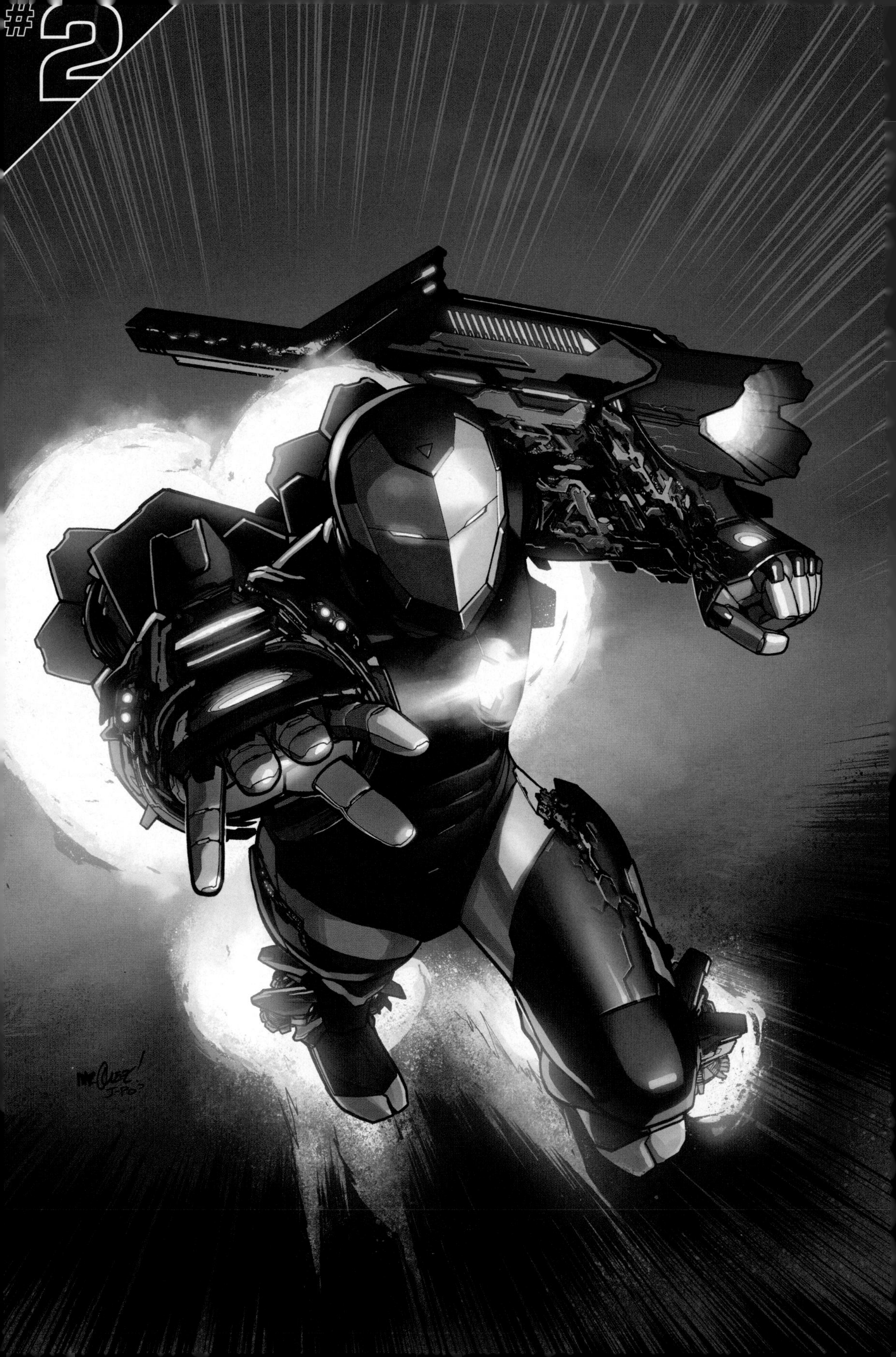
#2

YOU ARE VICTOR VON DOOM?

YES.

AND I ASSUME YOUR ARMOR SENSORS AND A.I. HAVE VERIFIED *MUCH* THE SAME THING.

THAT *IS* VICTOR VON DOOM.

SHUSH, FRIDAY. WHY ARE YOU NOT WEARING YOUR ARMOR?

THIS IS THE *NEW* ME.

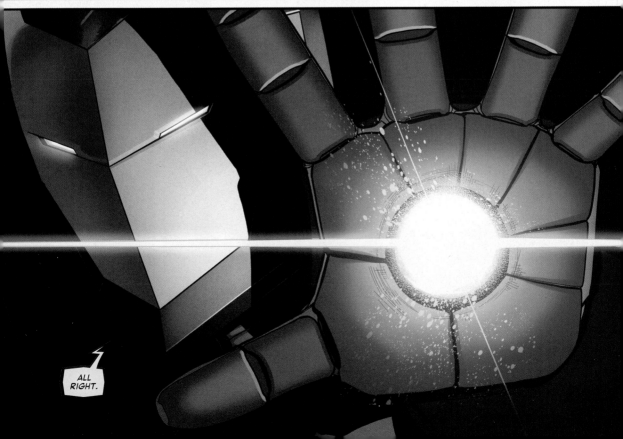

ALL RIGHT.

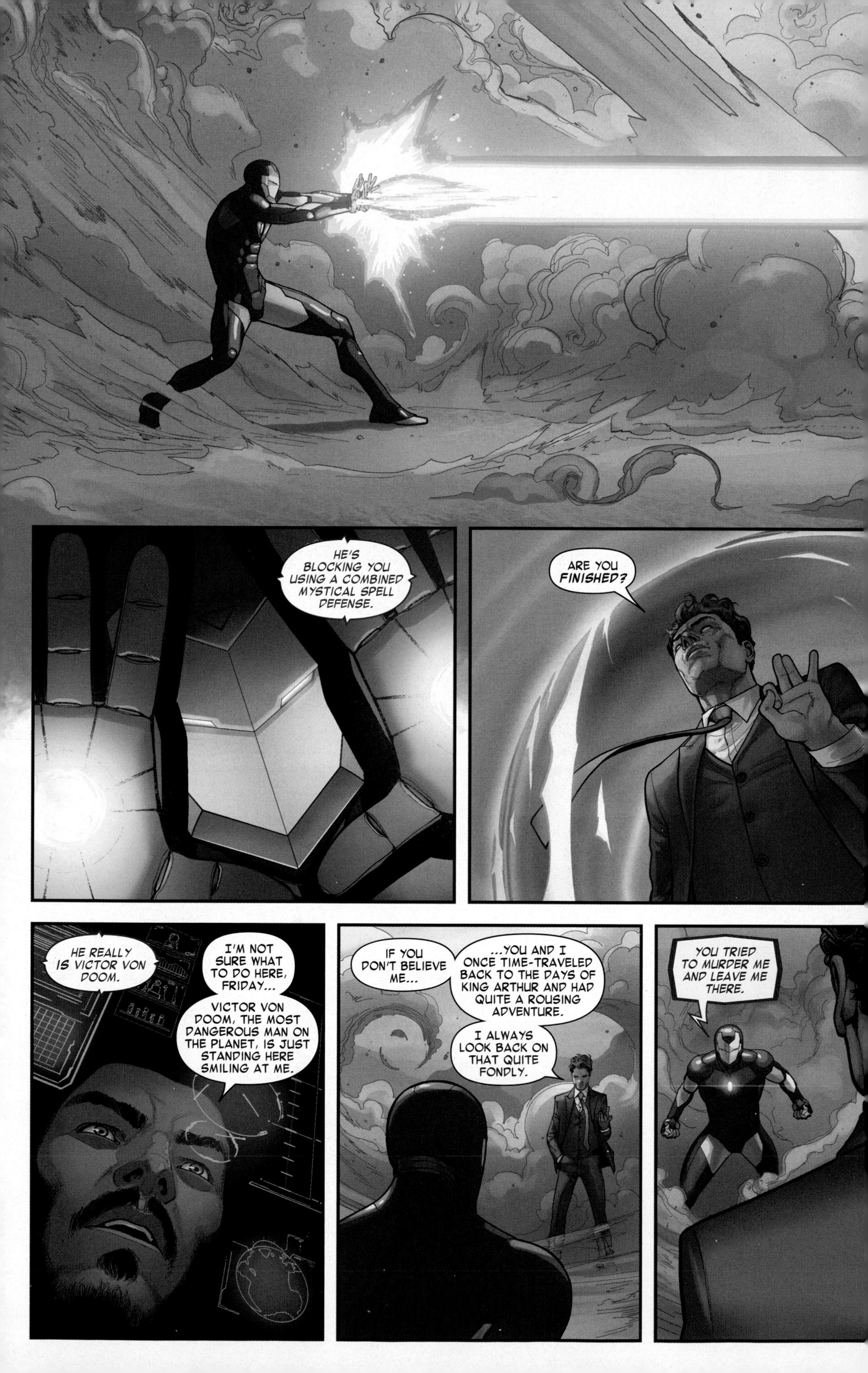

HE'S BLOCKING YOU USING A COMBINED MYSTICAL SPELL DEFENSE.
ARE YOU FINISHED?
HE REALLY IS VICTOR VON DOOM.
I'M NOT SURE WHAT TO DO HERE, FRIDAY...
VICTOR VON DOOM, THE MOST DANGEROUS MAN ON THE PLANET, IS JUST STANDING HERE SMILING AT ME.
IF YOU DON'T BELIEVE ME...
...YOU AND I ONCE TIME-TRAVELED BACK TO THE DAYS OF KING ARTHUR AND HAD QUITE A ROUSING ADVENTURE.
I ALWAYS LOOK BACK ON THAT QUITE FONDLY.
YOU TRIED TO MURDER ME AND LEAVE ME THERE.

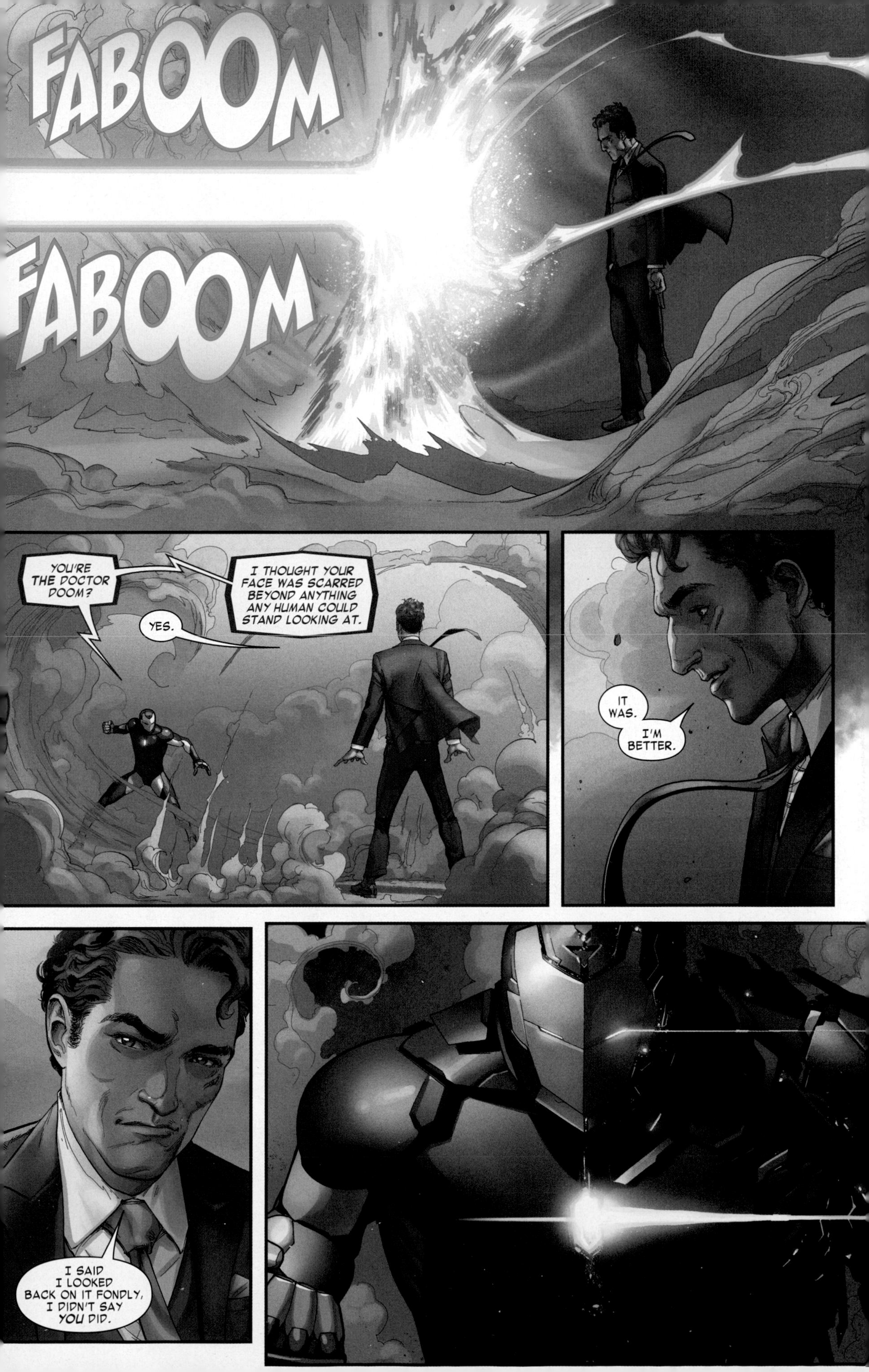
FABOOM
FABOOM
YOU'RE THE DOCTOR DOOM?
YES.
I THOUGHT YOUR FACE WAS SCARRED BEYOND ANYTHING ANY HUMAN COULD STAND LOOKING AT.
IT WAS.
I'M BETTER.
I SAID I LOOKED BACK ON IT FONDLY, I DIDN'T SAY YOU DID.

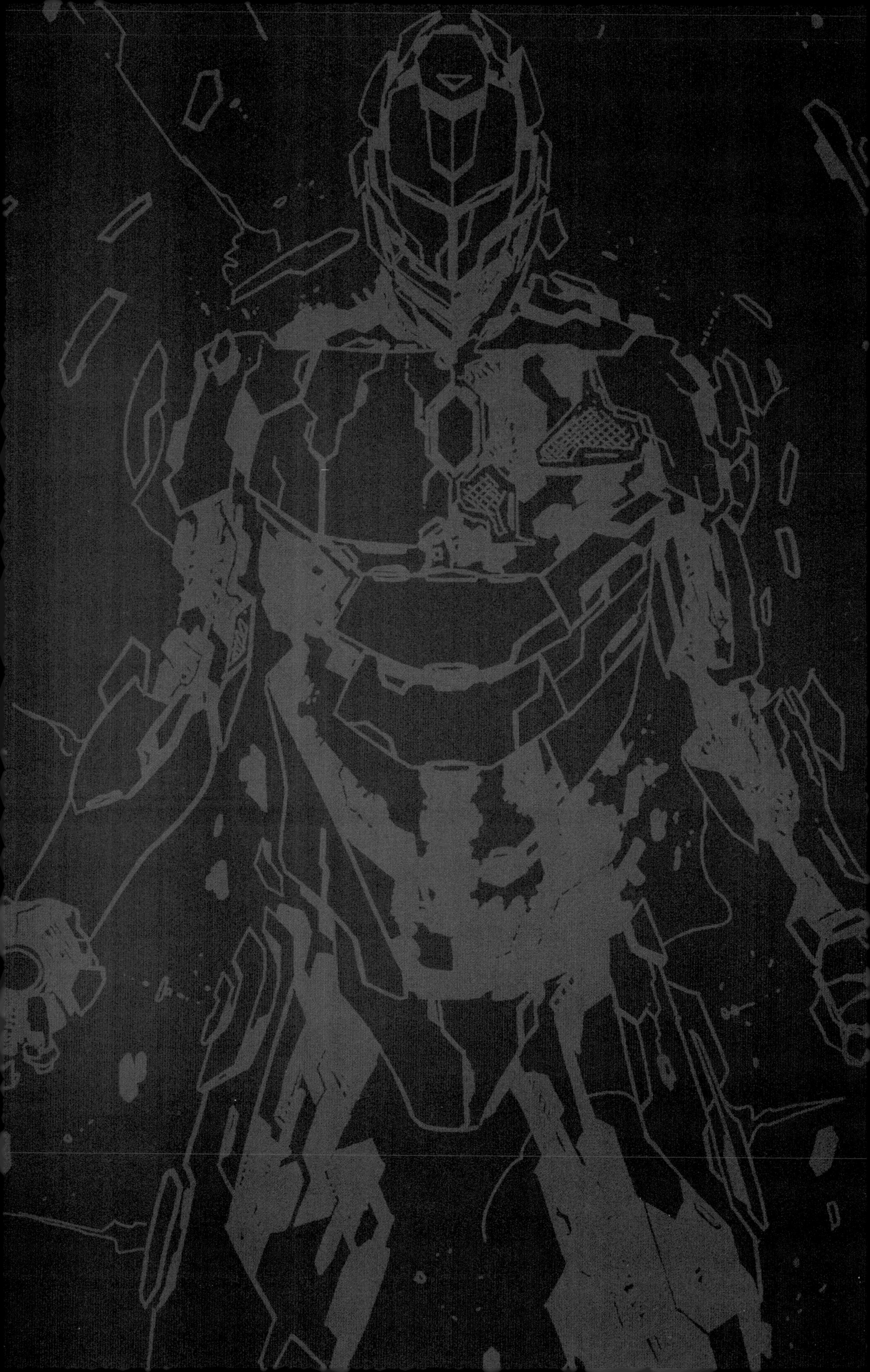

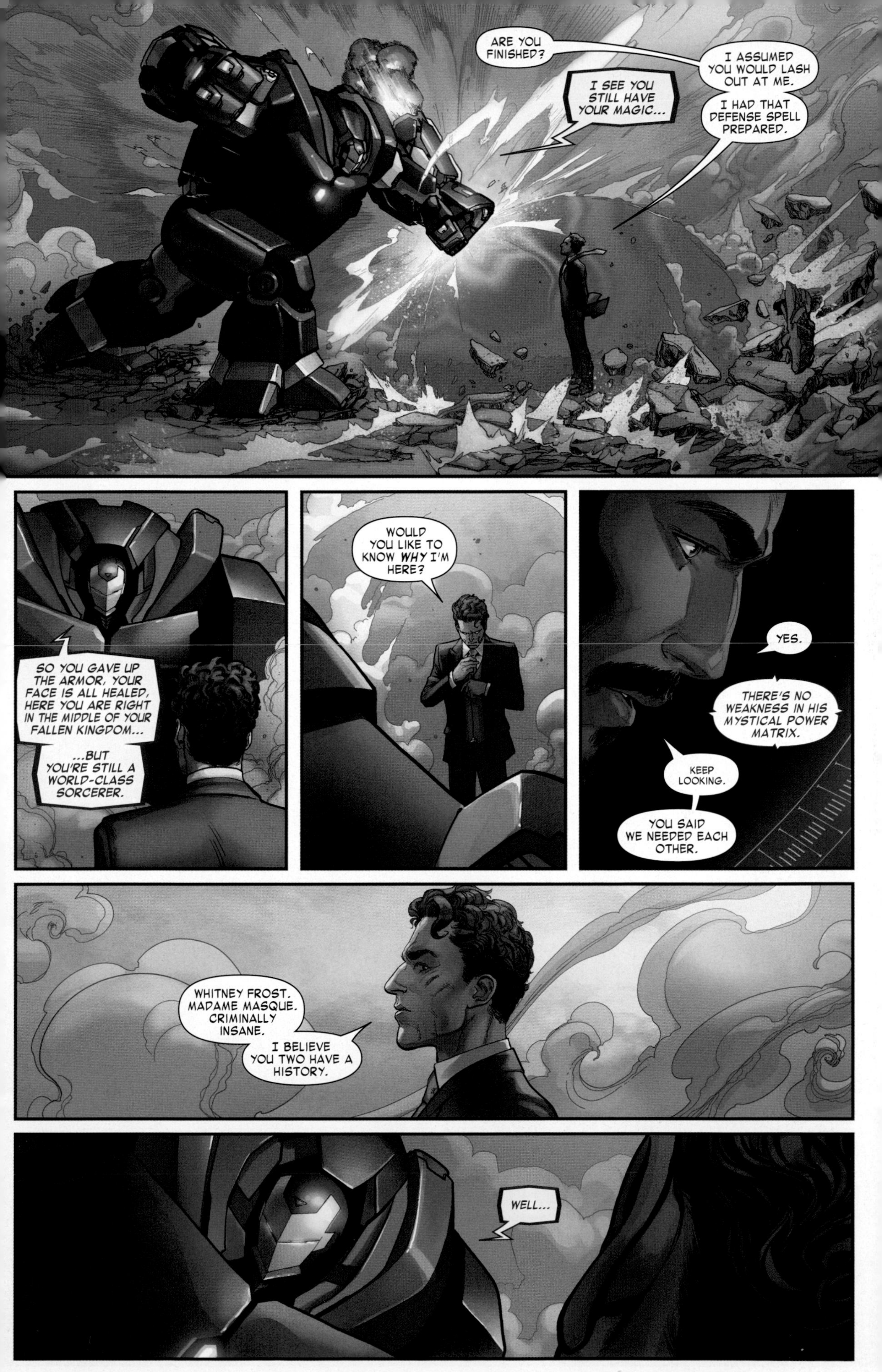
ARE YOU FINISHED?
I SEE YOU STILL HAVE YOUR MAGIC...
I ASSUMED YOU WOULD LASH OUT AT ME.
I HAD THAT DEFENSE SPELL PREPARED.
SO YOU GAVE UP THE ARMOR, YOUR FACE IS ALL HEALED, HERE YOU ARE RIGHT IN THE MIDDLE OF YOUR FALLEN KINGDOM...
...BUT YOU'RE STILL A WORLD-CLASS SORCERER.
WOULD YOU LIKE TO KNOW WHY I'M HERE?
YES.
THERE'S NO WEAKNESS IN HIS MYSTICAL POWER MATRIX.
KEEP LOOKING.
YOU SAID WE NEEDED EACH OTHER.
WHITNEY FROST. MADAME MASQUE. CRIMINALLY INSANE.
I BELIEVE YOU TWO HAVE A HISTORY.
WELL...

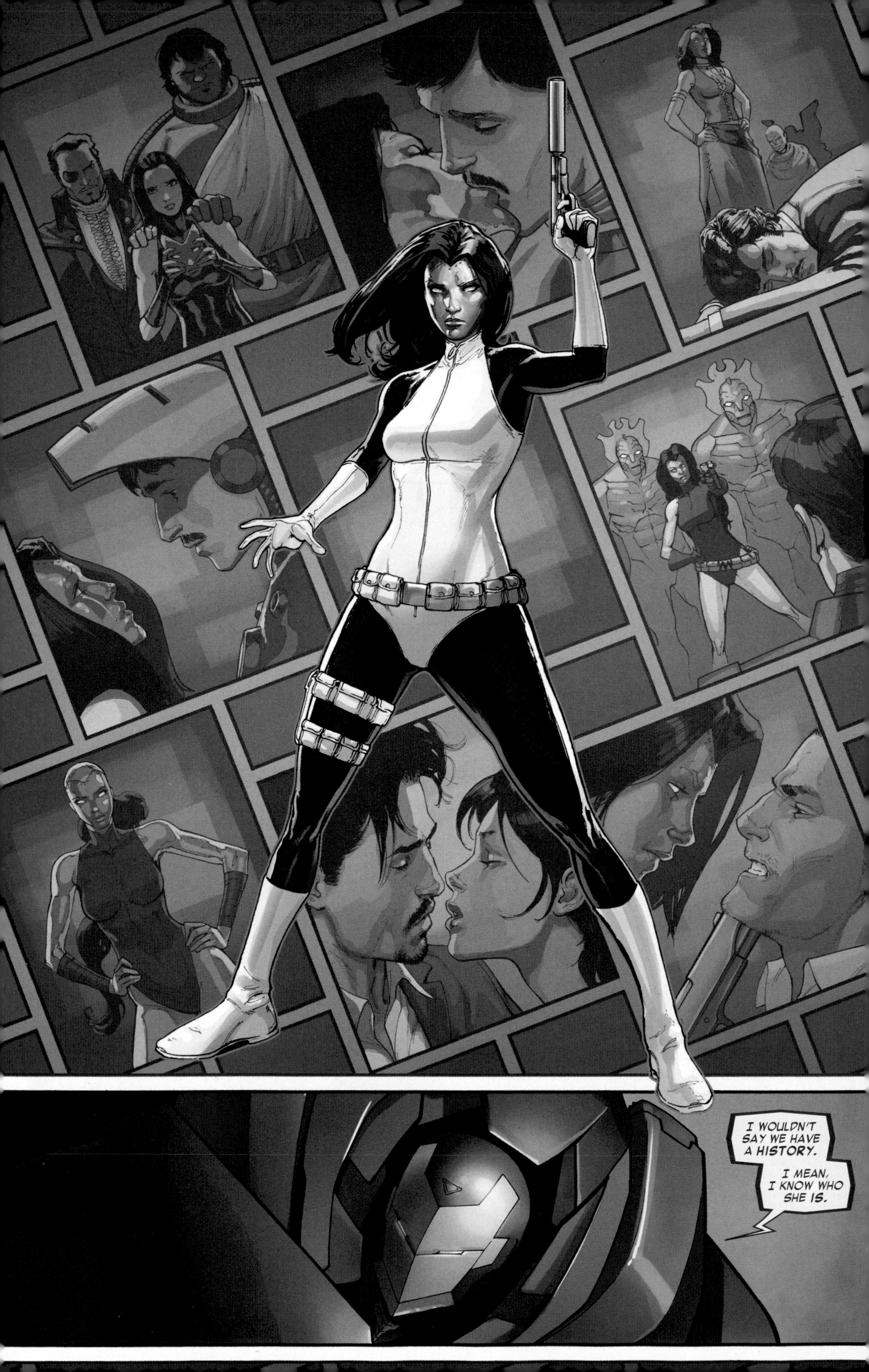
I WOULDN'T SAY WE HAVE A HISTORY.
I MEAN, I KNOW WHO SHE IS.

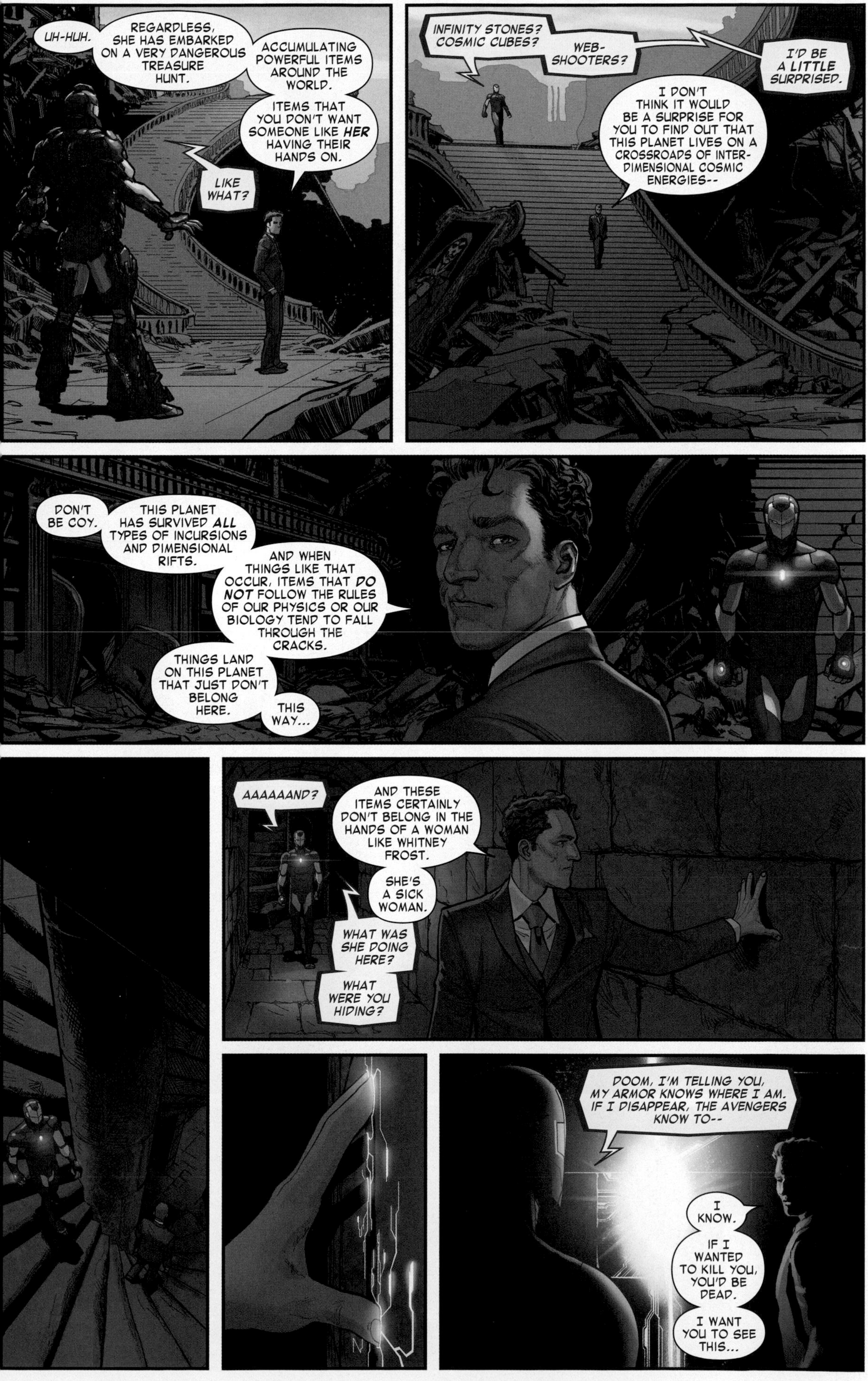
UH-HUH.
REGARDLESS, SHE HAS EMBARKED ON A VERY DANGEROUS TREASURE HUNT.
ACCUMULATING POWERFUL ITEMS AROUND THE WORLD.
ITEMS THAT YOU DON'T WANT SOMEONE LIKE HER HAVING THEIR HANDS ON.
LIKE WHAT?
INFINITY STONES? COSMIC CUBES?
WEB-SHOOTERS?
I'D BE A LITTLE SURPRISED.
I DON'T THINK IT WOULD BE A SURPRISE FOR YOU TO FIND OUT THAT THIS PLANET LIVES ON A CROSSROADS OF INTER-DIMENSIONAL COSMIC ENERGIES--
DON'T BE COY.
THIS PLANET HAS SURVIVED ALL TYPES OF INCURSIONS AND DIMENSIONAL RIFTS.
AND WHEN THINGS LIKE THAT OCCUR, ITEMS THAT DO NOT FOLLOW THE RULES OF OUR PHYSICS OR OUR BIOLOGY TEND TO FALL THROUGH THE CRACKS.
THINGS LAND ON THIS PLANET THAT JUST DON'T BELONG HERE.
THIS WAY...
AAAAAAND?
AND THESE ITEMS CERTAINLY DON'T BELONG IN THE HANDS OF A WOMAN LIKE WHITNEY FROST.
SHE'S A SICK WOMAN.
WHAT WAS SHE DOING HERE?
WHAT WERE YOU HIDING?
DOOM, I'M TELLING YOU, MY ARMOR KNOWS WHERE I AM. IF I DISAPPEAR, THE AVENGERS KNOW TO--
I KNOW.
IF I WANTED TO KILL YOU, YOU'D BE DEAD.
I WANT YOU TO SEE THIS...

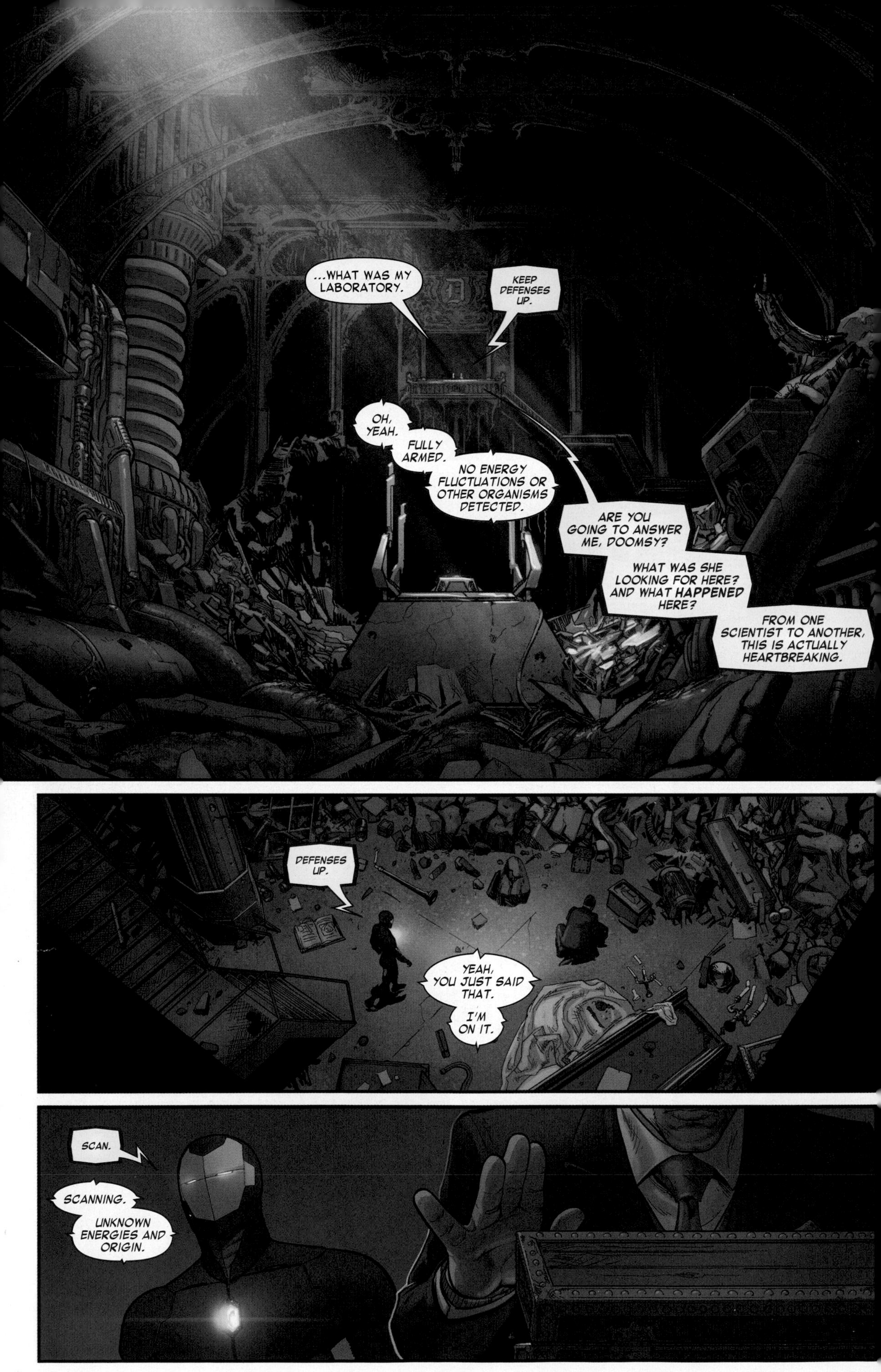
...WHAT WAS MY LABORATORY.
KEEP DEFENSES UP.
OH, YEAH.
FULLY ARMED.
NO ENERGY FLUCTUATIONS OR OTHER ORGANISMS DETECTED.
ARE YOU GOING TO ANSWER ME, DOOMSY?
WHAT WAS SHE LOOKING FOR HERE? AND WHAT HAPPENED HERE?
FROM ONE SCIENTIST TO ANOTHER, THIS IS ACTUALLY HEARTBREAKING.
DEFENSES UP.
YEAH, YOU JUST SAID THAT.
I'M ON IT.
SCAN.
SCANNING.
UNKNOWN ENERGIES AND ORIGIN.

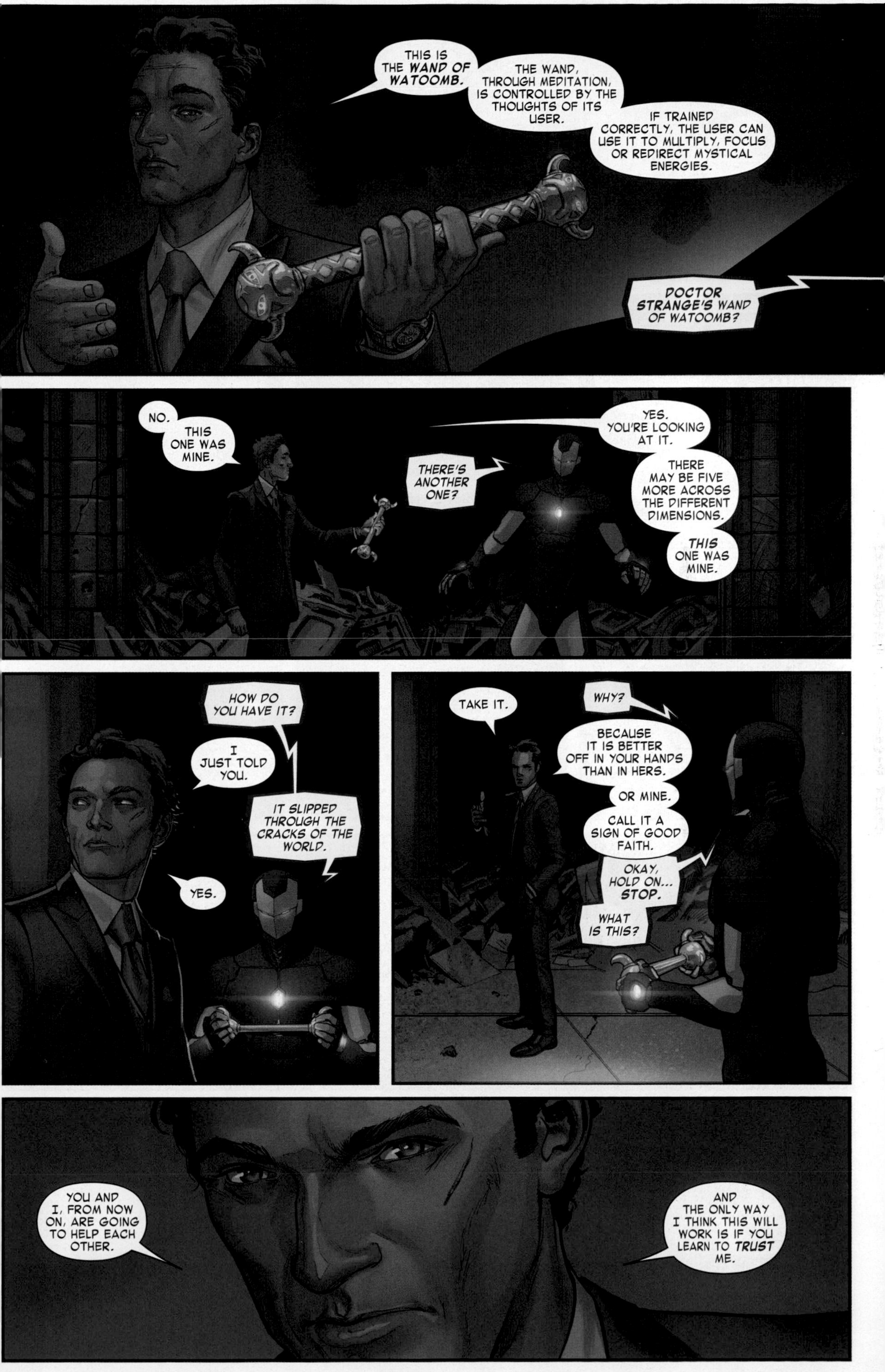
THIS IS THE WAND OF WATOOMB.
THE WAND, THROUGH MEDITATION, IS CONTROLLED BY THE THOUGHTS OF ITS USER.
IF TRAINED CORRECTLY, THE USER CAN USE IT TO MULTIPLY, FOCUS OR REDIRECT MYSTICAL ENERGIES.
DOCTOR STRANGE'S WAND OF WATOOMB?
NO. THIS ONE WAS MINE.
THERE'S ANOTHER ONE?
YES. YOU'RE LOOKING AT IT.
THERE MAY BE FIVE MORE ACROSS THE DIFFERENT DIMENSIONS.
THIS ONE WAS MINE.
HOW DO YOU HAVE IT?
I JUST TOLD YOU.
IT SLIPPED THROUGH THE CRACKS OF THE WORLD.
YES.
TAKE IT.
WHY?
BECAUSE IT IS BETTER OFF IN YOUR HANDS THAN IN HERS.
OR MINE.
CALL IT A SIGN OF GOOD FAITH.
OKAY, HOLD ON... STOP.
WHAT IS THIS?
YOU AND I, FROM NOW ON, ARE GOING TO HELP EACH OTHER.
AND THE ONLY WAY I THINK THIS WILL WORK IS IF YOU LEARN TO TRUST ME.

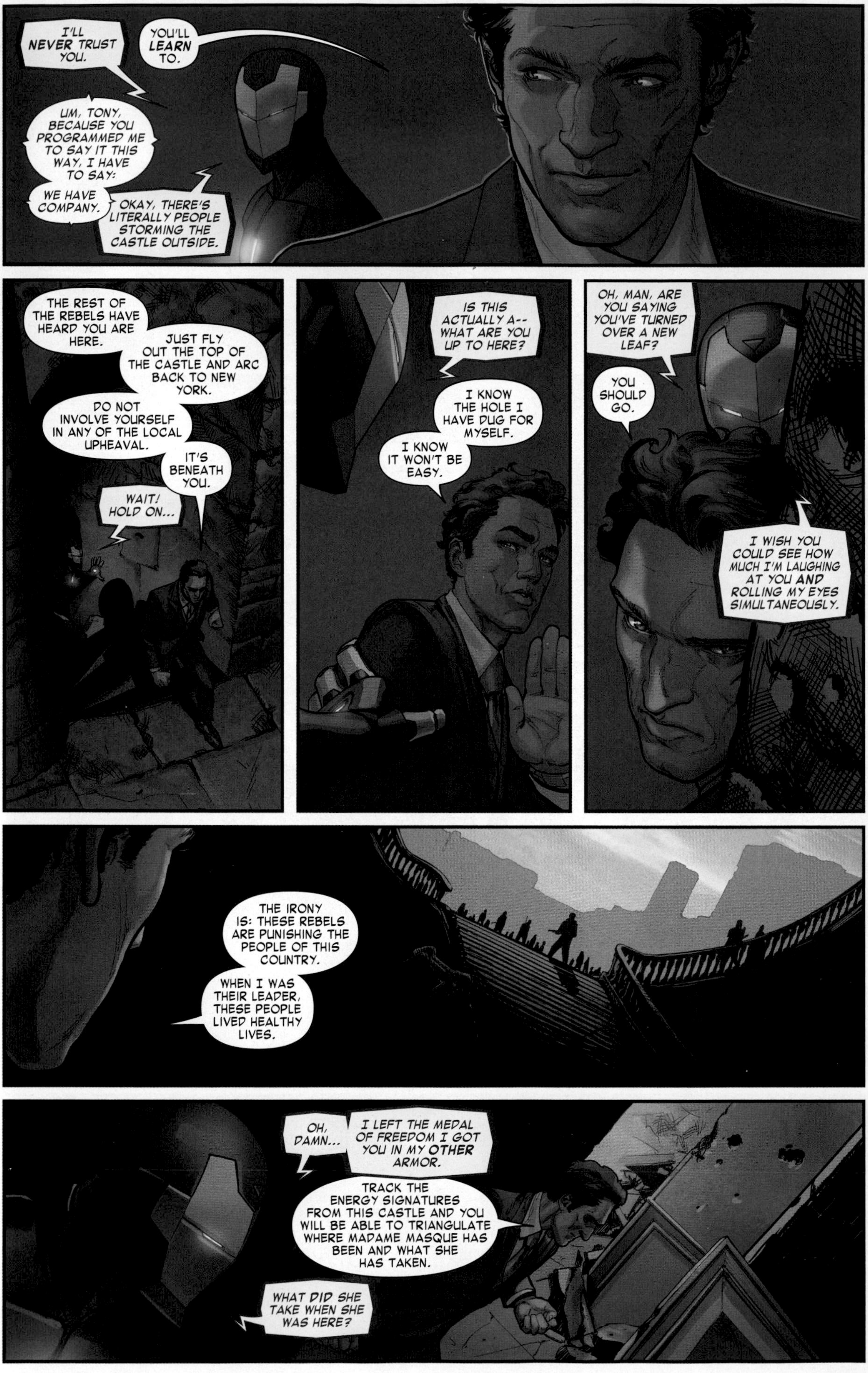
I'LL NEVER TRUST YOU.
YOU'LL LEARN TO.
UM, TONY, BECAUSE YOU PROGRAMMED ME TO SAY IT THIS WAY, I HAVE TO SAY:
WE HAVE COMPANY.
OKAY, THERE'S LITERALLY PEOPLE STORMING THE CASTLE OUTSIDE.
THE REST OF THE REBELS HAVE HEARD YOU ARE HERE.
JUST FLY OUT THE TOP OF THE CASTLE AND ARC BACK TO NEW YORK.
DO NOT INVOLVE YOURSELF IN ANY OF THE LOCAL UPHEAVAL.
IT'S BENEATH YOU.
WAIT! HOLD ON...
IS THIS ACTUALLY A-- WHAT ARE YOU UP TO HERE?
I KNOW THE HOLE I HAVE DUG FOR MYSELF.
I KNOW IT WON'T BE EASY.
OH, MAN, ARE YOU SAYING YOU'VE TURNED OVER A NEW LEAF?
YOU SHOULD GO.
I WISH YOU COULD SEE HOW MUCH I'M LAUGHING AT YOU AND ROLLING MY EYES SIMULTANEOUSLY.
THE IRONY IS: THESE REBELS ARE PUNISHING THE PEOPLE OF THIS COUNTRY.
WHEN I WAS THEIR LEADER, THESE PEOPLE LIVED HEALTHY LIVES.
OH, DAMN...
I LEFT THE MEDAL OF FREEDOM I GOT YOU IN MY OTHER ARMOR.
TRACK THE ENERGY SIGNATURES FROM THIS CASTLE AND YOU WILL BE ABLE TO TRIANGULATE WHERE MADAME MASQUE HAS BEEN AND WHAT SHE HAS TAKEN.
WHAT DID SHE TAKE WHEN SHE WAS HERE?

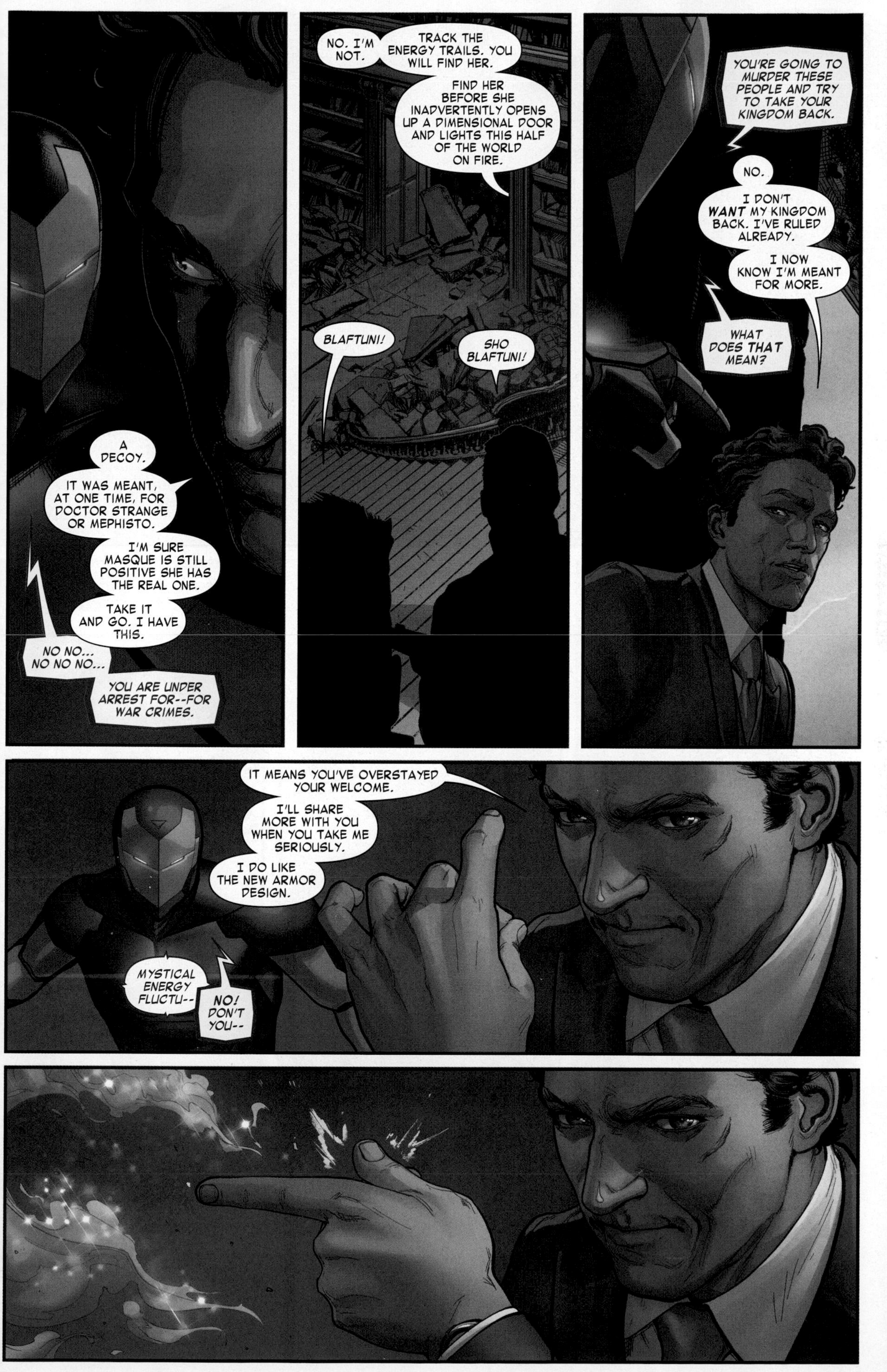
A DECOY.
IT WAS MEANT, AT ONE TIME, FOR DOCTOR STRANGE OR MEPHISTO.
I'M SURE MASQUE IS STILL POSITIVE SHE HAS THE REAL ONE.
TAKE IT AND GO. I HAVE THIS.
NO NO... NO NO NO...
YOU ARE UNDER ARREST FOR--FOR WAR CRIMES.
NO. I'M NOT.
TRACK THE ENERGY TRAILS. YOU WILL FIND HER.
FIND HER BEFORE SHE INADVERTENTLY OPENS UP A DIMENSIONAL DOOR AND LIGHTS THIS HALF OF THE WORLD ON FIRE.
BLAFTUNI!
SHO BLAFTUNI!
YOU'RE GOING TO MURDER THESE PEOPLE AND TRY TO TAKE YOUR KINGDOM BACK.
NO.
I DON'T WANT MY KINGDOM BACK. I'VE RULED ALREADY.
I NOW KNOW I'M MEANT FOR MORE.
WHAT DOES THAT MEAN?
IT MEANS YOU'VE OVERSTAYED YOUR WELCOME.
I'LL SHARE MORE WITH YOU WHEN YOU TAKE ME SERIOUSLY.
I DO LIKE THE NEW ARMOR DESIGN.
MYSTICAL ENERGY FLUCTU--
NO! DON'T YOU--

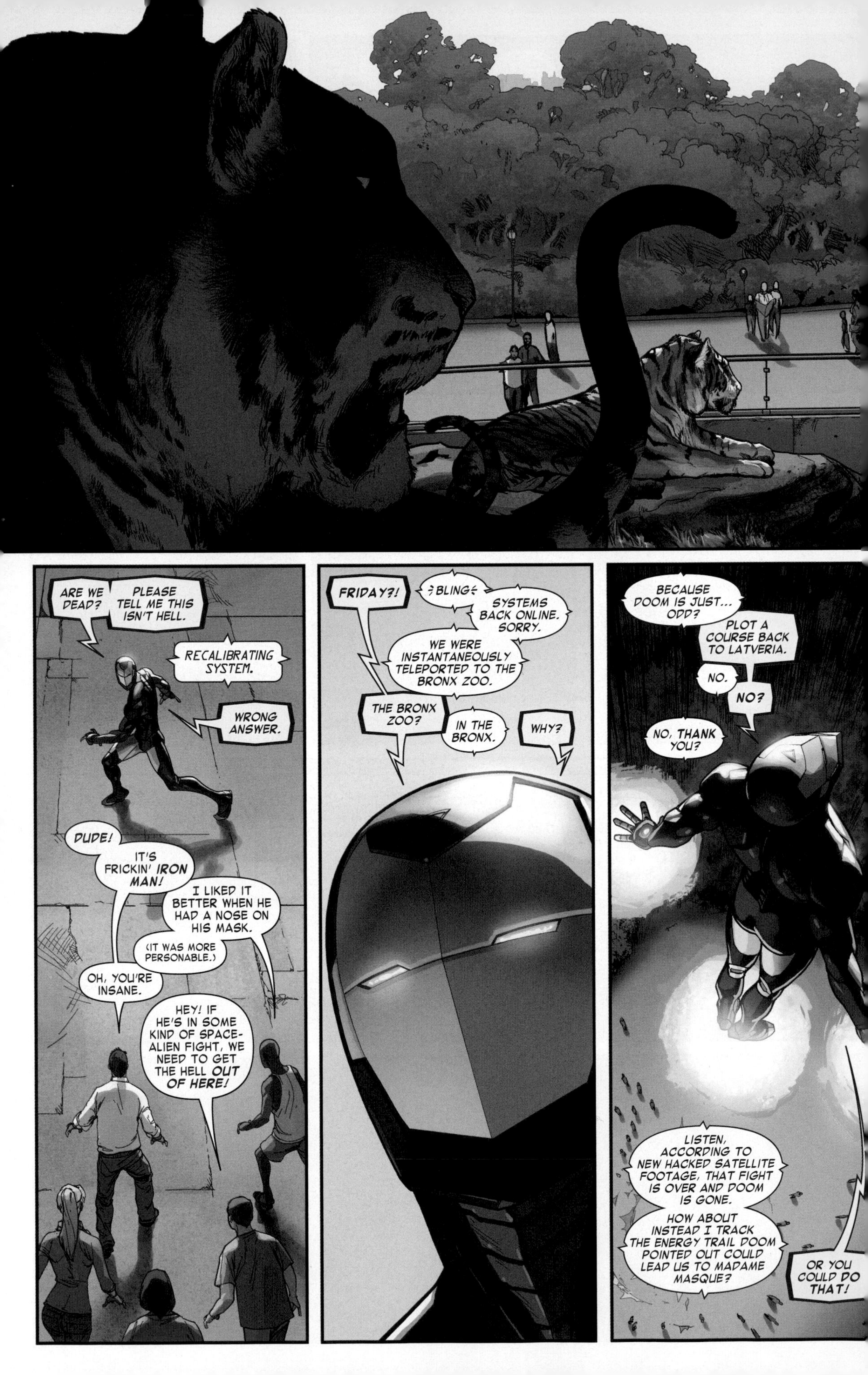
ARE WE DEAD?
PLEASE TELL ME THIS ISN'T HELL.
RECALIBRATING SYSTEM.
WRONG ANSWER.
DUDE!
IT'S FRICKIN' IRON MAN!
I LIKED IT BETTER WHEN HE HAD A NOSE ON HIS MASK.
(IT WAS MORE PERSONABLE.)
OH, YOU'RE INSANE.
HEY! IF HE'S IN SOME KIND OF SPACE-ALIEN FIGHT, WE NEED TO GET THE HELL OUT OF HERE!
FRIDAY?!
BLING
SYSTEMS BACK ONLINE. SORRY.
WE WERE INSTANTANEOUSLY TELEPORTED TO THE BRONX ZOO.
THE BRONX ZOO?
IN THE BRONX.
WHY?
BECAUSE DOOM IS JUST... ODD?
PLOT A COURSE BACK TO LATVERIA.
NO.
NO?
NO, THANK YOU?
LISTEN, ACCORDING TO NEW HACKED SATELLITE FOOTAGE, THAT FIGHT IS OVER AND DOOM IS GONE.
HOW ABOUT INSTEAD I TRACK THE ENERGY TRAIL DOOM POINTED OUT COULD LEAD US TO MADAME MASQUE?
OR YOU COULD DO THAT!

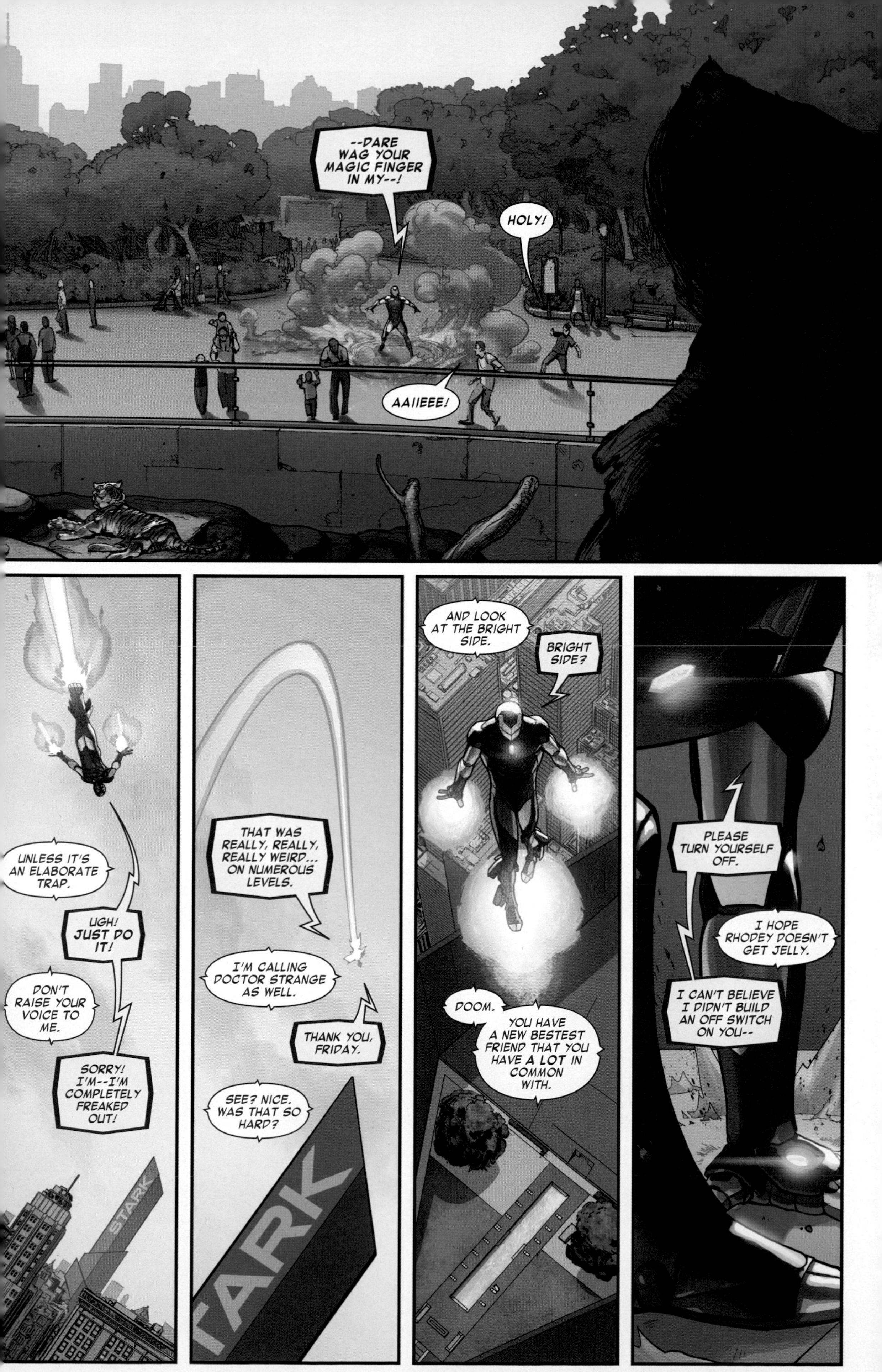
--DARE WAG YOUR MAGIC FINGER IN MY--!
HOLY!
AAIIEEE!
UNLESS IT'S AN ELABORATE TRAP.
UGH! JUST DO IT!
DON'T RAISE YOUR VOICE TO ME.
SORRY! I'M--I'M COMPLETELY FREAKED OUT!
STARK
THAT WAS REALLY, REALLY, REALLY WEIRD... ON NUMEROUS LEVELS.
I'M CALLING DOCTOR STRANGE AS WELL.
THANK YOU, FRIDAY.
SEE? NICE. WAS THAT SO HARD?
TARK
AND LOOK AT THE BRIGHT SIDE.
BRIGHT SIDE?
DOOM.
YOU HAVE A NEW BESTEST FRIEND THAT YOU HAVE A LOT IN COMMON WITH.
PLEASE TURN YOURSELF OFF.
I HOPE RHODEY DOESN'T GET JELLY.
I CAN'T BELIEVE I DIDN'T BUILD AN OFF SWITCH ON YOU--

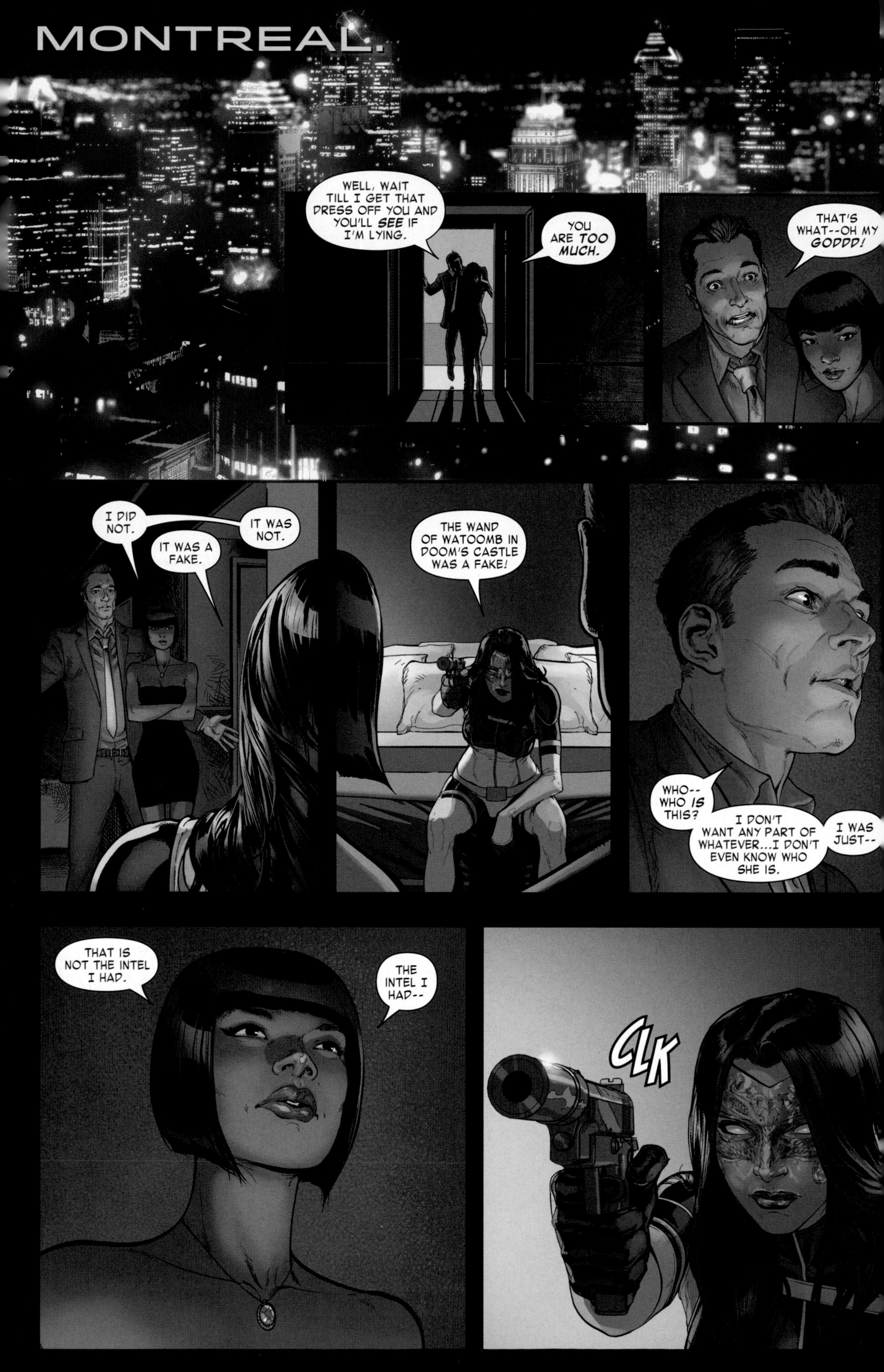
MONTREAL.
WELL, WAIT TILL I GET THAT DRESS OFF YOU AND YOU'LL SEE IF I'M LYING.
YOU ARE TOO MUCH.
THAT'S WHAT--OH MY GODDD!
I DID NOT.
IT WAS NOT.
IT WAS A FAKE.
THE WAND OF WATOOMB IN DOOM'S CASTLE WAS A FAKE!
WHO-- WHO IS THIS?
I DON'T WANT ANY PART OF WHATEVER...I DON'T EVEN KNOW WHO SHE IS.
I WAS JUST--
THAT IS NOT THE INTEL I HAD.
THE INTEL I HAD--
CLK

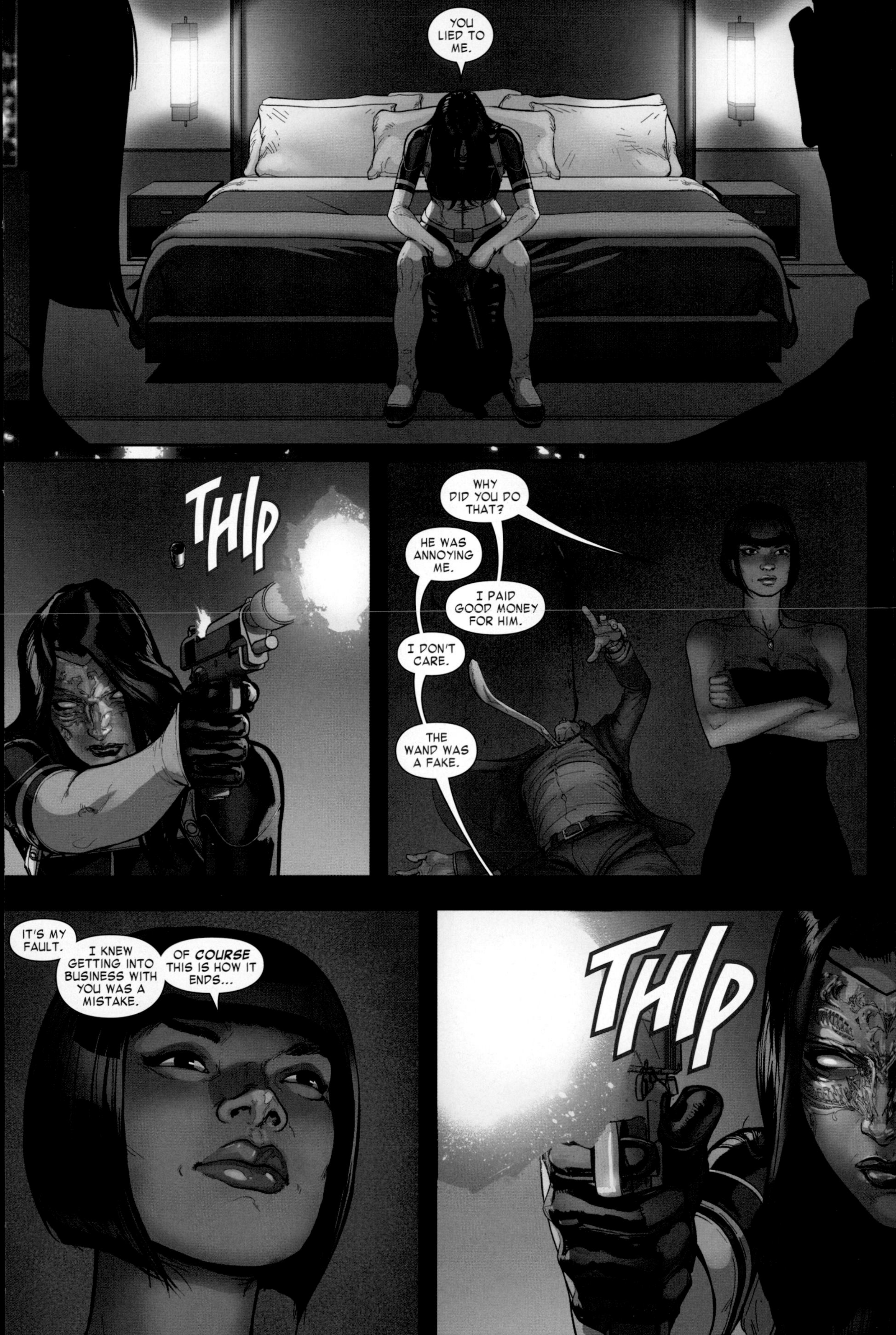
YOU LIED TO ME.
THIP
WHY DID YOU DO THAT?
HE WAS ANNOYING ME.
I PAID GOOD MONEY FOR HIM.
I DON'T CARE.
THE WAND WAS A FAKE.
IT'S MY FAULT.
I KNEW GETTING INTO BUSINESS WITH YOU WAS A MISTAKE.
OF COURSE THIS IS HOW IT ENDS...
THIP

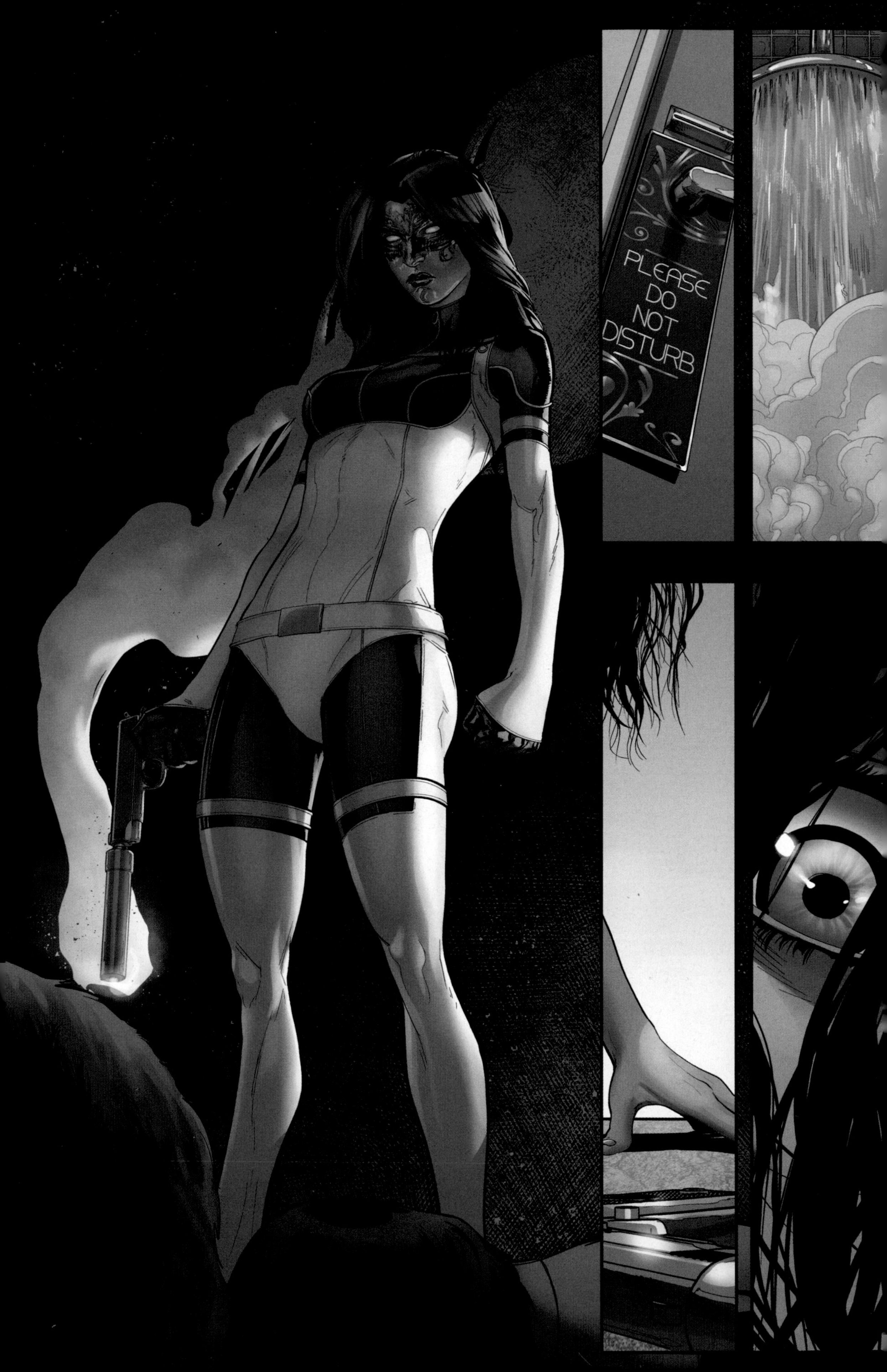

PLEASE DO NOT DISTURB

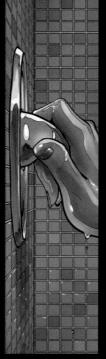

I TOOK THE BULLETS.

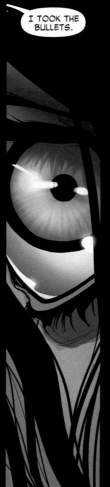

DON'T RUN.

LET'S TALK.

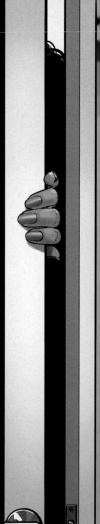

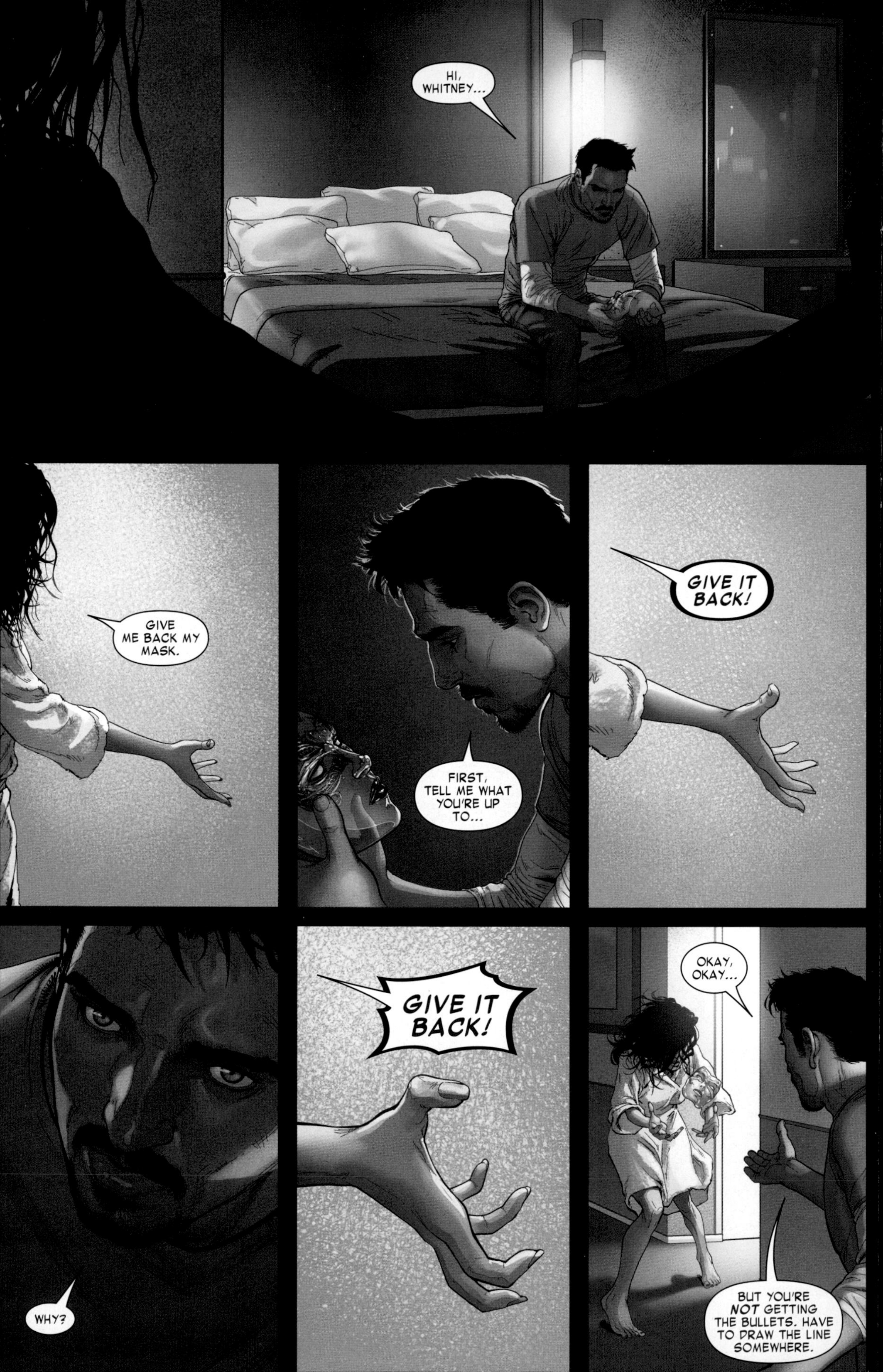
HI, WHITNEY...
GIVE ME BACK MY MASK.
FIRST, TELL ME WHAT YOU'RE UP TO...
GIVE IT BACK!
WHY?
GIVE IT BACK!
OKAY, OKAY...
BUT YOU'RE *NOT* GETTING THE BULLETS. HAVE TO DRAW THE LINE SOMEWHERE.

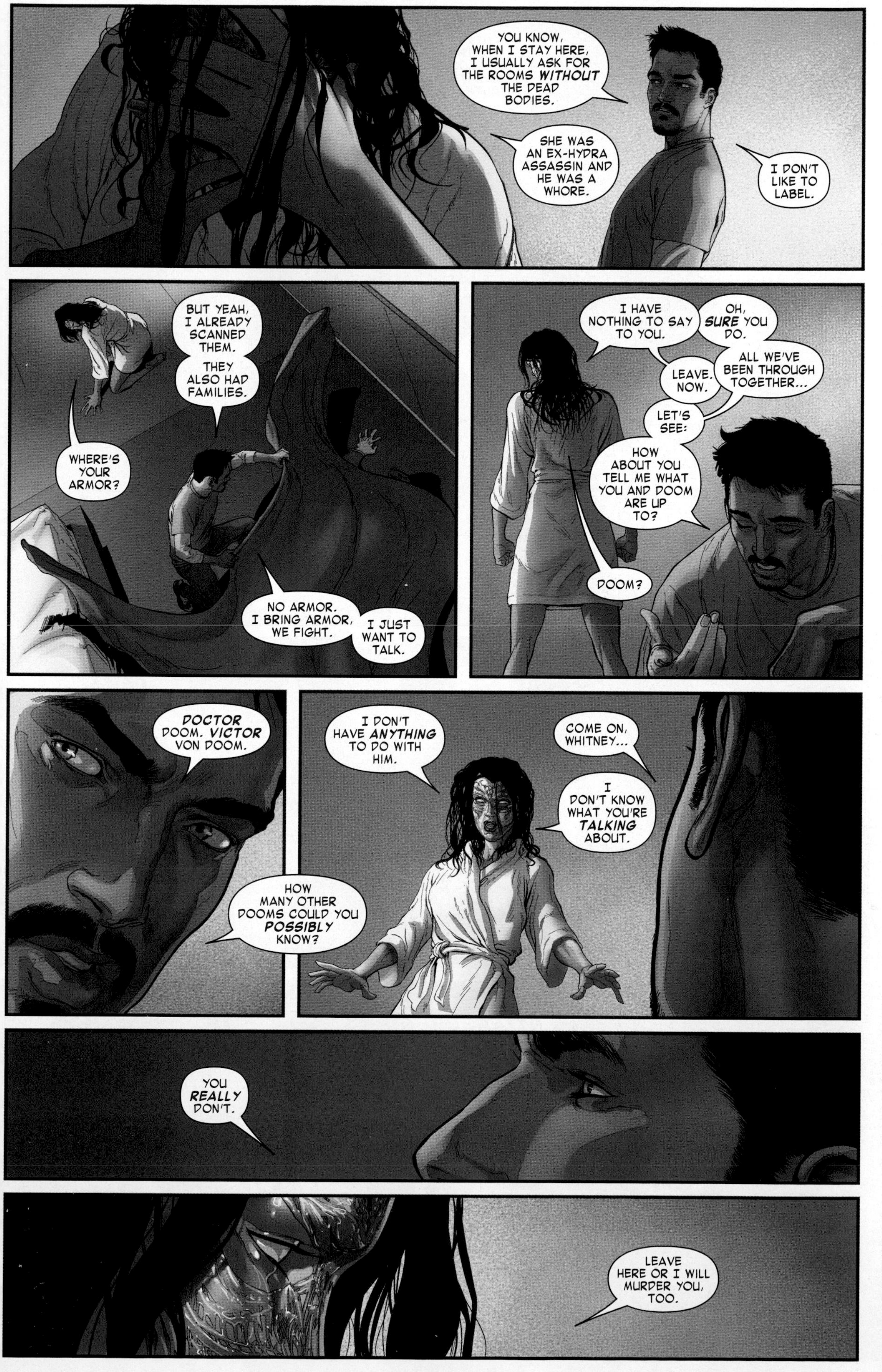
YOU KNOW, WHEN I STAY HERE, I USUALLY ASK FOR THE ROOMS WITHOUT THE DEAD BODIES.
SHE WAS AN EX-HYDRA ASSASSIN AND HE WAS A WHORE.
I DON'T LIKE TO LABEL.
BUT YEAH, I ALREADY SCANNED THEM.
THEY ALSO HAD FAMILIES.
WHERE'S YOUR ARMOR?
NO ARMOR. I BRING ARMOR, WE FIGHT.
I JUST WANT TO TALK.
I HAVE NOTHING TO SAY TO YOU.
OH, SURE YOU DO.
LEAVE. NOW.
ALL WE'VE BEEN THROUGH TOGETHER...
LET'S SEE:
HOW ABOUT YOU TELL ME WHAT YOU AND DOOM ARE UP TO?
DOOM?
DOCTOR DOOM. VICTOR VON DOOM.
HOW MANY OTHER DOOMS COULD YOU POSSIBLY KNOW?
I DON'T HAVE ANYTHING TO DO WITH HIM.
COME ON, WHITNEY...
I DON'T KNOW WHAT YOU'RE TALKING ABOUT.
YOU REALLY DON'T.
LEAVE HERE OR I WILL MURDER YOU, TOO.

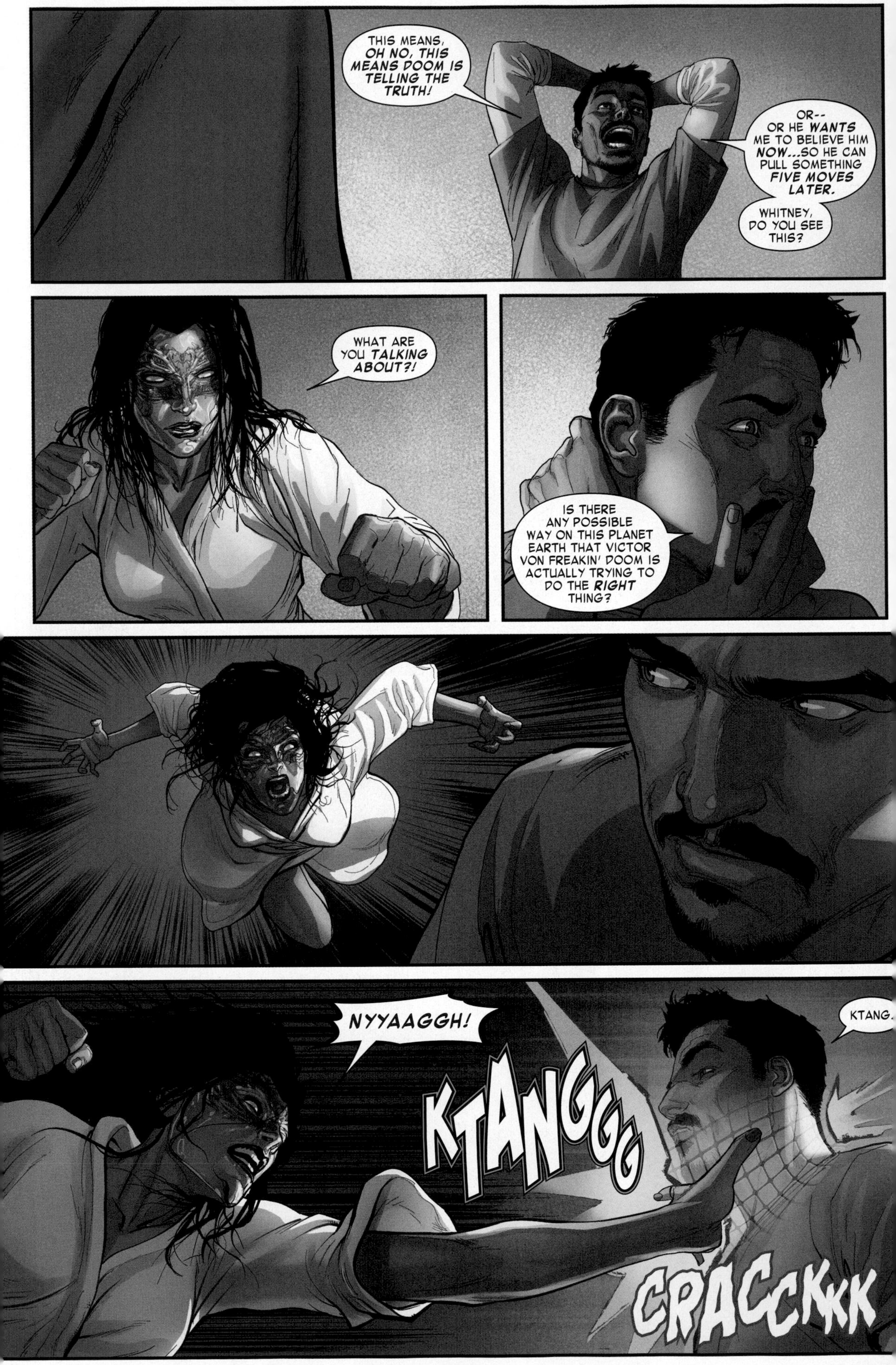
THIS MEANS, OH NO, THIS MEANS DOOM IS TELLING THE TRUTH!
OR-- OR HE WANTS ME TO BELIEVE HIM NOW...SO HE CAN PULL SOMETHING FIVE MOVES LATER.
WHITNEY, DO YOU SEE THIS?
WHAT ARE YOU TALKING ABOUT?!
IS THERE ANY POSSIBLE WAY ON THIS PLANET EARTH THAT VICTOR VON FREAKIN' DOOM IS ACTUALLY TRYING TO DO THE RIGHT THING?
NYYAAGGH!
KTANGGG
KTANG.
CRACCKKK

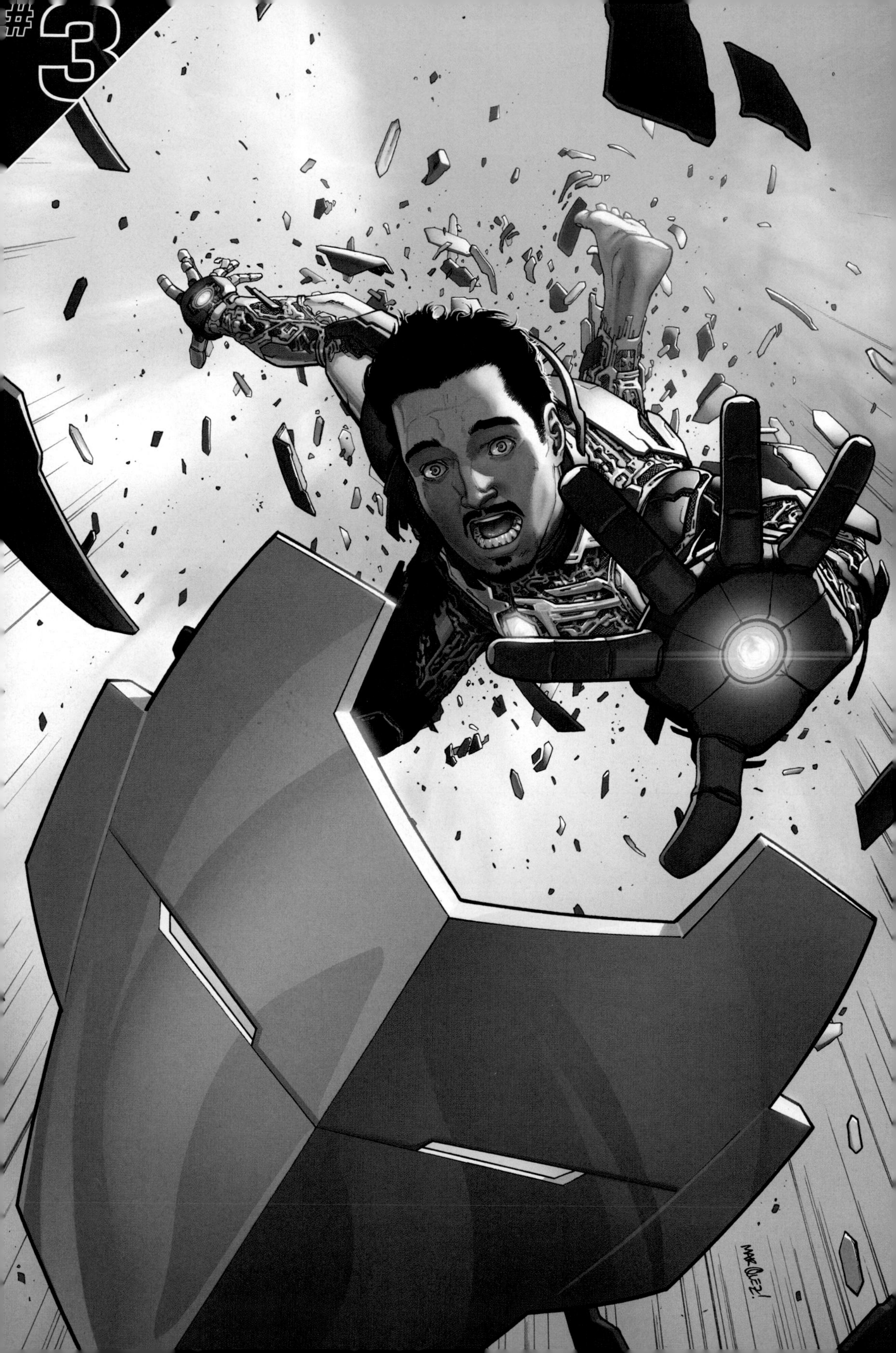
#3

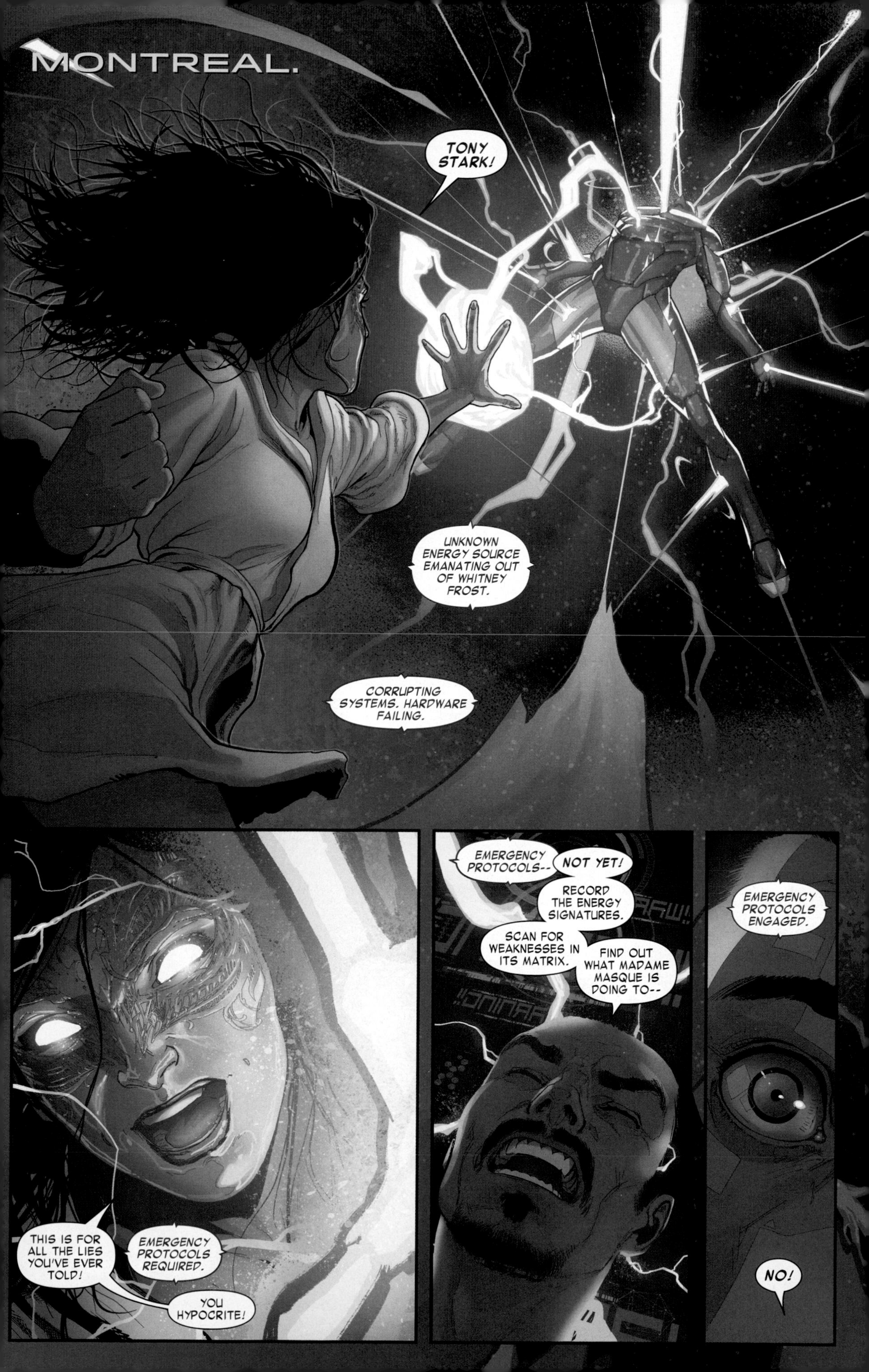
MONTREAL.
TONY STARK!
UNKNOWN ENERGY SOURCE EMANATING OUT OF WHITNEY FROST.
CORRUPTING SYSTEMS. HARDWARE FAILING.
THIS IS FOR ALL THE LIES YOU'VE EVER TOLD!
EMERGENCY PROTOCOLS REQUIRED.
YOU HYPOCRITE!
EMERGENCY PROTOCOLS--
NOT YET!
RECORD THE ENERGY SIGNATURES.
SCAN FOR WEAKNESSES IN ITS MATRIX.
FIND OUT WHAT MADAME MASQUE IS DOING TO--
EMERGENCY PROTOCOLS ENGAGED.
NO!

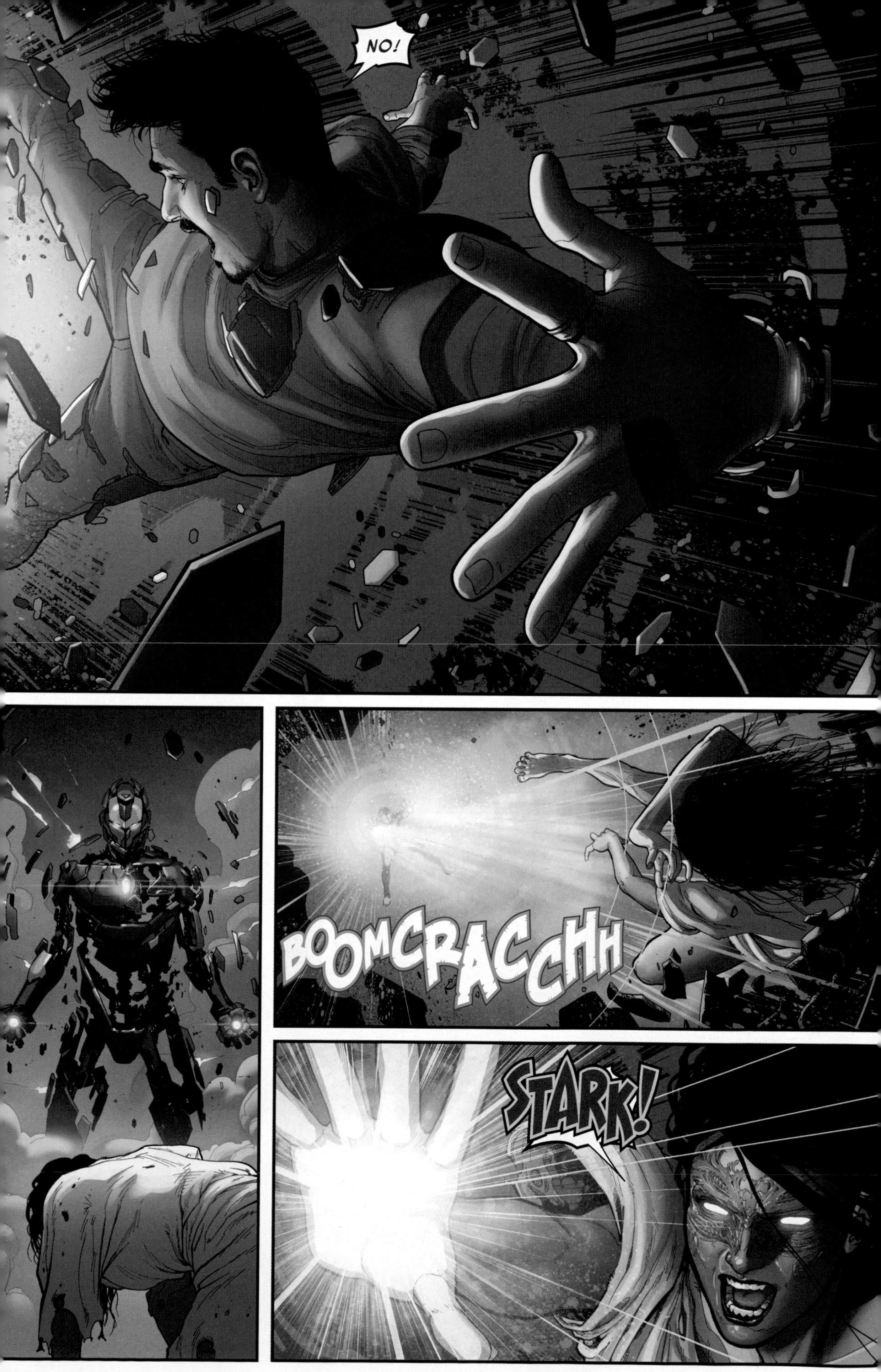
NO!
BOOMCRACCHH
STARK!

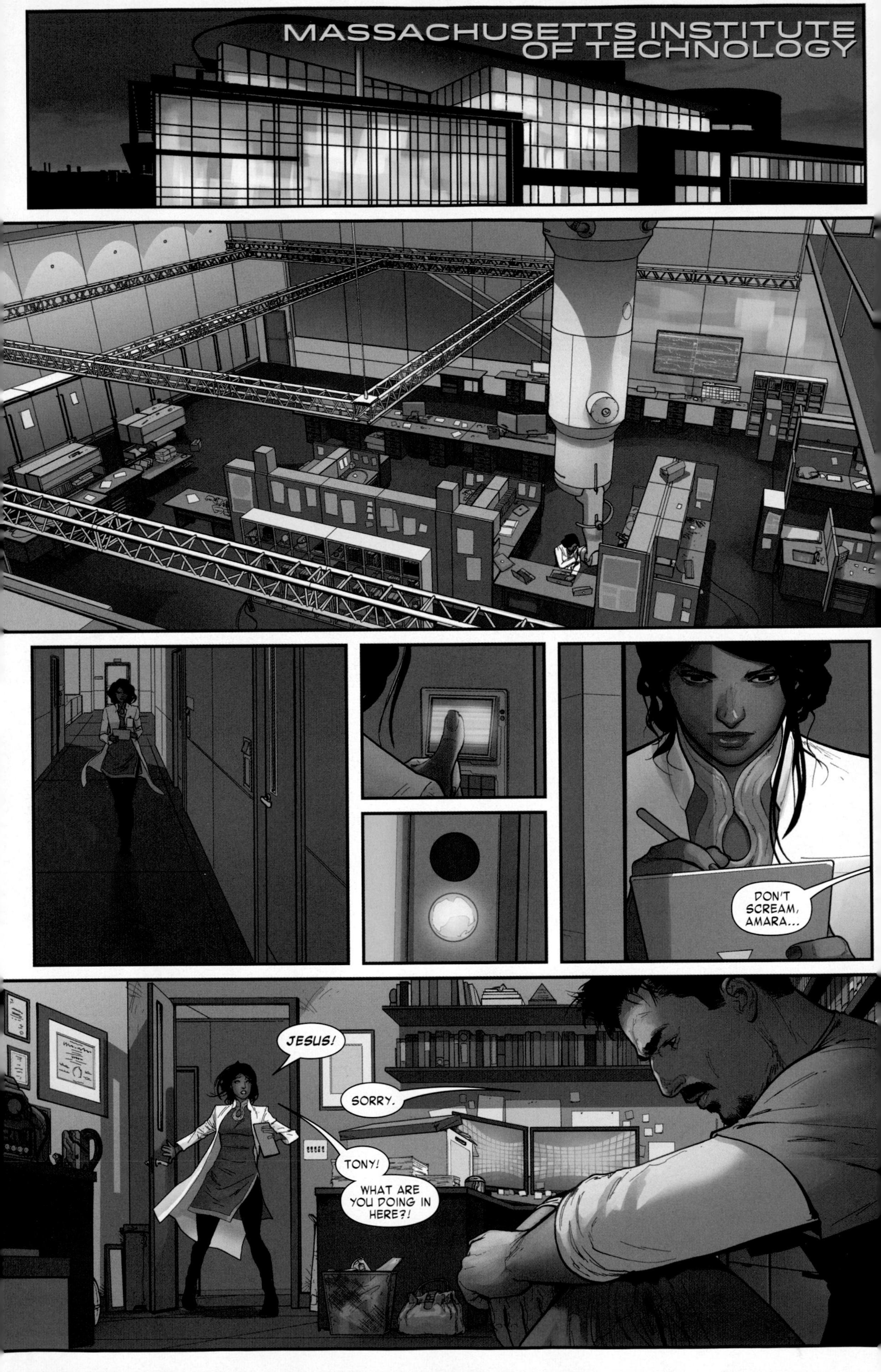
MASSACHUSETTS INSTITUTE OF TECHNOLOGY
DON'T SCREAM, AMARA...
JESUS!
SORRY.
TONY!
WHAT ARE YOU DOING IN HERE?!

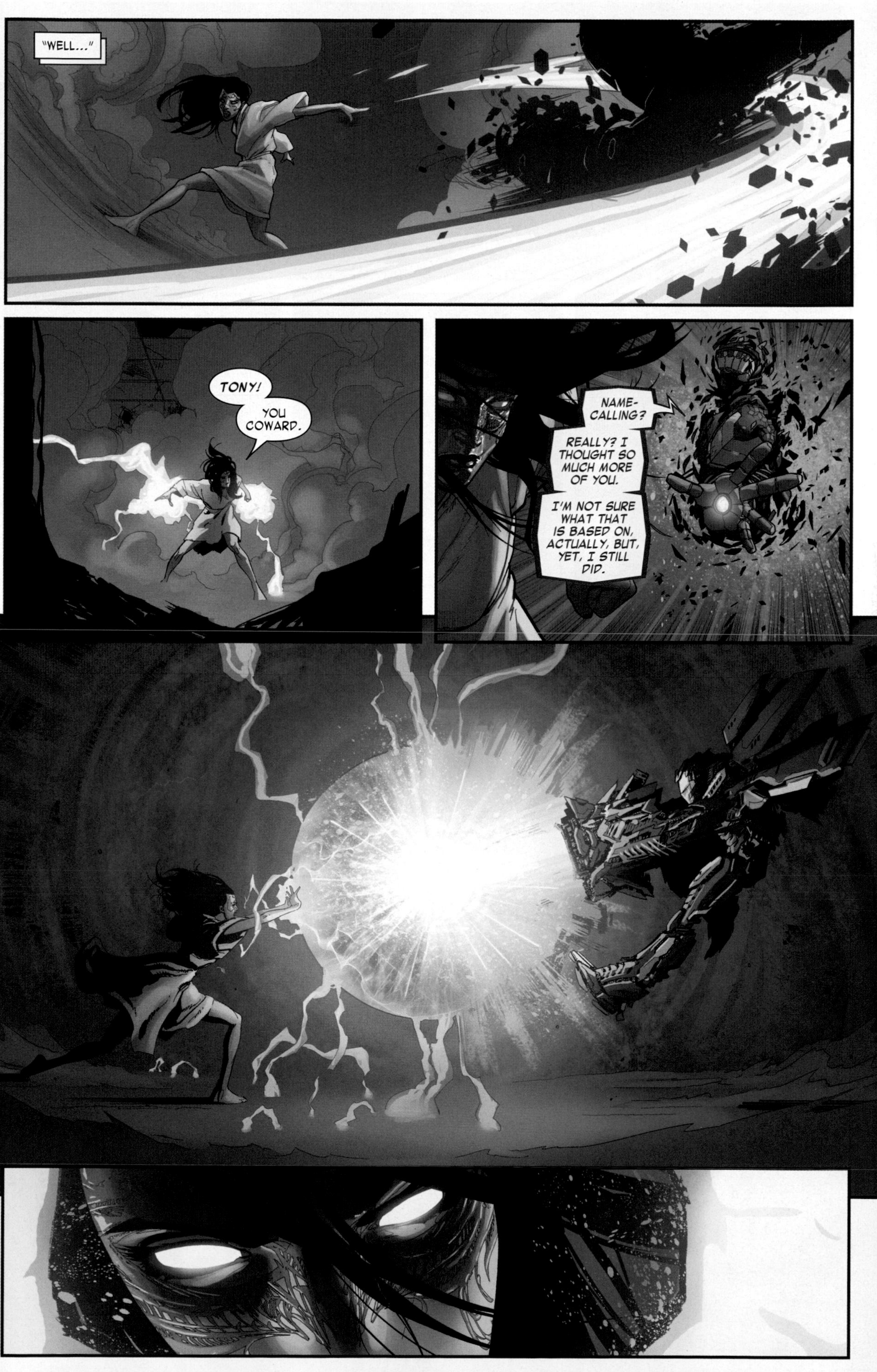
"WELL..."
TONY!
YOU COWARD.
NAME-CALLING?
REALLY? I THOUGHT SO MUCH MORE OF YOU.
I'M NOT SURE WHAT THAT IS BASED ON, ACTUALLY, BUT, YET, I STILL DID.

WHAT IS GOING ON WITH YOU, WHITNEY?
YOU'RE RUNNING AROUND MURDERING AND STEALING...
HOW DO YOU THINK IT'S GOING TO END FOR YOU IF YOU KEEP MESSING AROUND LIKE THIS?
RRRAAGGHH!
SMAAASSHH
SIGNAL LOST ...REACQUIRING...
RUDE.

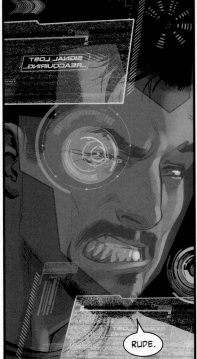

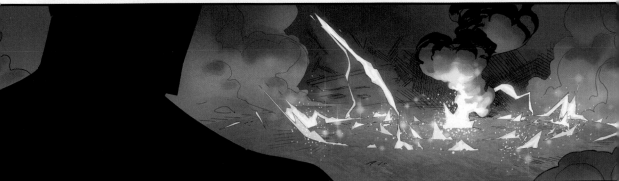

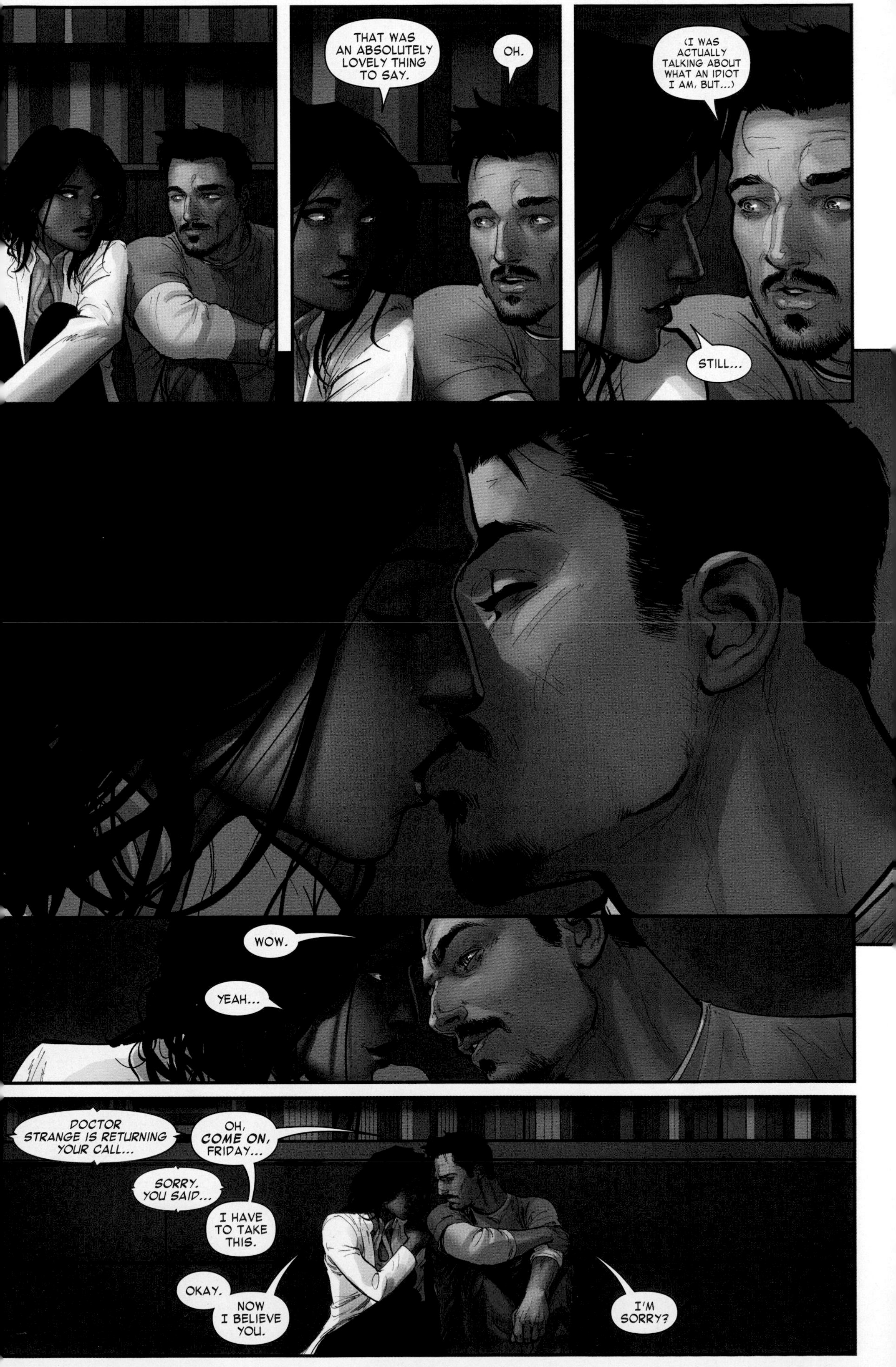
THAT WAS AN ABSOLUTELY LOVELY THING TO SAY.
OH.
(I WAS ACTUALLY TALKING ABOUT WHAT AN IDIOT I AM, BUT...)
STILL...
WOW.
YEAH...
DOCTOR STRANGE IS RETURNING YOUR CALL...
OH, COME ON, FRIDAY...
SORRY. YOU SAID...
I HAVE TO TAKE THIS.
OKAY.
NOW I BELIEVE YOU.
I'M SORRY?

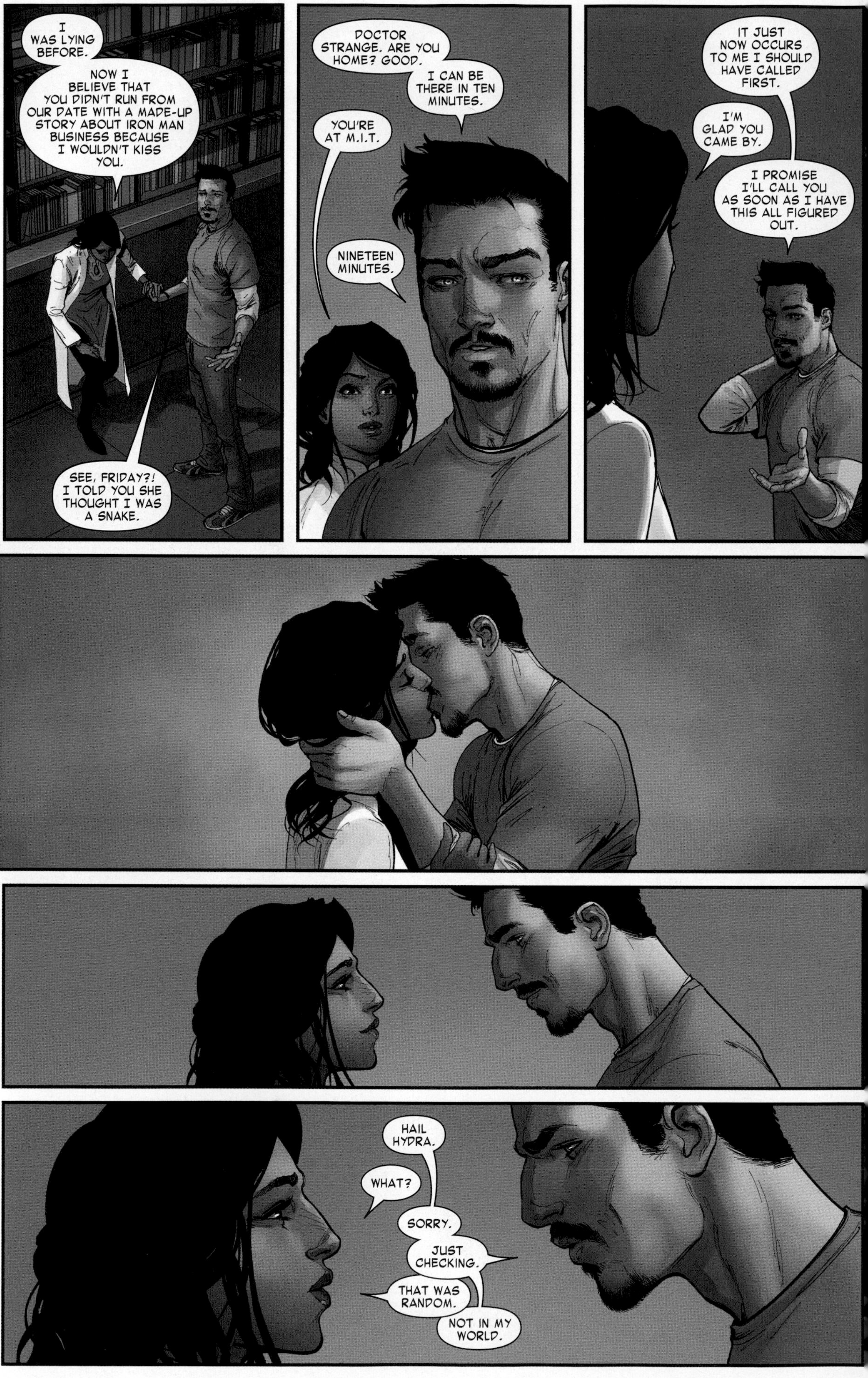

I WAS LYING BEFORE.
NOW I BELIEVE THAT YOU DIDN'T RUN FROM OUR DATE WITH A MADE-UP STORY ABOUT IRON MAN BUSINESS BECAUSE I WOULDN'T KISS YOU.
SEE, FRIDAY?! I TOLD YOU SHE THOUGHT I WAS A SNAKE.
DOCTOR STRANGE. ARE YOU HOME? GOOD.
I CAN BE THERE IN TEN MINUTES.
YOU'RE AT M.I.T.
NINETEEN MINUTES.
IT JUST NOW OCCURS TO ME I SHOULD HAVE CALLED FIRST.
I'M GLAD YOU CAME BY.
I PROMISE I'LL CALL YOU AS SOON AS I HAVE THIS ALL FIGURED OUT.
HAIL HYDRA.
WHAT?
SORRY.
JUST CHECKING.
THAT WAS RANDOM.
NOT IN MY WORLD.

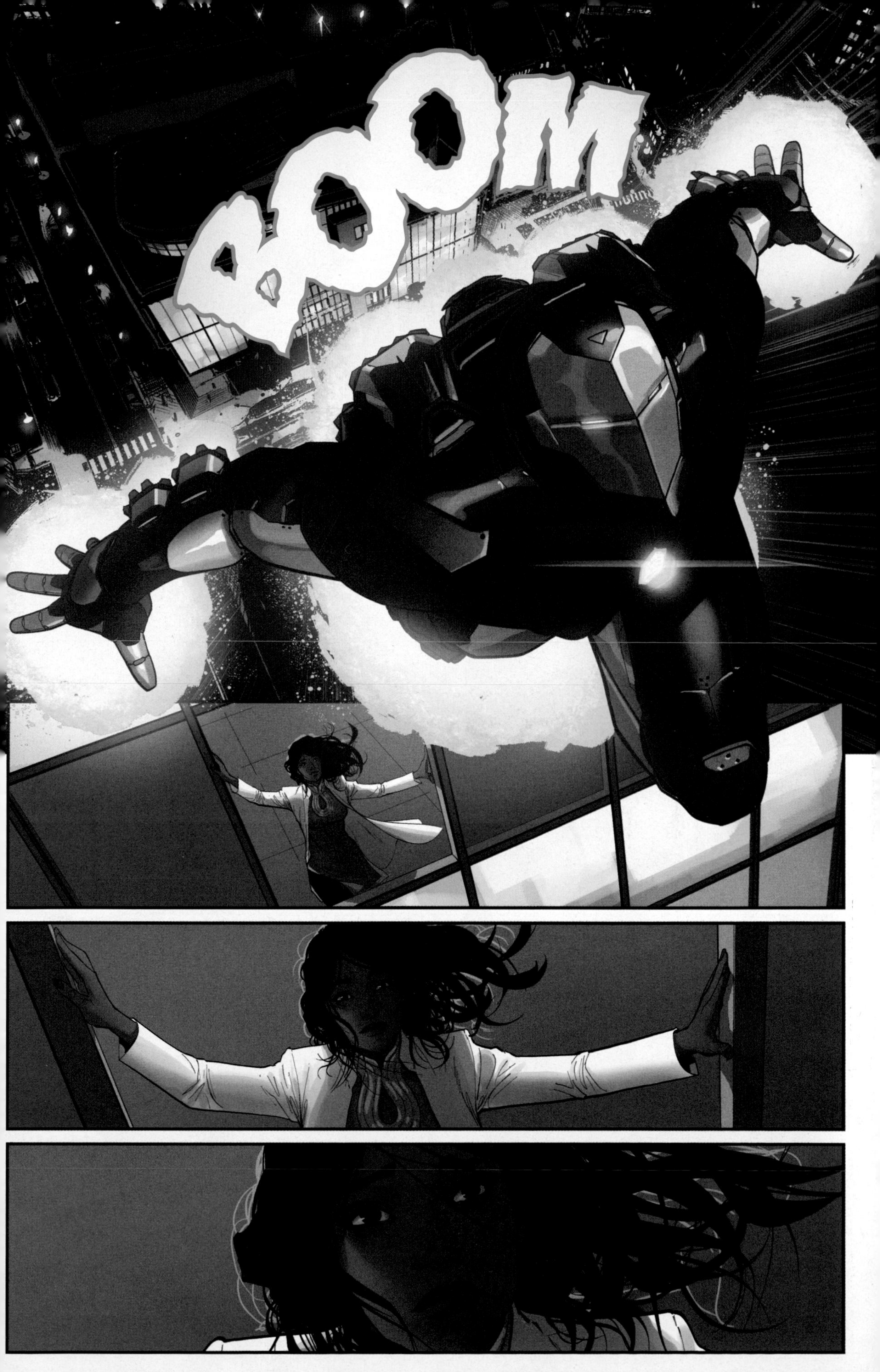
BOOM

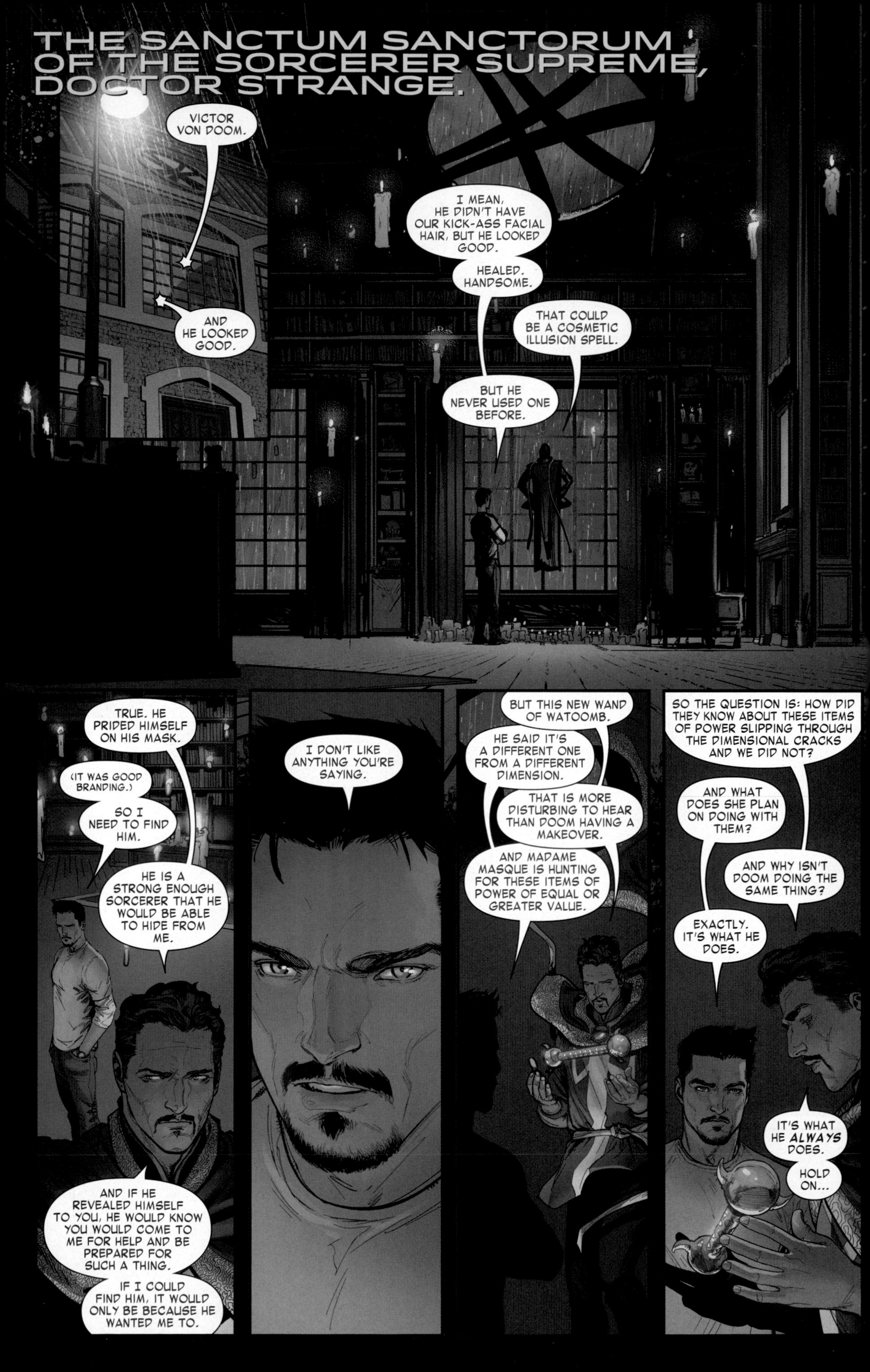
THE SANCTUM SANCTORUM OF THE SORCERER SUPREME, DOCTOR STRANGE.
VICTOR VON DOOM.
AND HE LOOKED GOOD.
I MEAN, HE DIDN'T HAVE OUR KICK-ASS FACIAL HAIR, BUT HE LOOKED GOOD.
HEALED. HANDSOME.
THAT COULD BE A COSMETIC ILLUSION SPELL.
BUT HE NEVER USED ONE BEFORE.
TRUE. HE PRIDED HIMSELF ON HIS MASK.
(IT WAS GOOD BRANDING.)
SO I NEED TO FIND HIM.
HE IS A STRONG ENOUGH SORCERER THAT HE WOULD BE ABLE TO HIDE FROM ME.
AND IF HE REVEALED HIMSELF TO YOU, HE WOULD KNOW YOU WOULD COME TO ME FOR HELP AND BE PREPARED FOR SUCH A THING.
IF I COULD FIND HIM, IT WOULD ONLY BE BECAUSE HE WANTED ME TO.
I DON'T LIKE ANYTHING YOU'RE SAYING.
BUT THIS NEW WAND OF WATOOMB.
HE SAID IT'S A DIFFERENT ONE FROM A DIFFERENT DIMENSION.
THAT IS MORE DISTURBING TO HEAR THAN DOOM HAVING A MAKEOVER.
AND MADAME MASQUE IS HUNTING FOR THESE ITEMS OF POWER OF EQUAL OR GREATER VALUE.
SO THE QUESTION IS: HOW DID THEY KNOW ABOUT THESE ITEMS OF POWER SLIPPING THROUGH THE DIMENSIONAL CRACKS AND WE DID NOT?
AND WHAT DOES SHE PLAN ON DOING WITH THEM?
AND WHY ISN'T DOOM DOING THE SAME THING?
EXACTLY. IT'S WHAT HE DOES.
IT'S WHAT HE *ALWAYS* DOES.
HOLD ON...

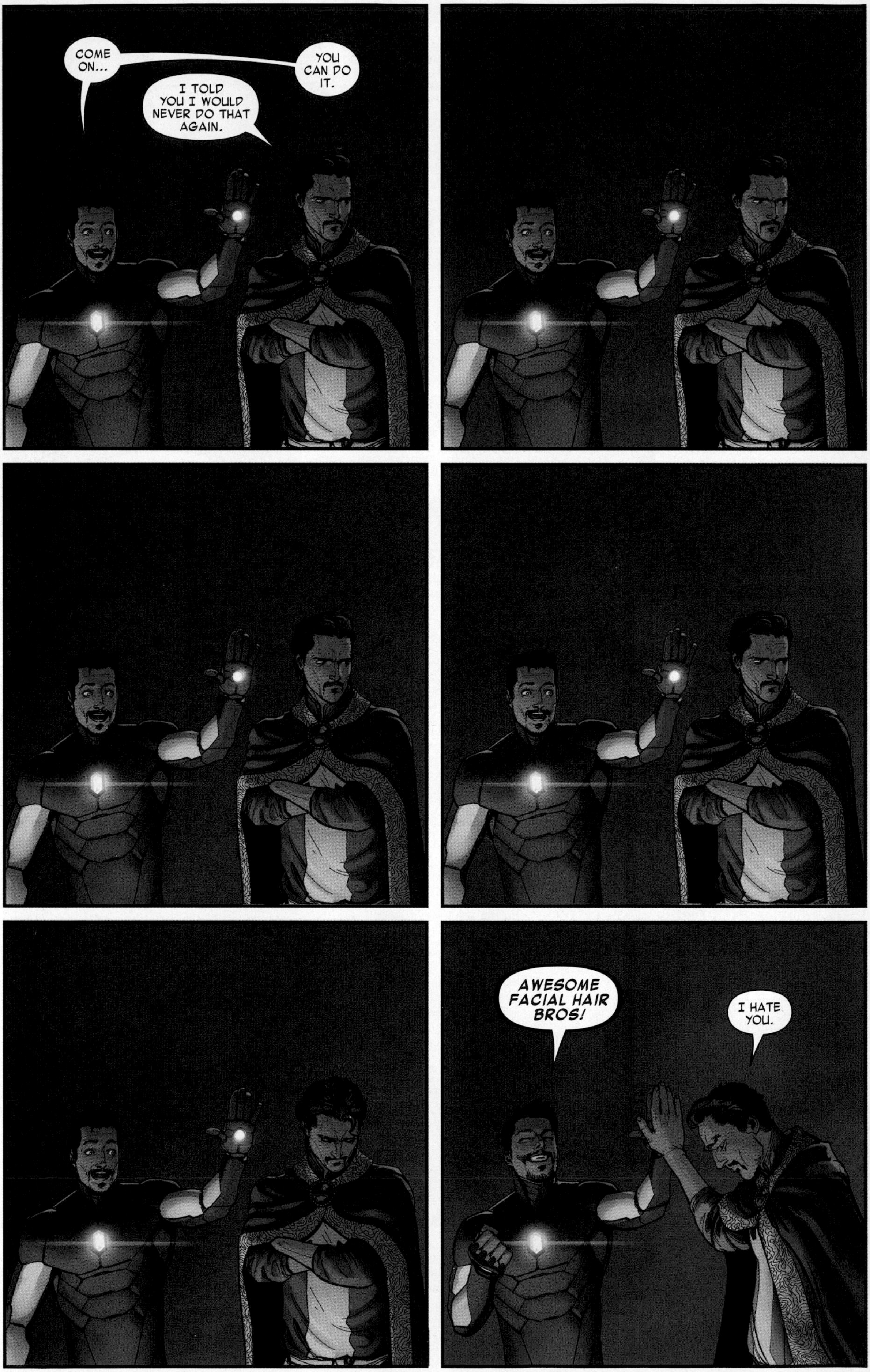
COME ON...
I TOLD YOU I WOULD NEVER DO THAT AGAIN.
YOU CAN DO IT.
AWESOME FACIAL HAIR BROS!
I HATE YOU.

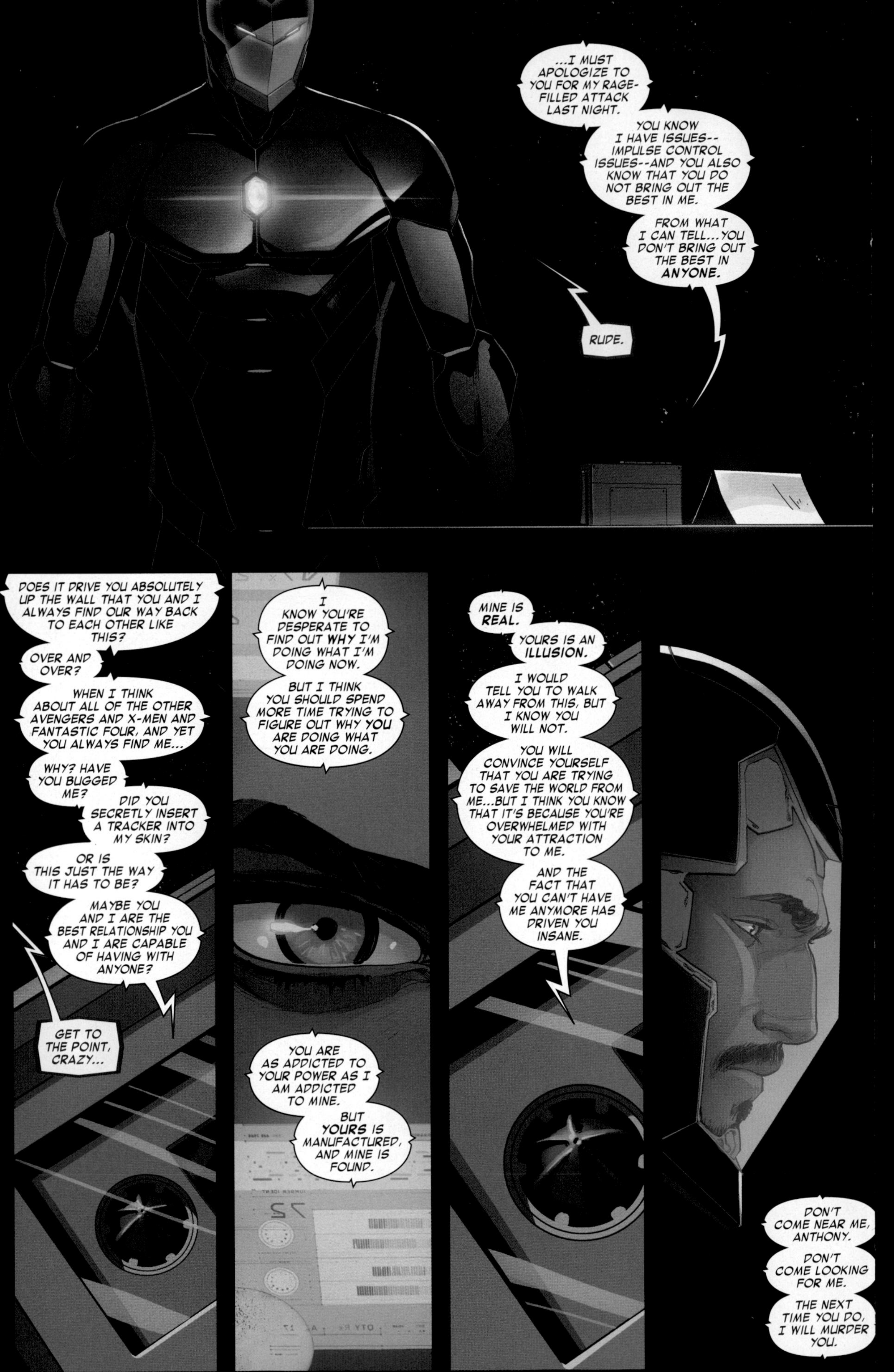
...I MUST APOLOGIZE TO YOU FOR MY RAGE-FILLED ATTACK LAST NIGHT.
YOU KNOW I HAVE ISSUES-- IMPULSE CONTROL ISSUES--AND YOU ALSO KNOW THAT YOU DO NOT BRING OUT THE BEST IN ME.
FROM WHAT I CAN TELL...YOU DON'T BRING OUT THE BEST IN ANYONE.
RUDE.
DOES IT DRIVE YOU ABSOLUTELY UP THE WALL THAT YOU AND I ALWAYS FIND OUR WAY BACK TO EACH OTHER LIKE THIS?
OVER AND OVER?
WHEN I THINK ABOUT ALL OF THE OTHER AVENGERS AND X-MEN AND FANTASTIC FOUR, AND YET YOU ALWAYS FIND ME...
WHY? HAVE YOU BUGGED ME?
DID YOU SECRETLY INSERT A TRACKER INTO MY SKIN?
OR IS THIS JUST THE WAY IT HAS TO BE?
MAYBE YOU AND I ARE THE BEST RELATIONSHIP YOU AND I ARE CAPABLE OF HAVING WITH ANYONE?
GET TO THE POINT, CRAZY...
I KNOW YOU'RE DESPERATE TO FIND OUT WHY I'M DOING WHAT I'M DOING NOW.
BUT I THINK YOU SHOULD SPEND MORE TIME TRYING TO FIGURE OUT WHY YOU ARE DOING WHAT YOU ARE DOING.
YOU ARE AS ADDICTED TO YOUR POWER AS I AM ADDICTED TO MINE.
BUT YOURS IS MANUFACTURED, AND MINE IS FOUND.
MINE IS REAL.
YOURS IS AN ILLUSION.
I WOULD TELL YOU TO WALK AWAY FROM THIS, BUT I KNOW YOU WILL NOT.
YOU WILL CONVINCE YOURSELF THAT YOU ARE TRYING TO SAVE THE WORLD FROM ME...BUT I THINK YOU KNOW THAT IT'S BECAUSE YOU'RE OVERWHELMED WITH YOUR ATTRACTION TO ME.
AND THE FACT THAT YOU CAN'T HAVE ME ANYMORE HAS DRIVEN YOU INSANE.
DON'T COME NEAR ME, ANTHONY.
DON'T COME LOOKING FOR ME.
THE NEXT TIME YOU DO, I WILL MURDER YOU.

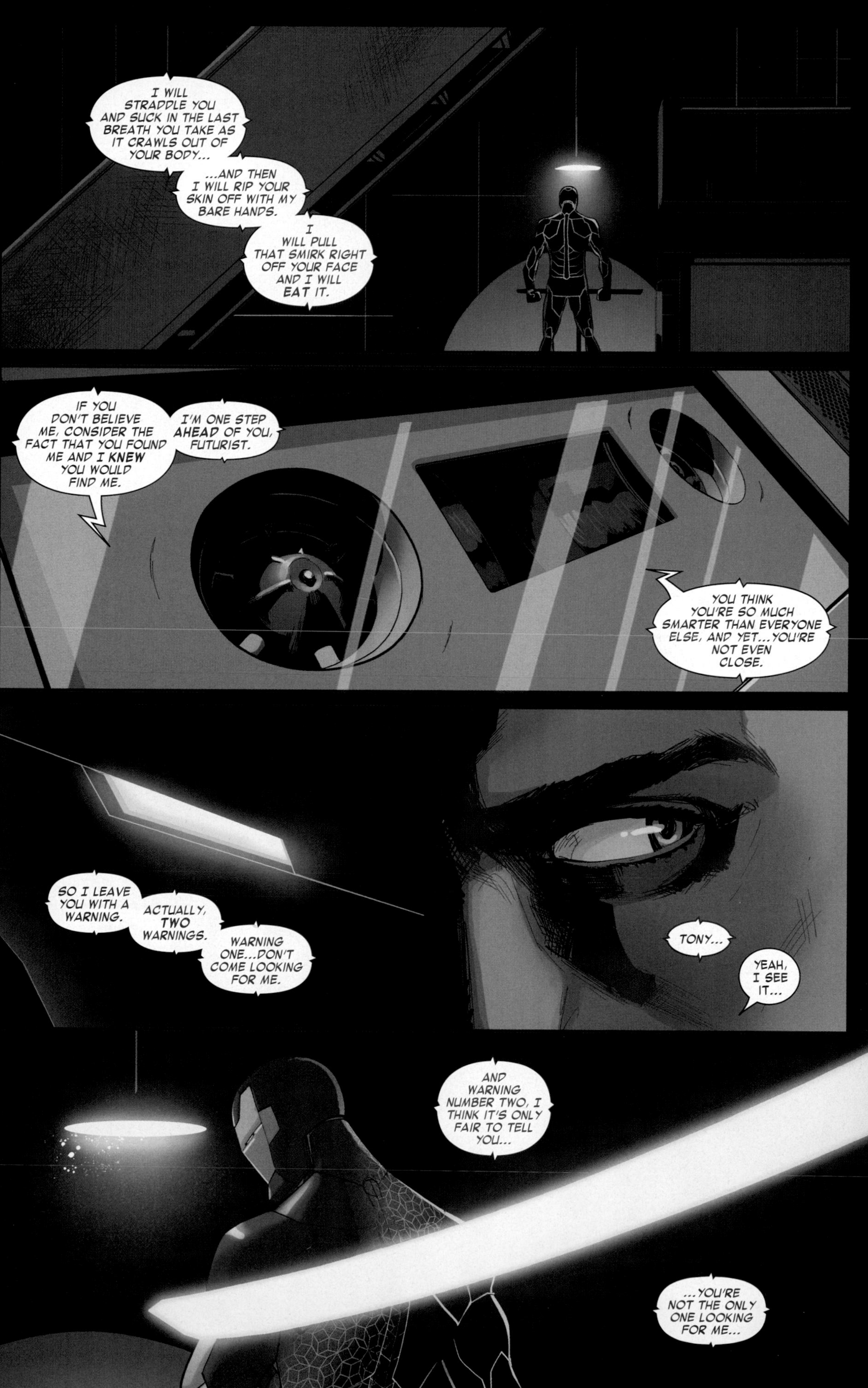
I WILL STRADDLE YOU AND SUCK IN THE LAST BREATH YOU TAKE AS IT CRAWLS OUT OF YOUR BODY...
...AND THEN I WILL RIP YOUR SKIN OFF WITH MY BARE HANDS.
I WILL PULL THAT SMIRK RIGHT OFF YOUR FACE AND I WILL EAT IT.
IF YOU DON'T BELIEVE ME, CONSIDER THE FACT THAT YOU FOUND ME AND I KNEW YOU WOULD FIND ME.
I'M ONE STEP AHEAD OF YOU, FUTURIST.
YOU THINK YOU'RE SO MUCH SMARTER THAN EVERYONE ELSE, AND YET...YOU'RE NOT EVEN CLOSE.
SO I LEAVE YOU WITH A WARNING.
ACTUALLY, TWO WARNINGS.
WARNING ONE...DON'T COME LOOKING FOR ME.
TONY...
YEAH, I SEE IT...
AND WARNING NUMBER TWO, I THINK IT'S ONLY FAIR TO TELL YOU...
...YOU'RE NOT THE ONLY ONE LOOKING FOR ME...

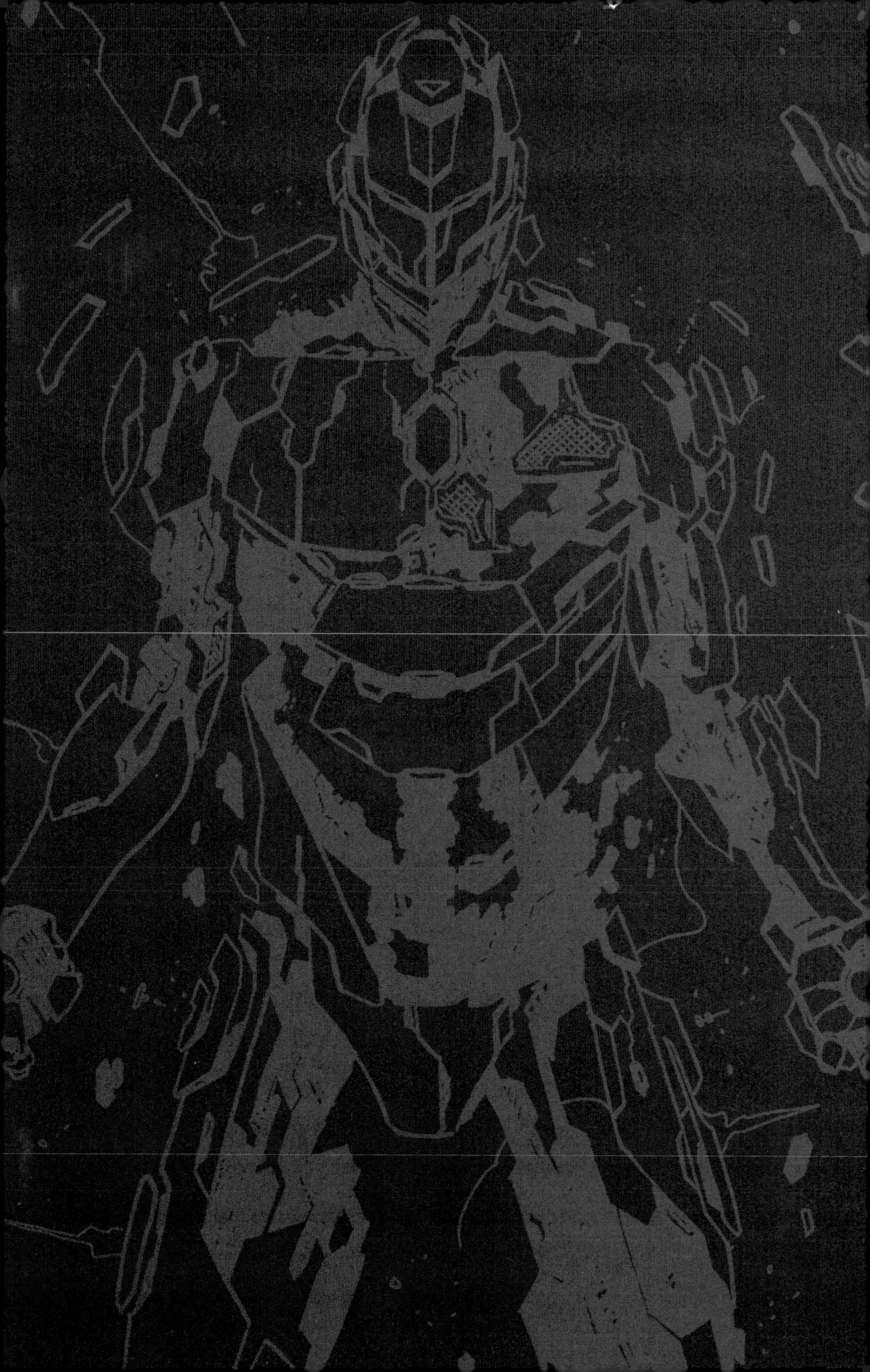

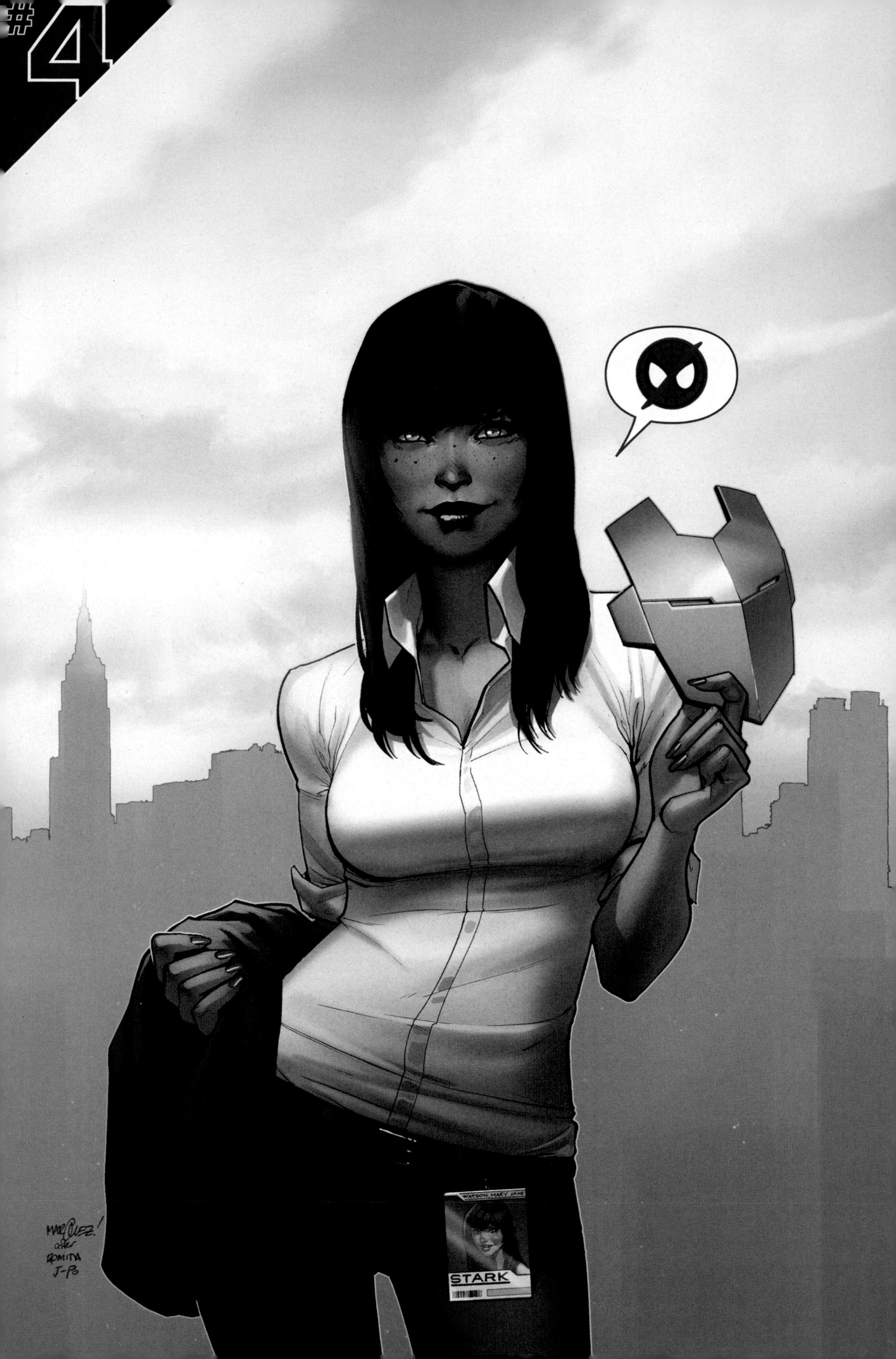
#4
WATSON MARY JANE
STARK
MARQUEZ! after ROMITA J-Po

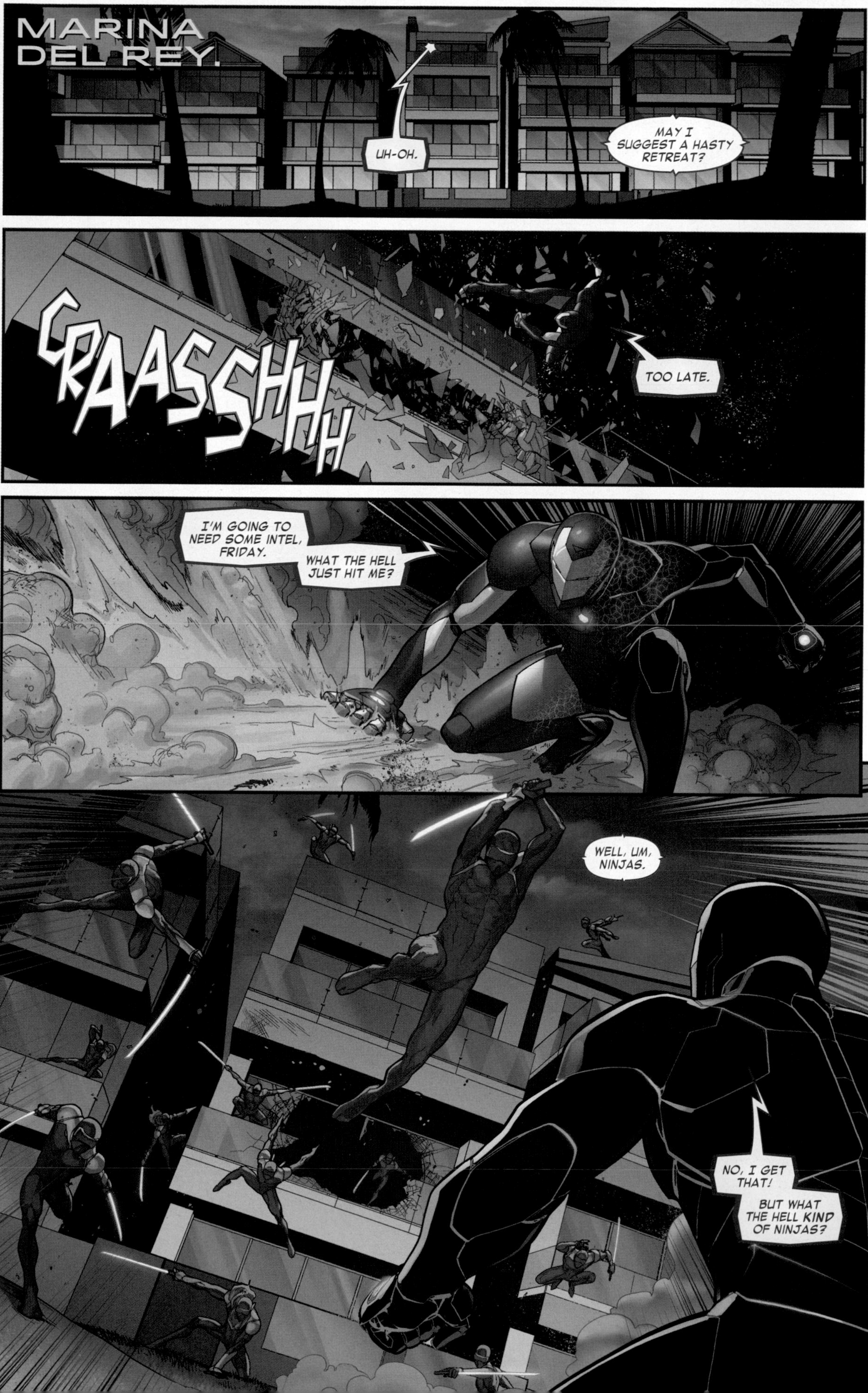
MARINA DEL REY.
UH-OH.
MAY I SUGGEST A HASTY RETREAT?
CRAASSHHH
TOO LATE.
I'M GOING TO NEED SOME INTEL, FRIDAY.
WHAT THE HELL JUST HIT ME?
WELL, UM, NINJAS.
NO, I GET THAT!
BUT WHAT THE HELL KIND OF NINJAS?

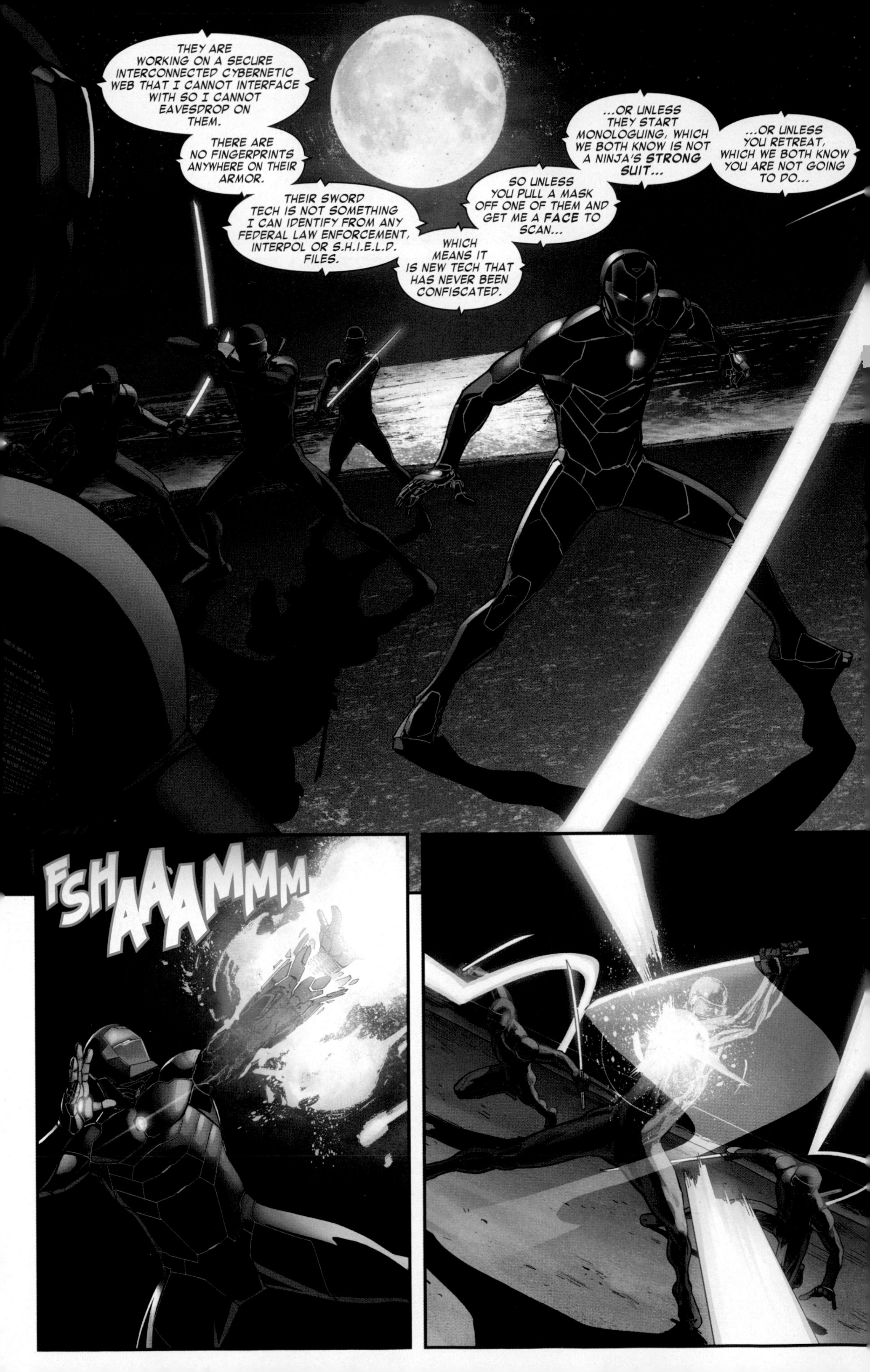

THEY ARE WORKING ON A SECURE INTERCONNECTED CYBERNETIC WEB THAT I CANNOT INTERFACE WITH SO I CANNOT EAVESDROP ON THEM.
THERE ARE NO FINGERPRINTS ANYWHERE ON THEIR ARMOR.
THEIR SWORD TECH IS NOT SOMETHING I CAN IDENTIFY FROM ANY FEDERAL LAW ENFORCEMENT, INTERPOL OR S.H.I.E.L.D. FILES.
WHICH MEANS IT IS NEW TECH THAT HAS NEVER BEEN CONFISCATED.
SO UNLESS YOU PULL A MASK OFF ONE OF THEM AND GET ME A FACE TO SCAN...
...OR UNLESS THEY START MONOLOGUING, WHICH WE BOTH KNOW IS NOT A NINJA'S STRONG SUIT...
...OR UNLESS YOU RETREAT, WHICH WE BOTH KNOW YOU ARE NOT GOING TO DO...
FSHAAAMMMM

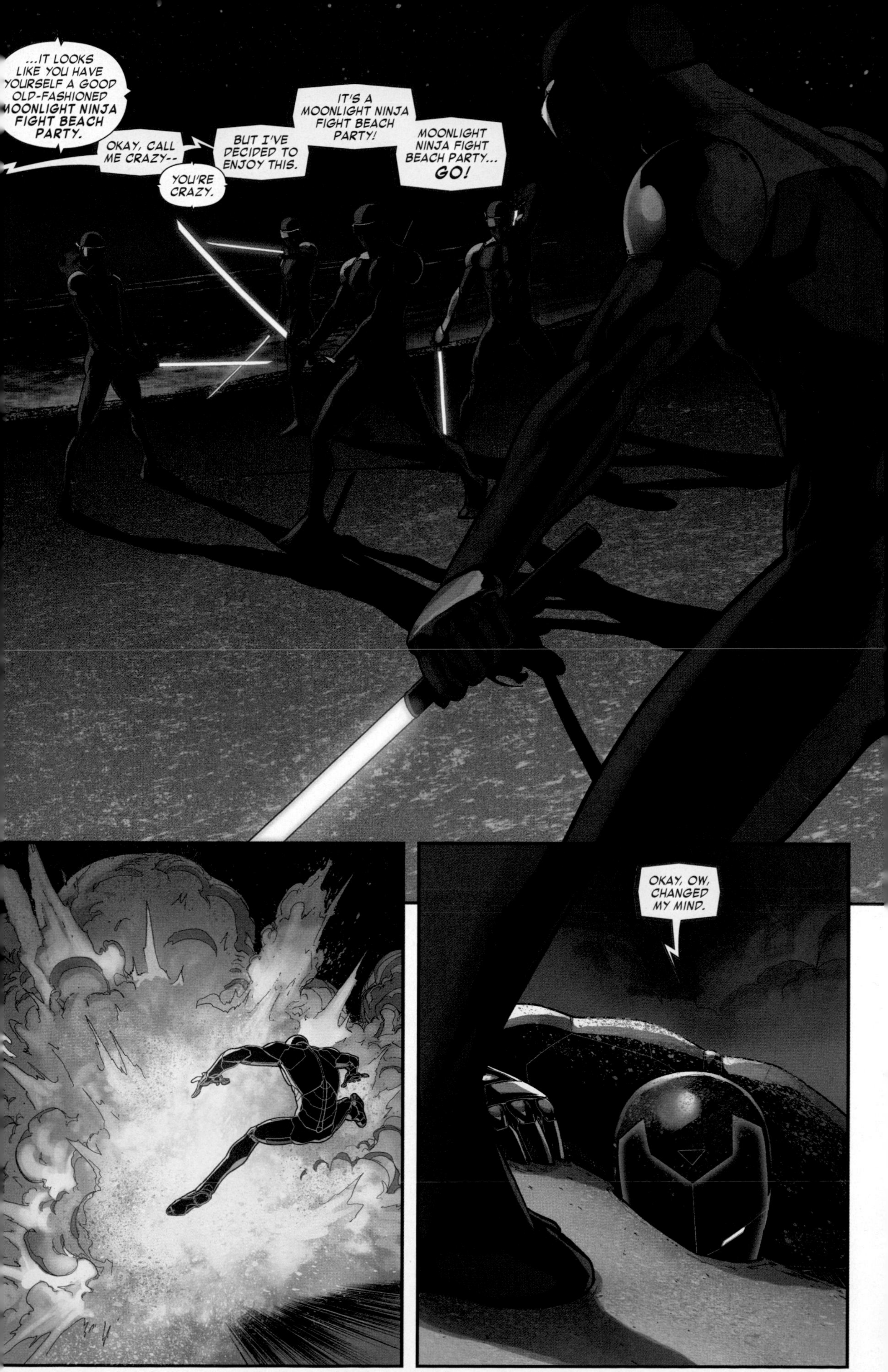
...IT LOOKS LIKE YOU HAVE YOURSELF A GOOD OLD-FASHIONED MOONLIGHT NINJA FIGHT BEACH PARTY.
OKAY, CALL ME CRAZY--
YOU'RE CRAZY.
BUT I'VE DECIDED TO ENJOY THIS.
IT'S A MOONLIGHT NINJA FIGHT BEACH PARTY!
MOONLIGHT NINJA FIGHT BEACH PARTY... GO!
OKAY, OW, CHANGED MY MIND.

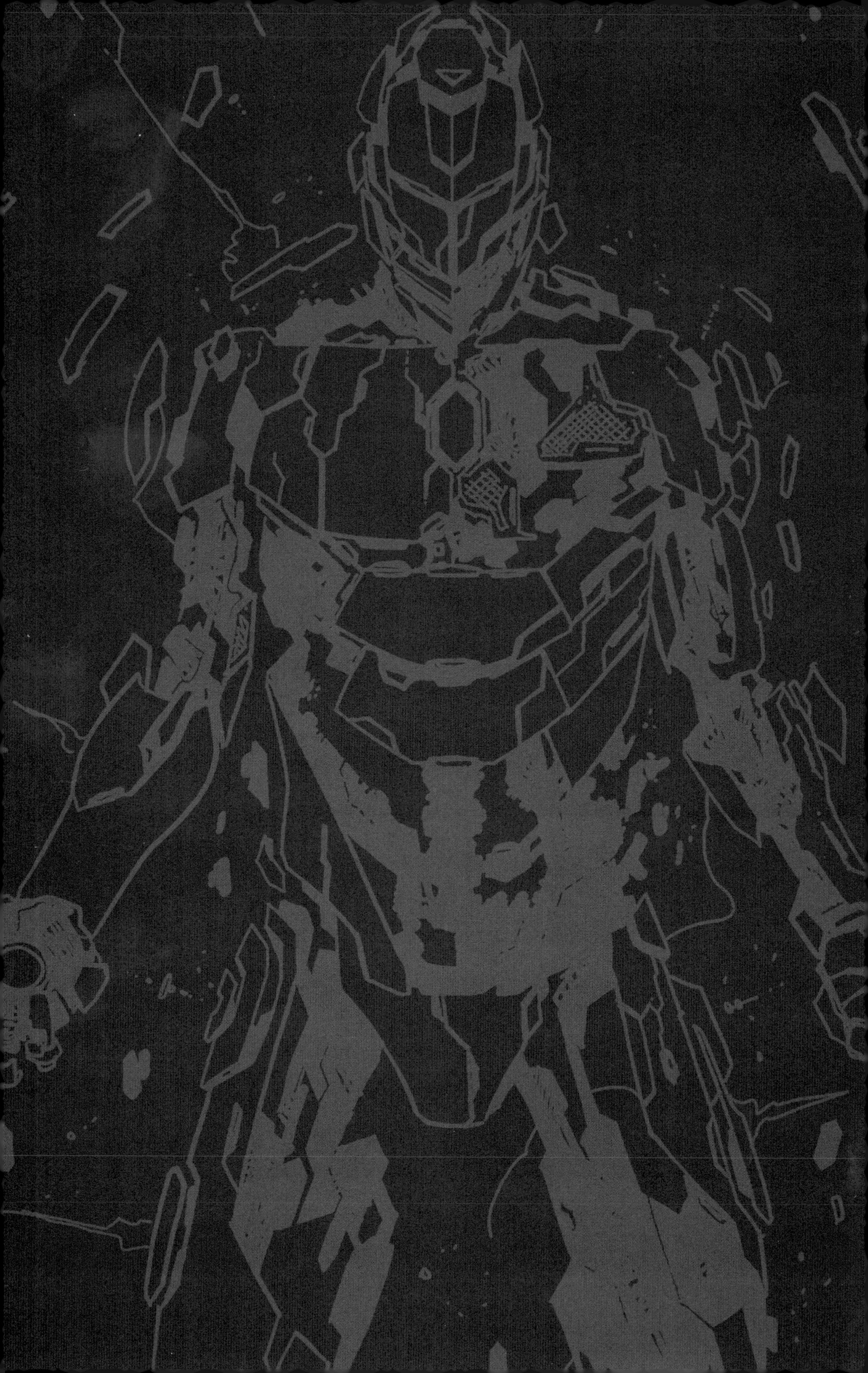

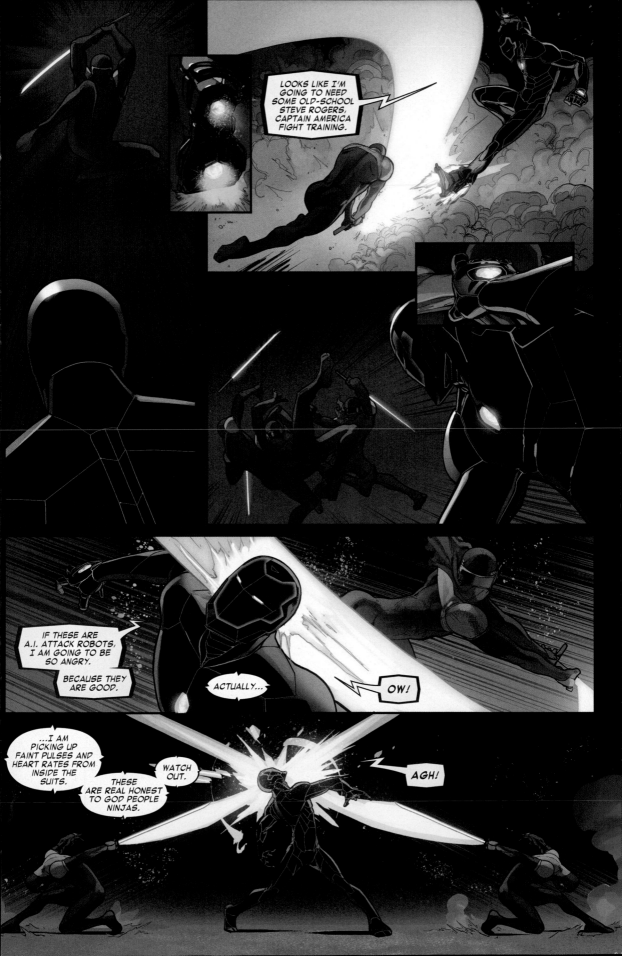

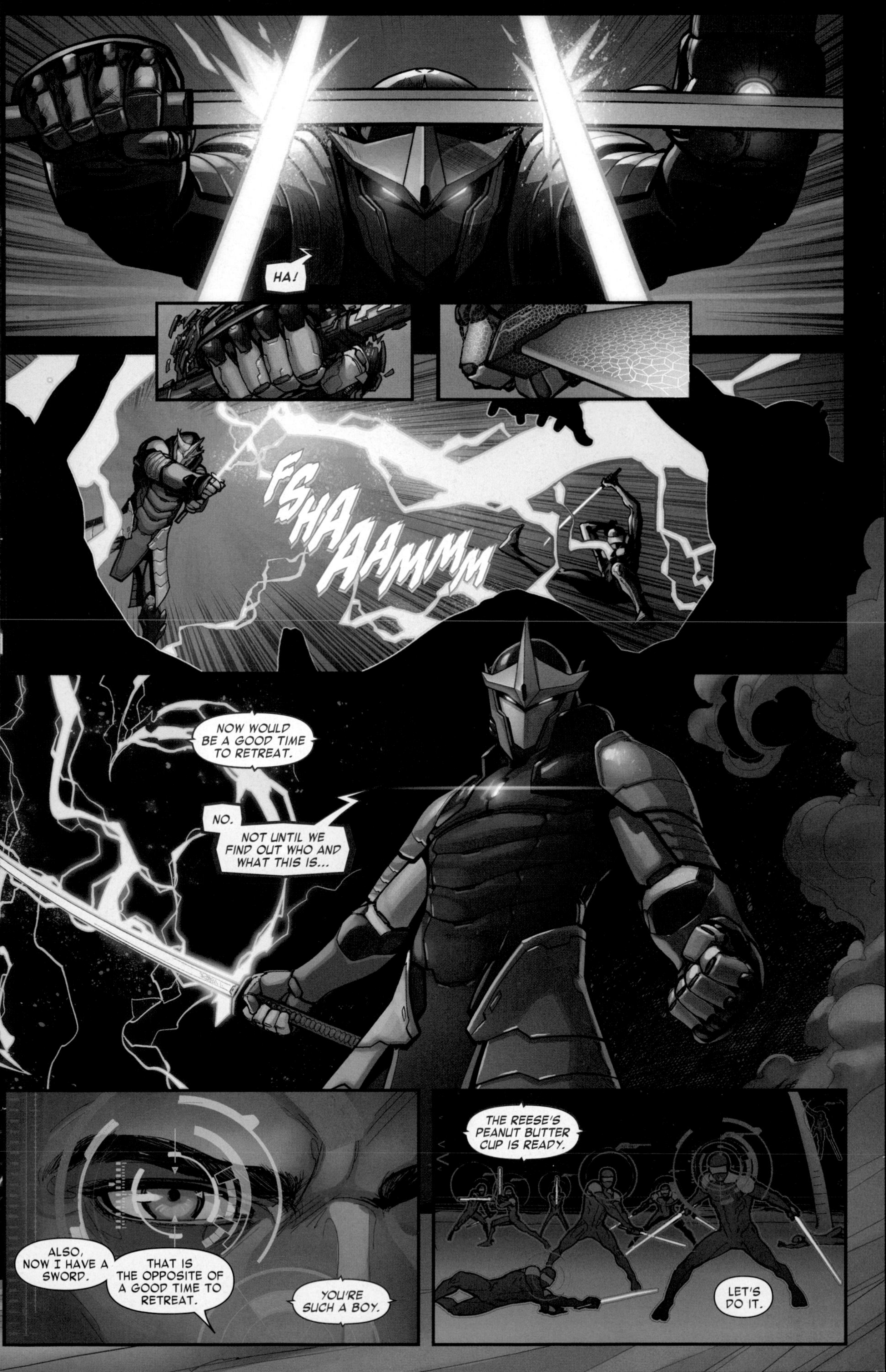
HA!
FSHAAAMMMM
NOW WOULD BE A GOOD TIME TO RETREAT.
NO.
NOT UNTIL WE FIND OUT WHO AND WHAT THIS IS...
ALSO, NOW I HAVE A SWORD.
THAT IS THE OPPOSITE OF A GOOD TIME TO RETREAT.
YOU'RE SUCH A BOY.
THE REESE'S PEANUT BUTTER CUP IS READY.
LET'S DO IT.

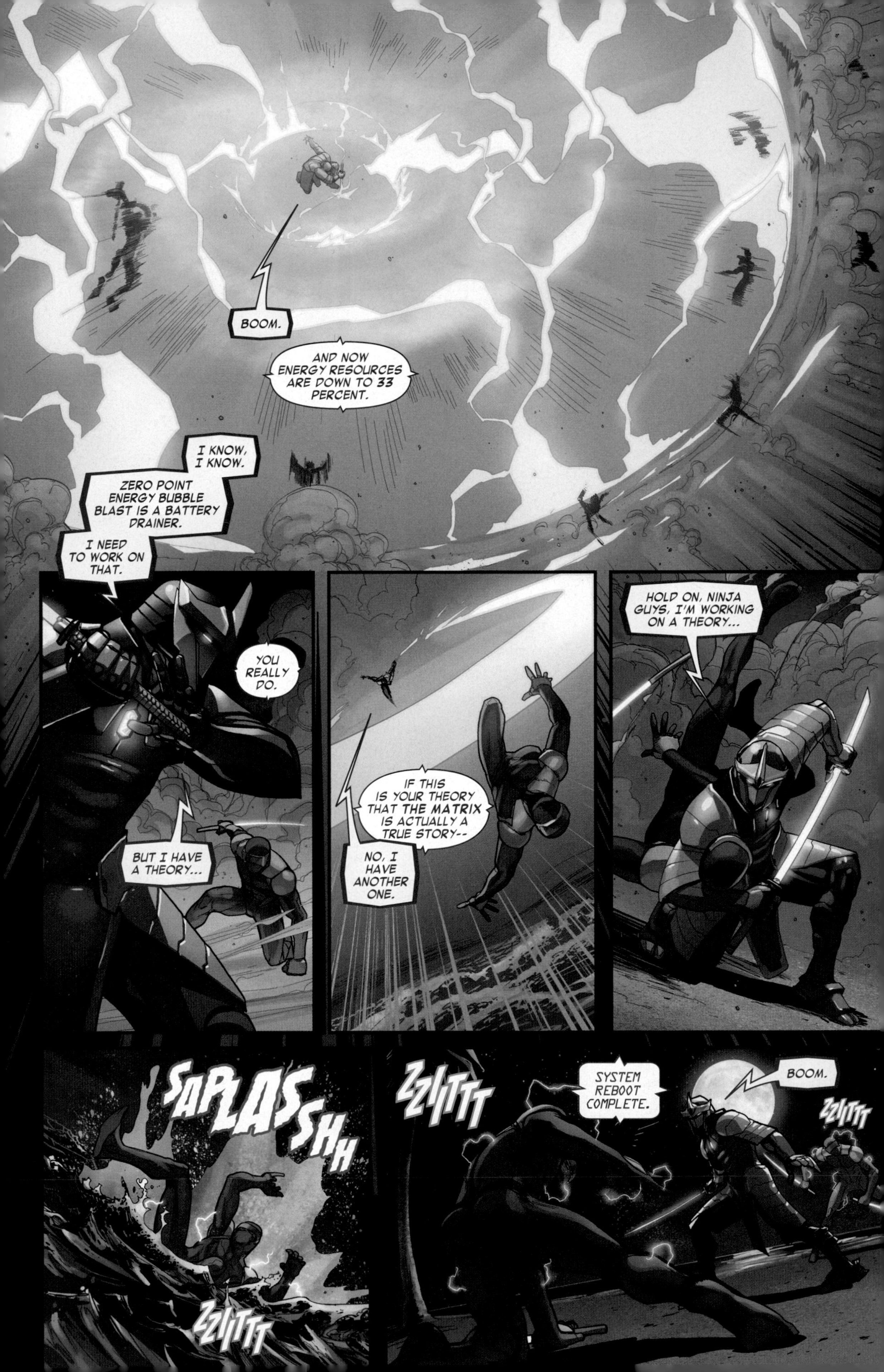
BOOM.
AND NOW ENERGY RESOURCES ARE DOWN TO 33 PERCENT.
I KNOW, I KNOW.
ZERO POINT ENERGY BUBBLE BLAST IS A BATTERY DRAINER.
I NEED TO WORK ON THAT.
YOU REALLY DO.
BUT I HAVE A THEORY...
IF THIS IS YOUR THEORY THAT THE MATRIX IS ACTUALLY A TRUE STORY--
NO, I HAVE ANOTHER ONE.
HOLD ON, NINJA GUYS, I'M WORKING ON A THEORY...
SPLASSHH
ZZIITTT
ZZIITTT
SYSTEM REBOOT COMPLETE.
BOOM.
ZZIITTT

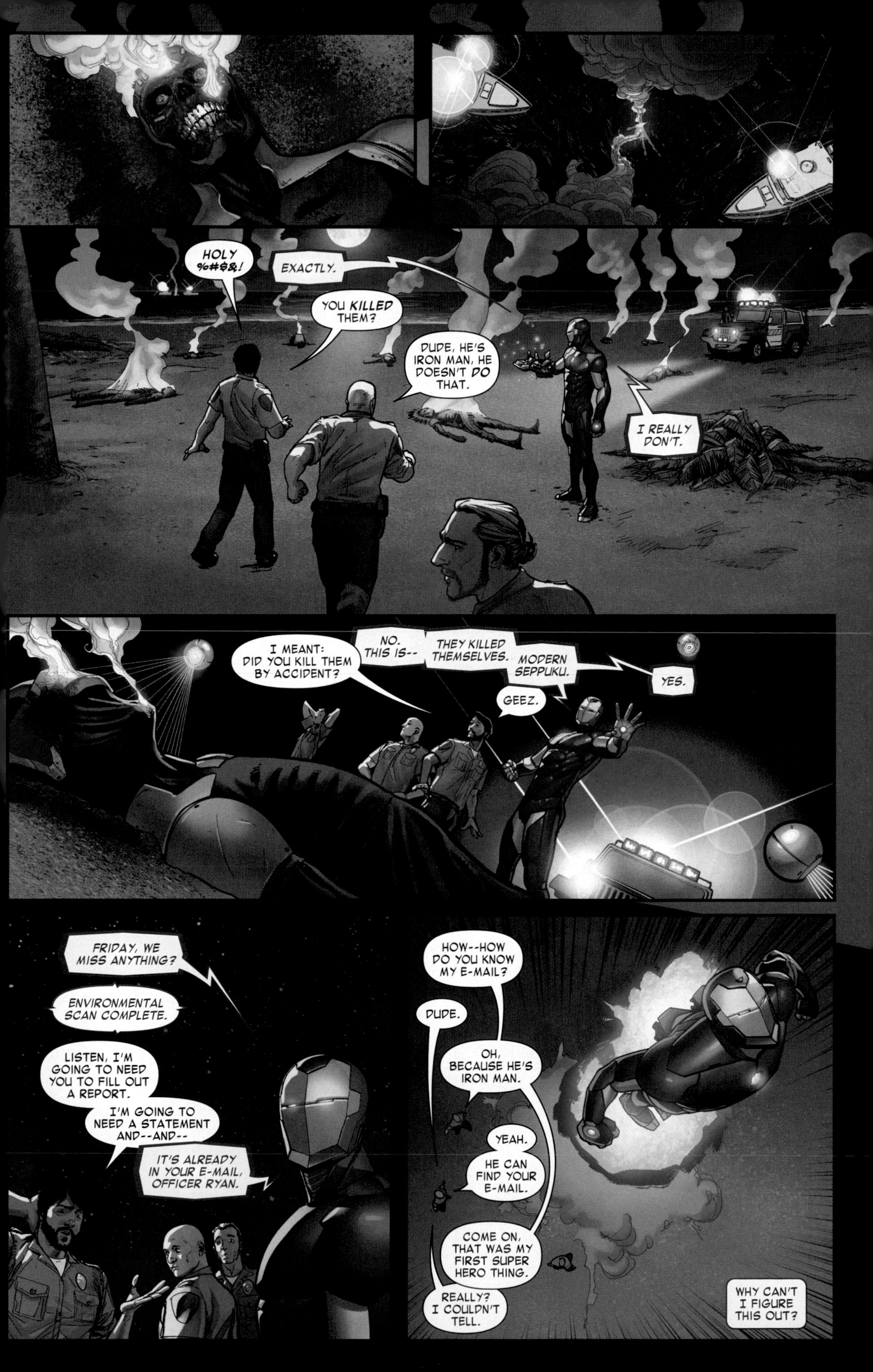
HOLY %#$&!
EXACTLY.
YOU KILLED THEM?
DUDE, HE'S IRON MAN, HE DOESN'T DO THAT.
I REALLY DON'T.
I MEANT: DID YOU KILL THEM BY ACCIDENT?
NO. THIS IS--
THEY KILLED THEMSELVES.
MODERN SEPPUKU.
YES.
GEEZ.
FRIDAY, WE MISS ANYTHING?
ENVIRONMENTAL SCAN COMPLETE.
LISTEN, I'M GOING TO NEED YOU TO FILL OUT A REPORT.
I'M GOING TO NEED A STATEMENT AND--AND--
IT'S ALREADY IN YOUR E-MAIL, OFFICER RYAN.
HOW--HOW DO YOU KNOW MY E-MAIL?
DUDE.
OH, BECAUSE HE'S IRON MAN.
YEAH.
HE CAN FIND YOUR E-MAIL.
COME ON, THAT WAS MY FIRST SUPER HERO THING.
REALLY? I COULDN'T TELL.
WHY CAN'T I FIGURE THIS OUT?

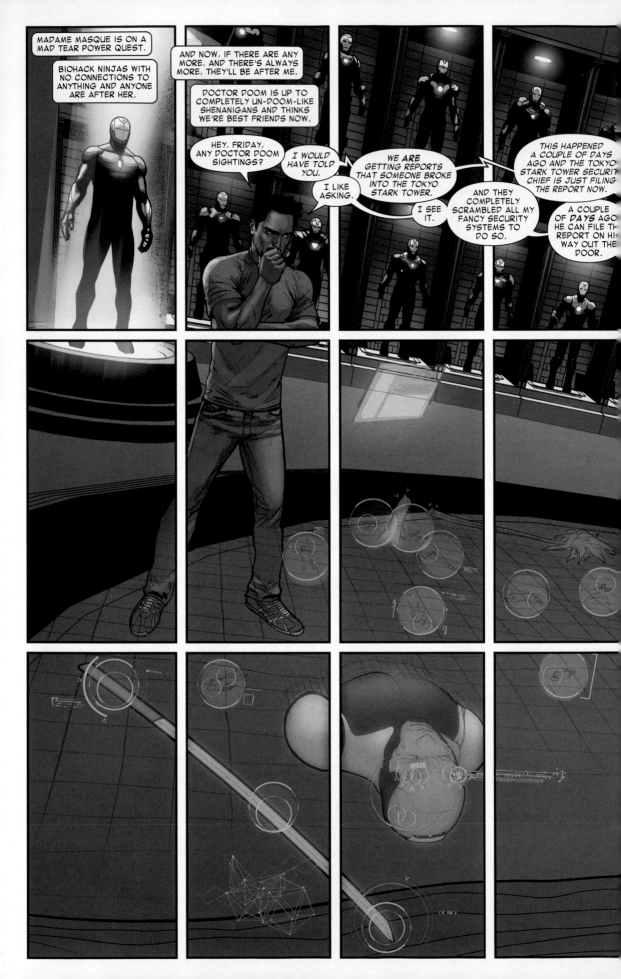

I BROUGHT A **BUNCH** OF THEM.

ALL RIGHT! YOU'RE, LIKE, MY **FAVORITE** AVENGER.

I'M NOT JUST SAYING THAT BECAUSE SPIDER-MAN ISN'T HERE.

ONE WHAT?

MAX.

YOU WANT TO TRY ONE ON?

THE ARMOR.

I'M TOO SMALL FOR THAT.

HMM, YOU'RE RIGHT.

I'M JUST NOW NOTICING HOW **INSANEL**Y SHORT YOU ARE.

I'M EIGHT.

DON'T TELL ME YOUR PROBLEMS.

ARMOR! RECONFIGURE!

WHOA...

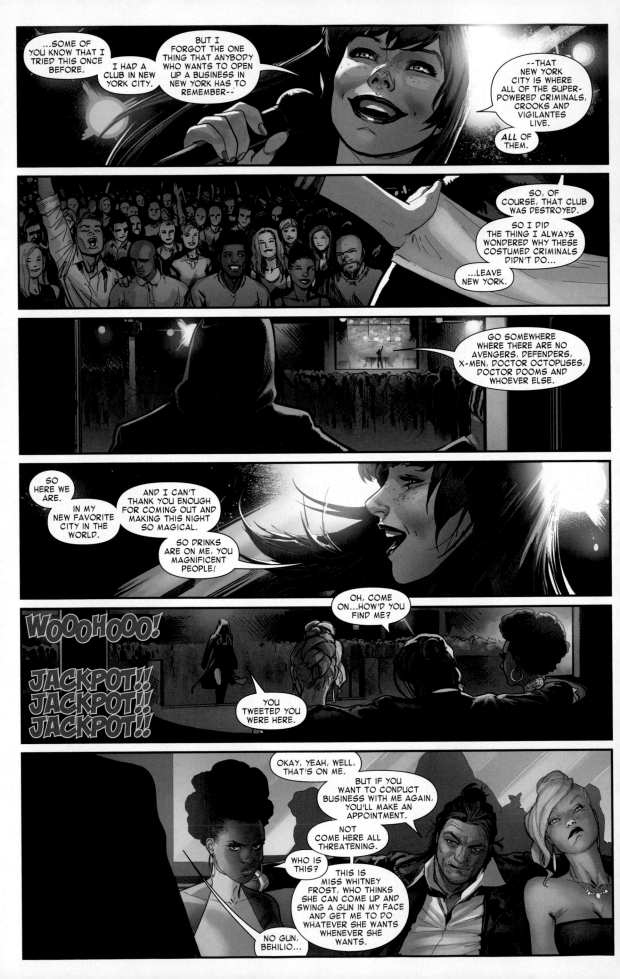

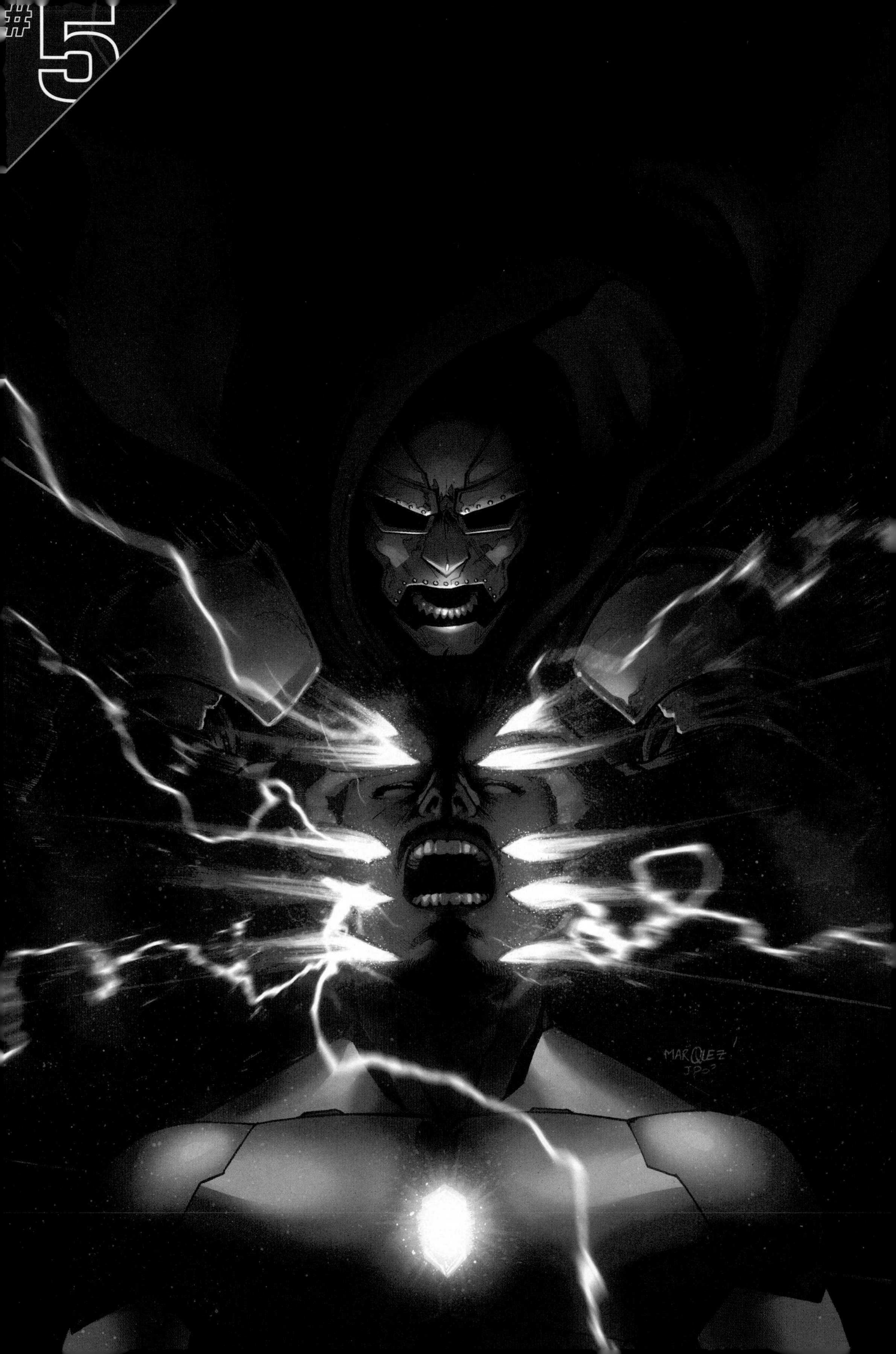
#5
MARQUEZ
JPO

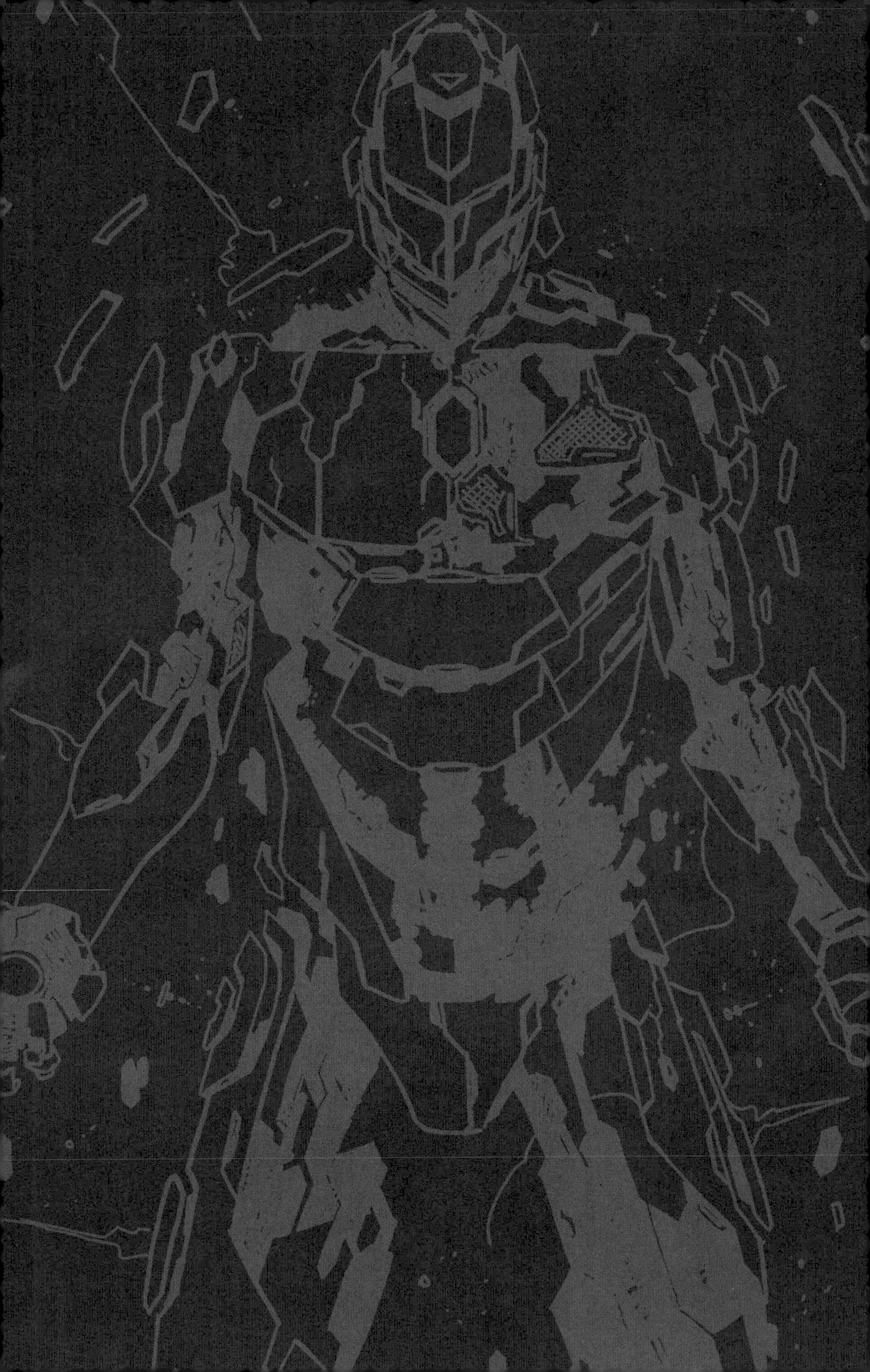

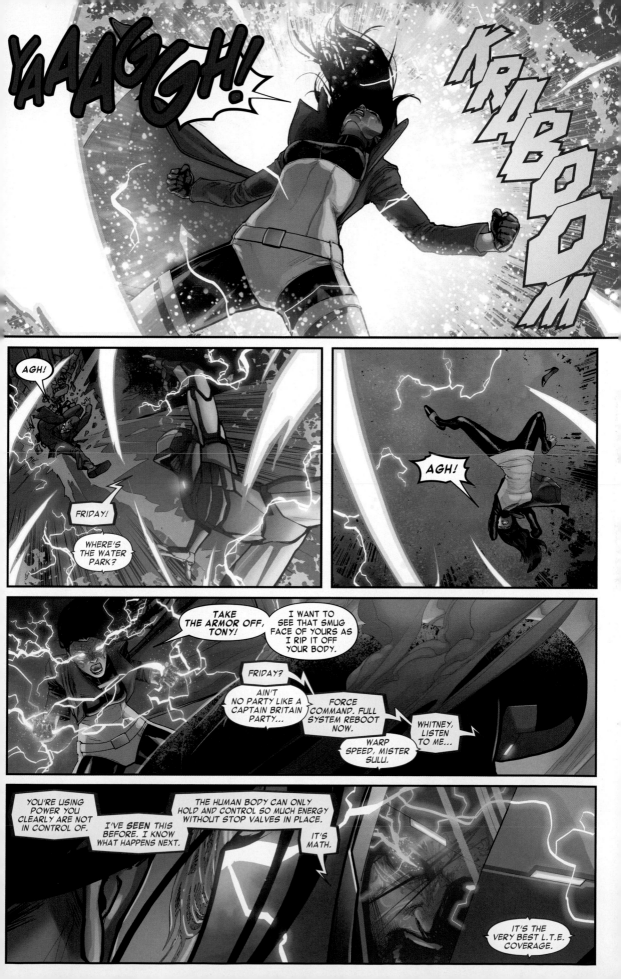

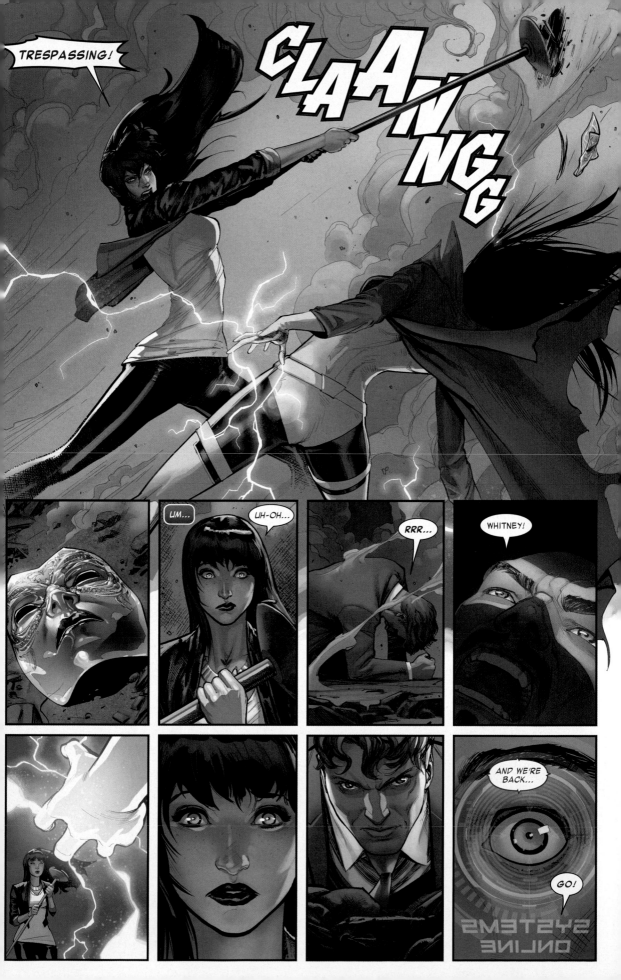

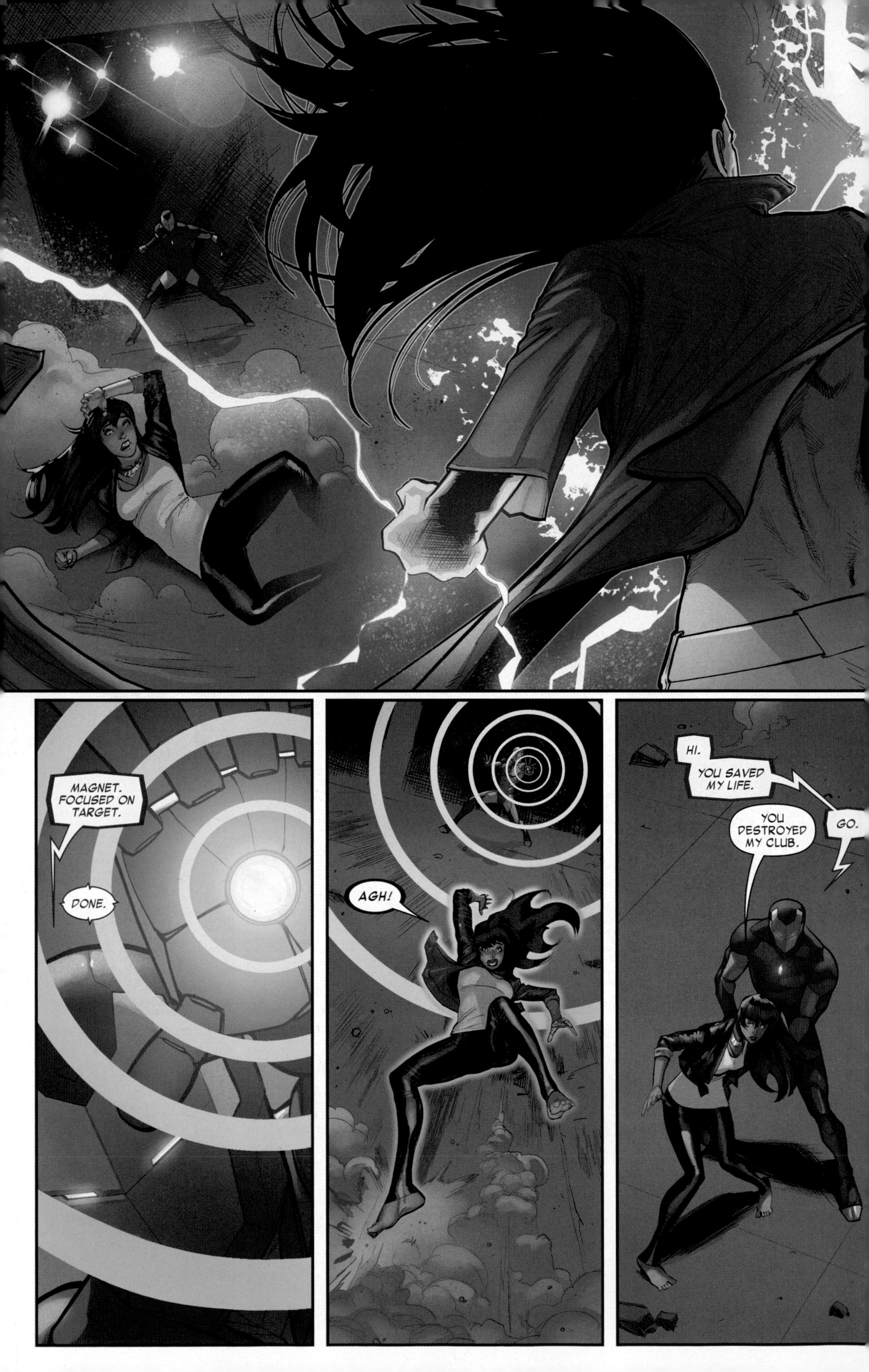
MAGNET. FOCUSED ON TARGET.
DONE.
AGH!
HI.
YOU SAVED MY LIFE.
GO.
YOU DESTROYED MY CLUB.

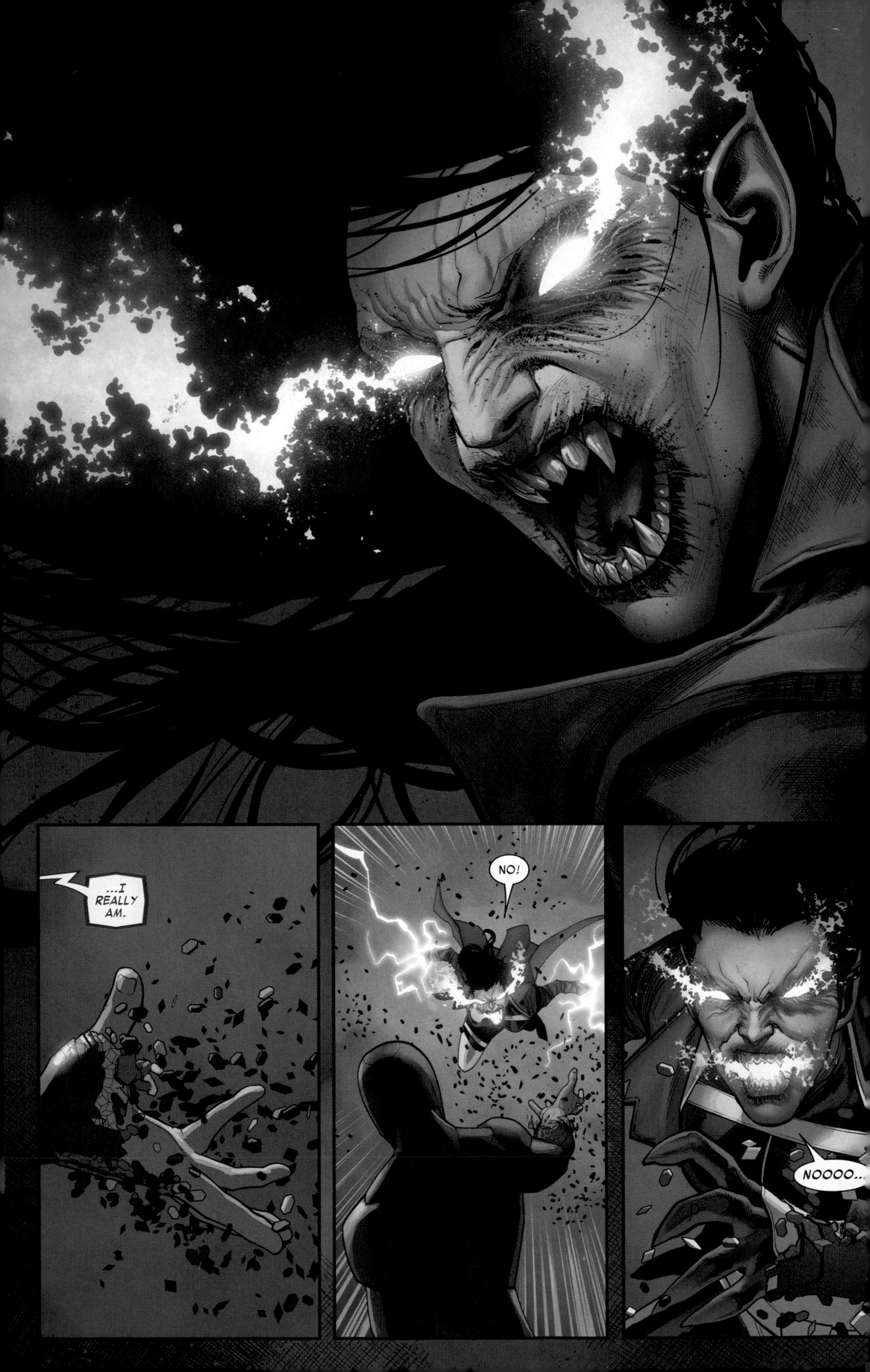
...I REALLY AM.
NO!
NOOOO...

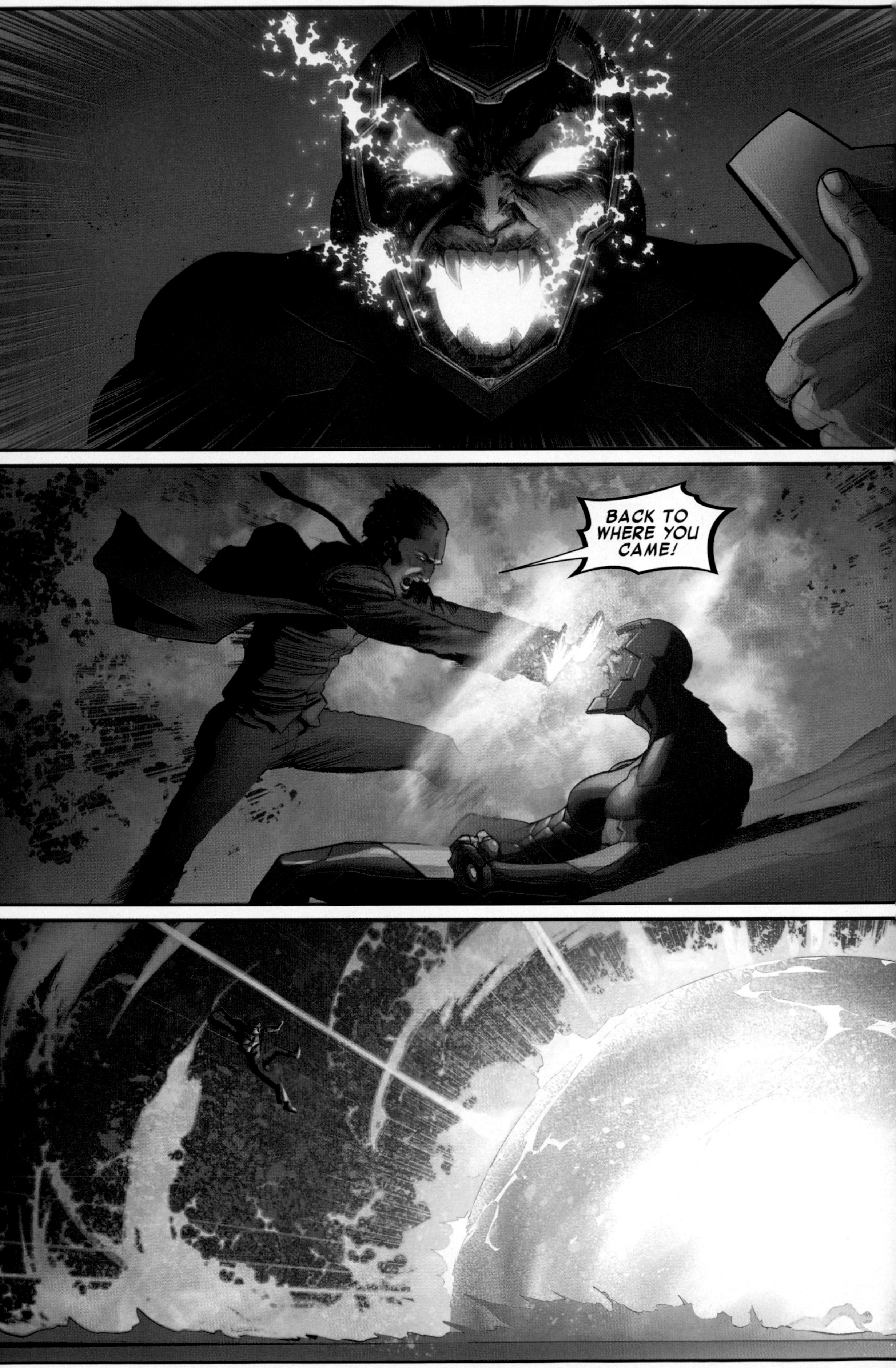
BACK TO WHERE YOU CAME!

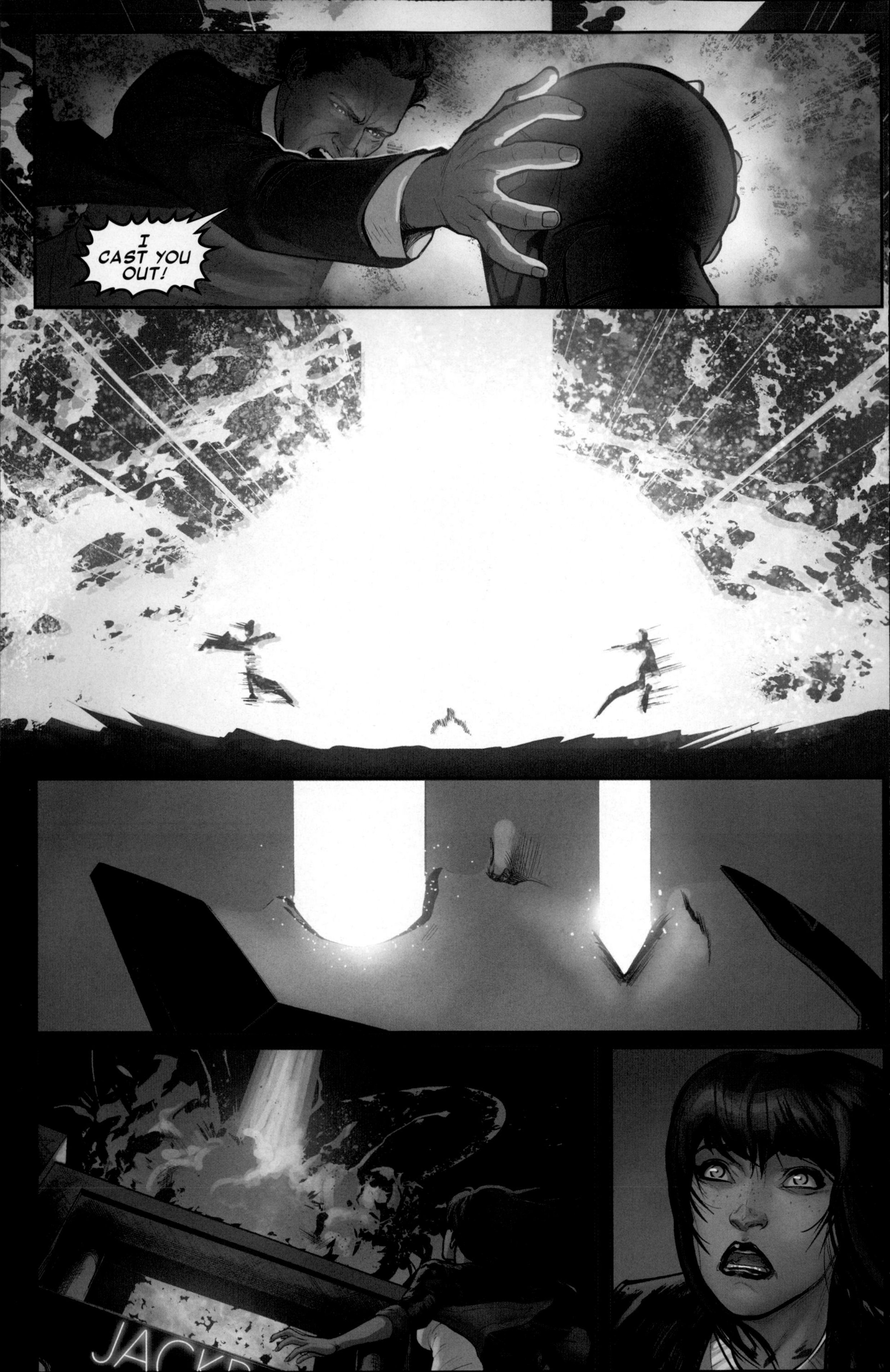
I CAST YOU OUT!

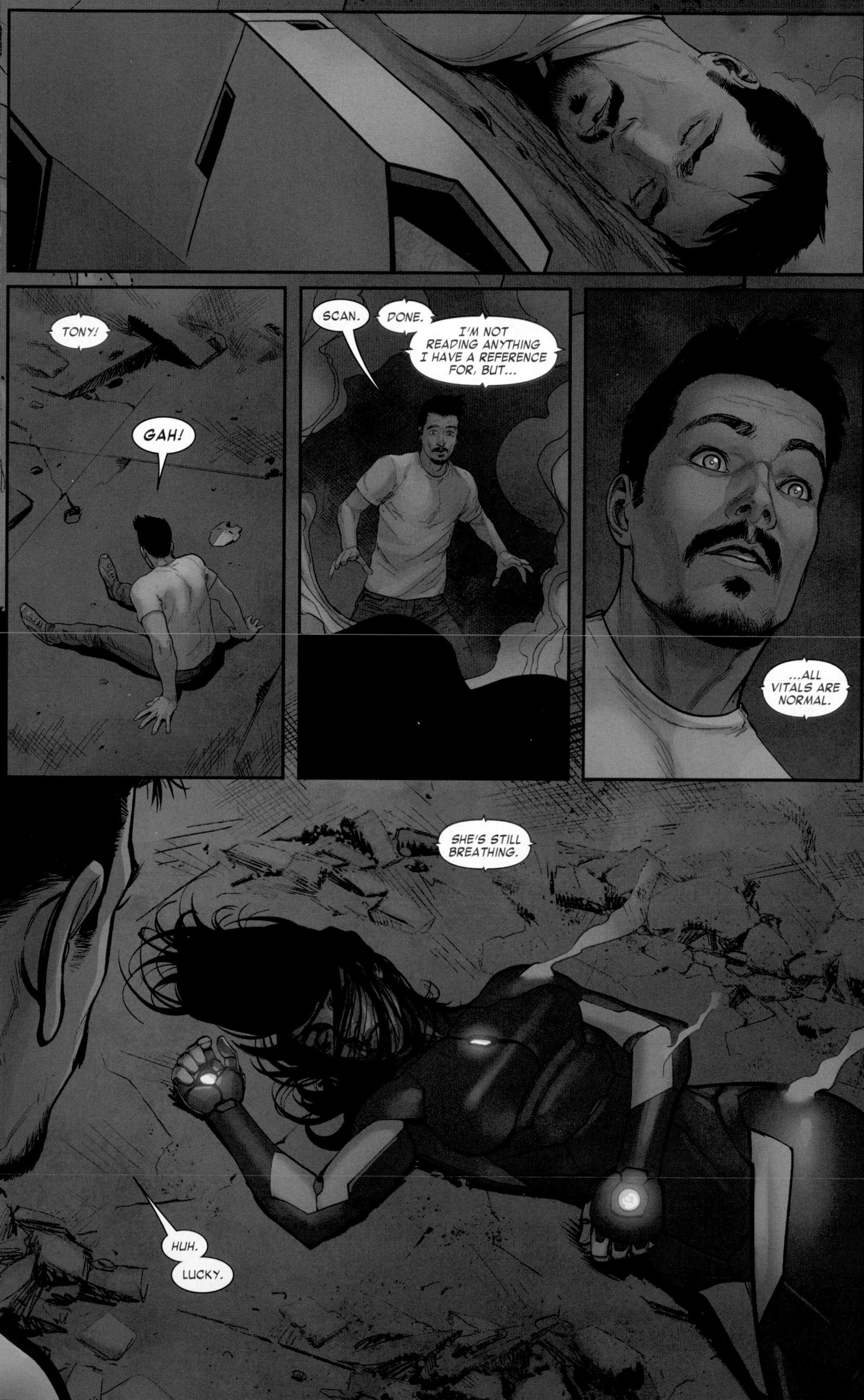
TONY!
GAH!
SCAN.
DONE.
I'M NOT READING ANYTHING I HAVE A REFERENCE FOR, BUT...
...ALL VITALS ARE NORMAL.
SHE'S STILL BREATHING.
HUH.
LUCKY.

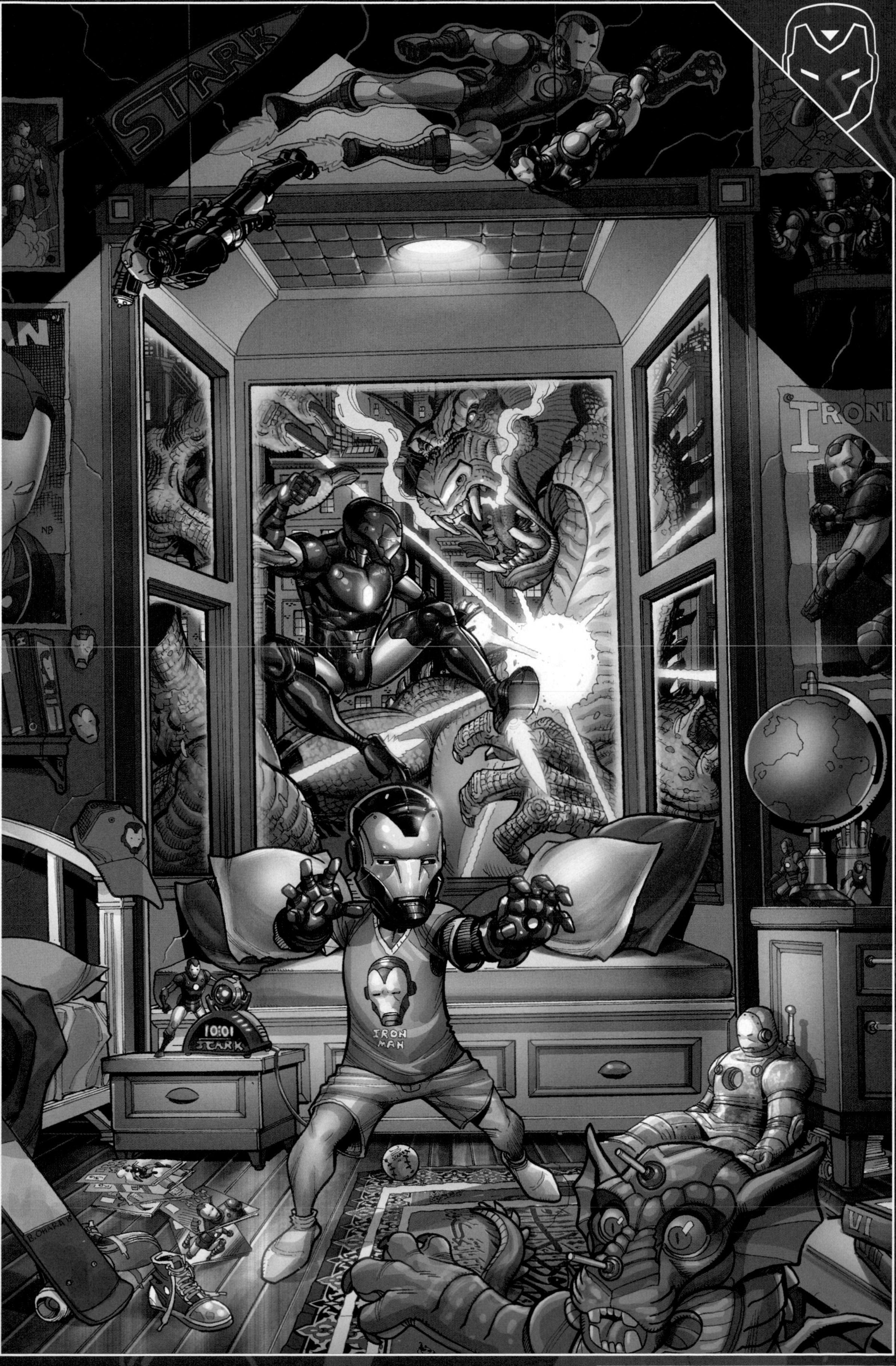
STARK
IRON
IRON
MAN
10:01
STARK

#1 YOUNG GUNS VARIANT BY NICK BRADSHAW & PAUL MOUNTS

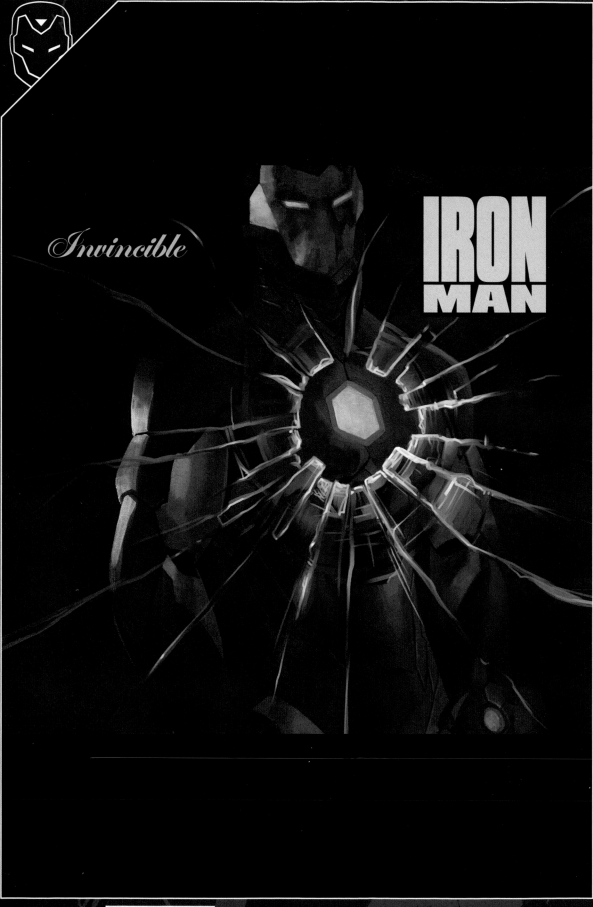

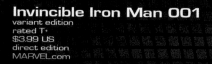

Invincible Iron Man 001
variant edition
rated T+
$3.99 US
direct edition
MARVEL.com

series

INVINCIBLE **IRON MAN**

IRON MAN

transformational mark ⬡

#1 ACTION FIGURE VARIANT BY JOHN TYLER CHRISTOPHER

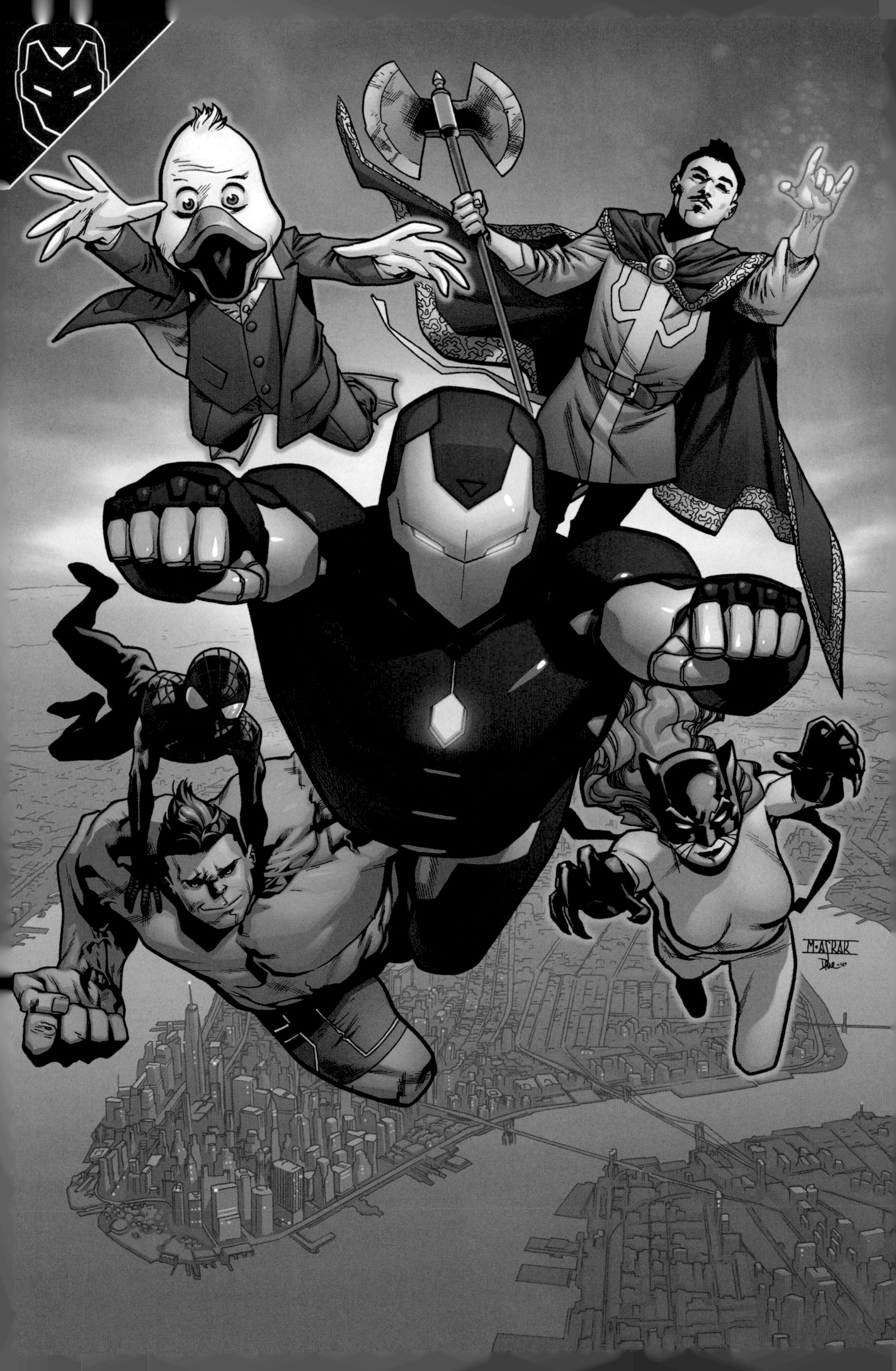
M·ASRAK

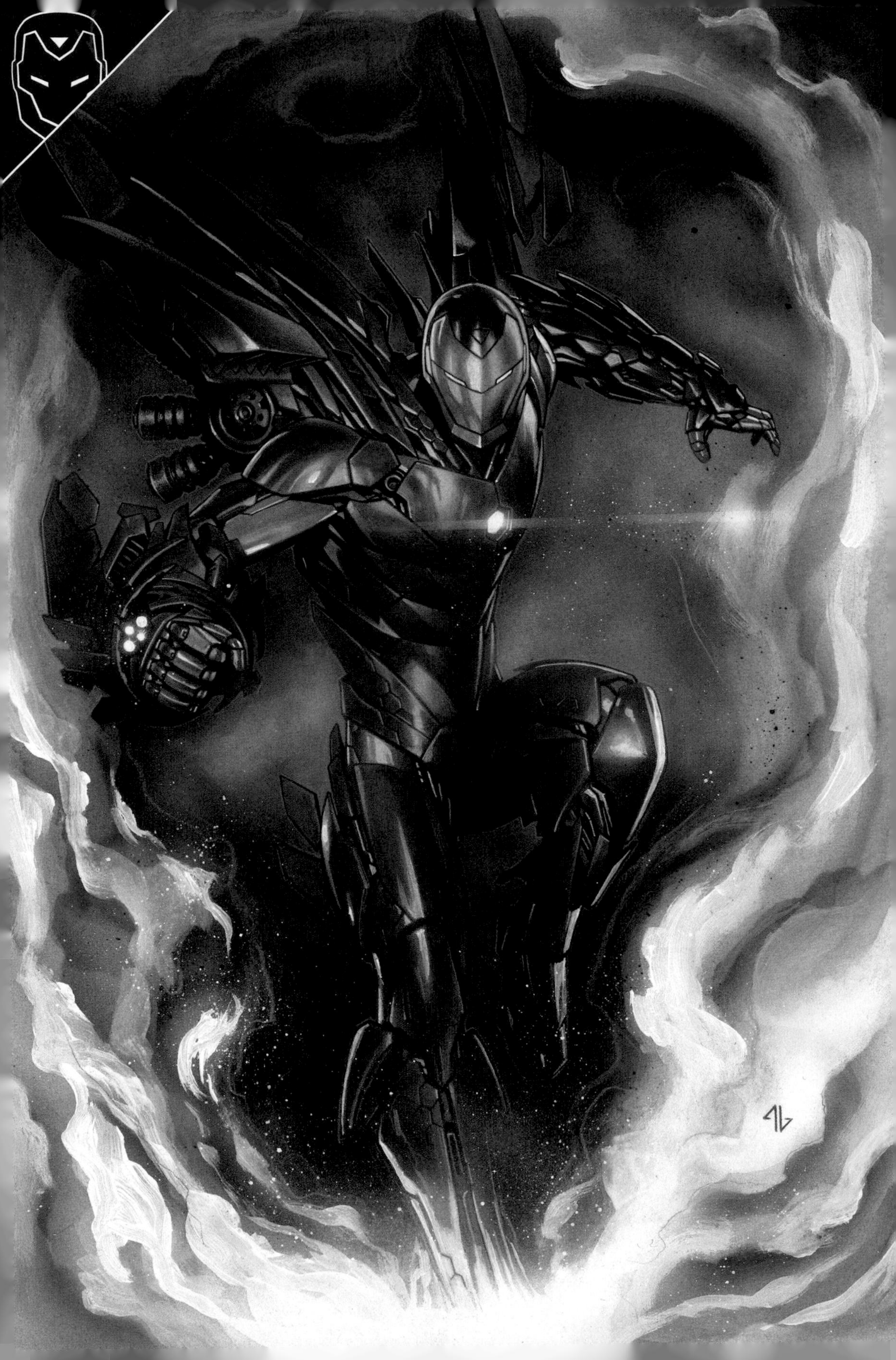

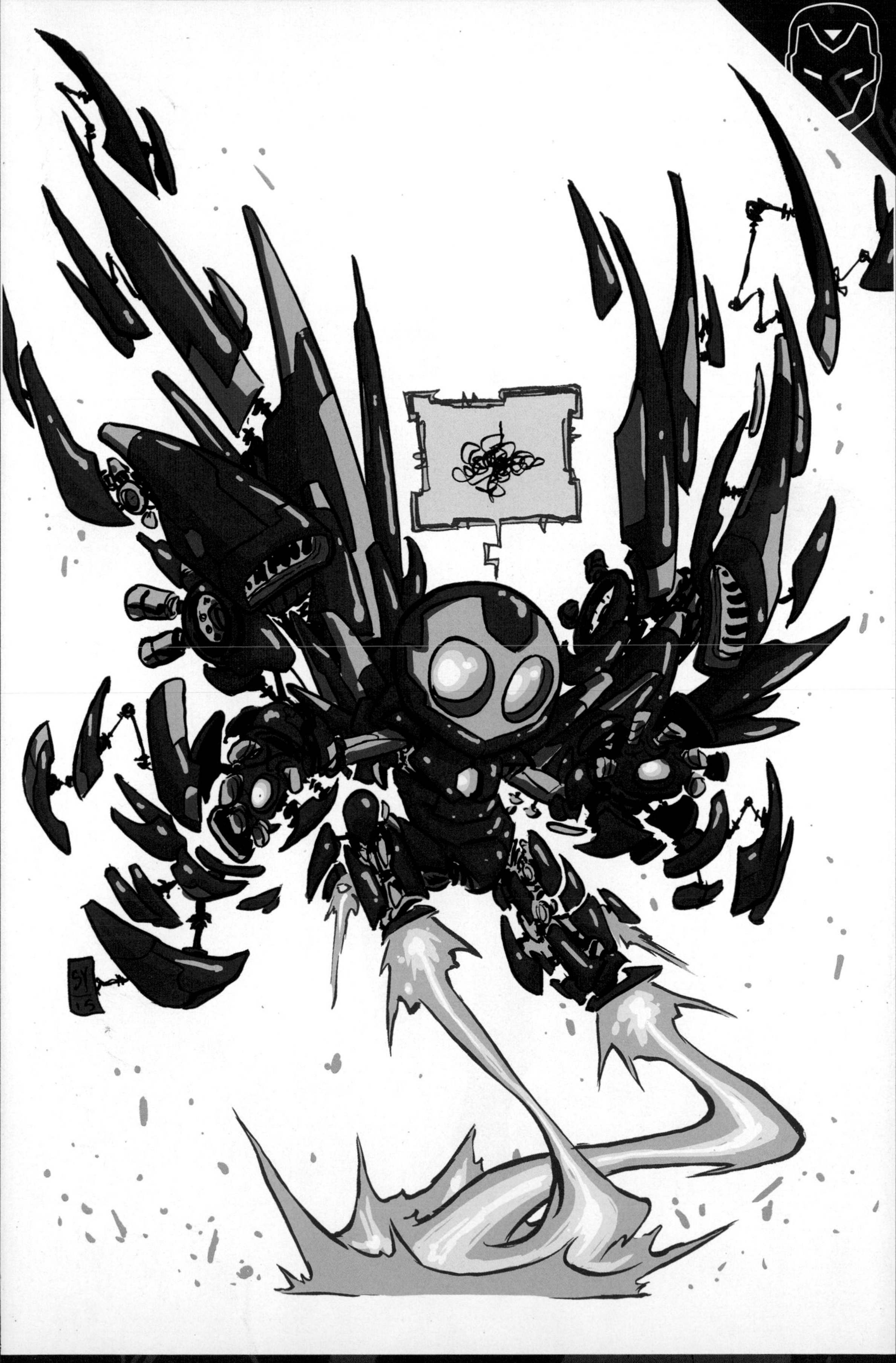

#1 VARIANT BY SKOTTIE YOUNG

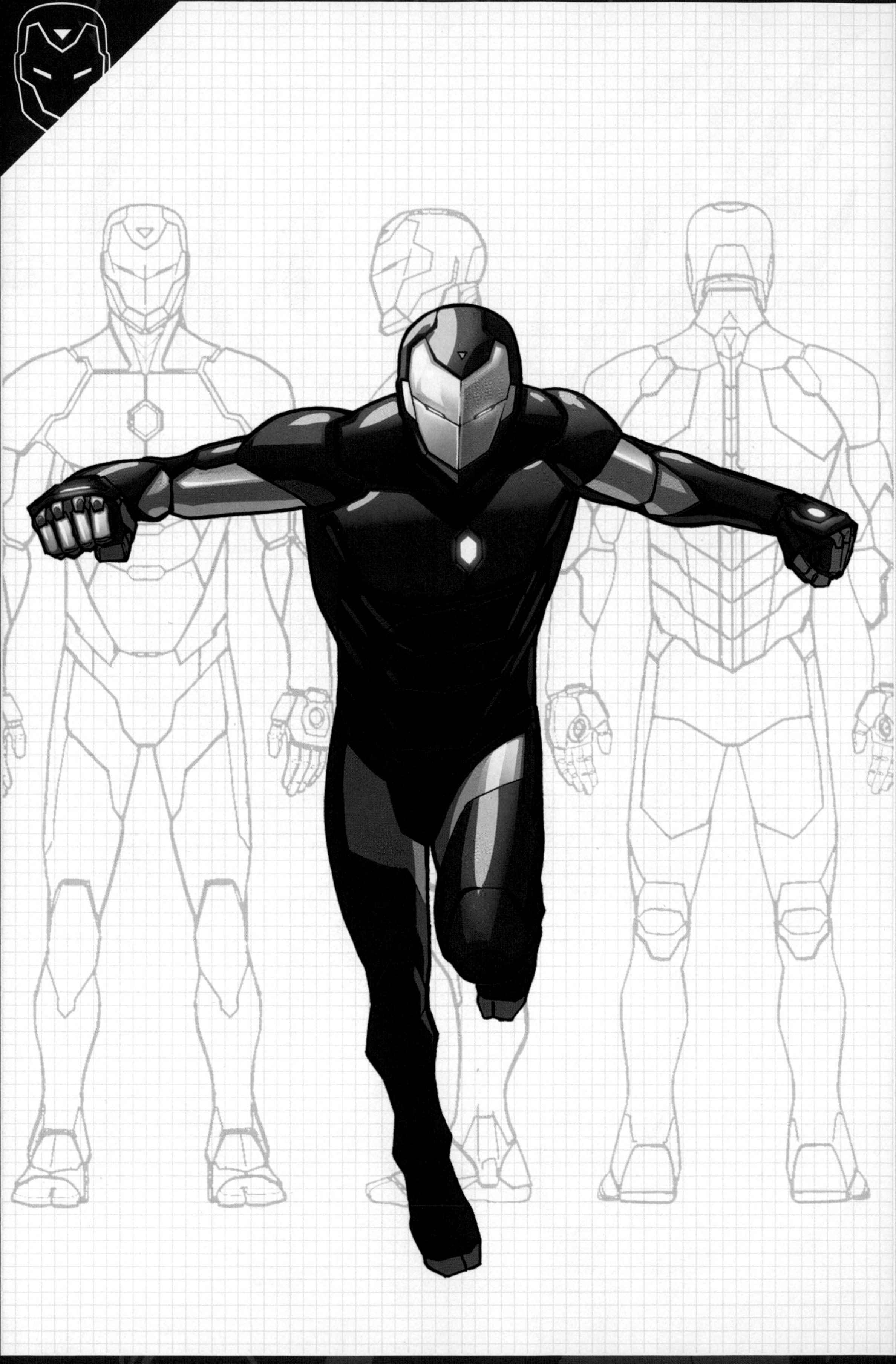

#1 YOUNG GUNS VARIANT BY DAVID MARQUEZ & MATTHEW WILSON

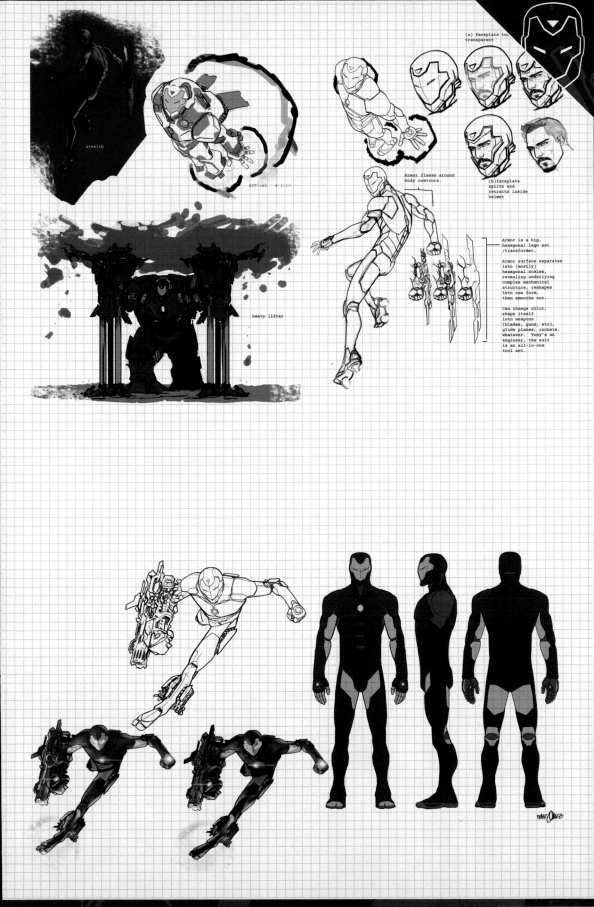

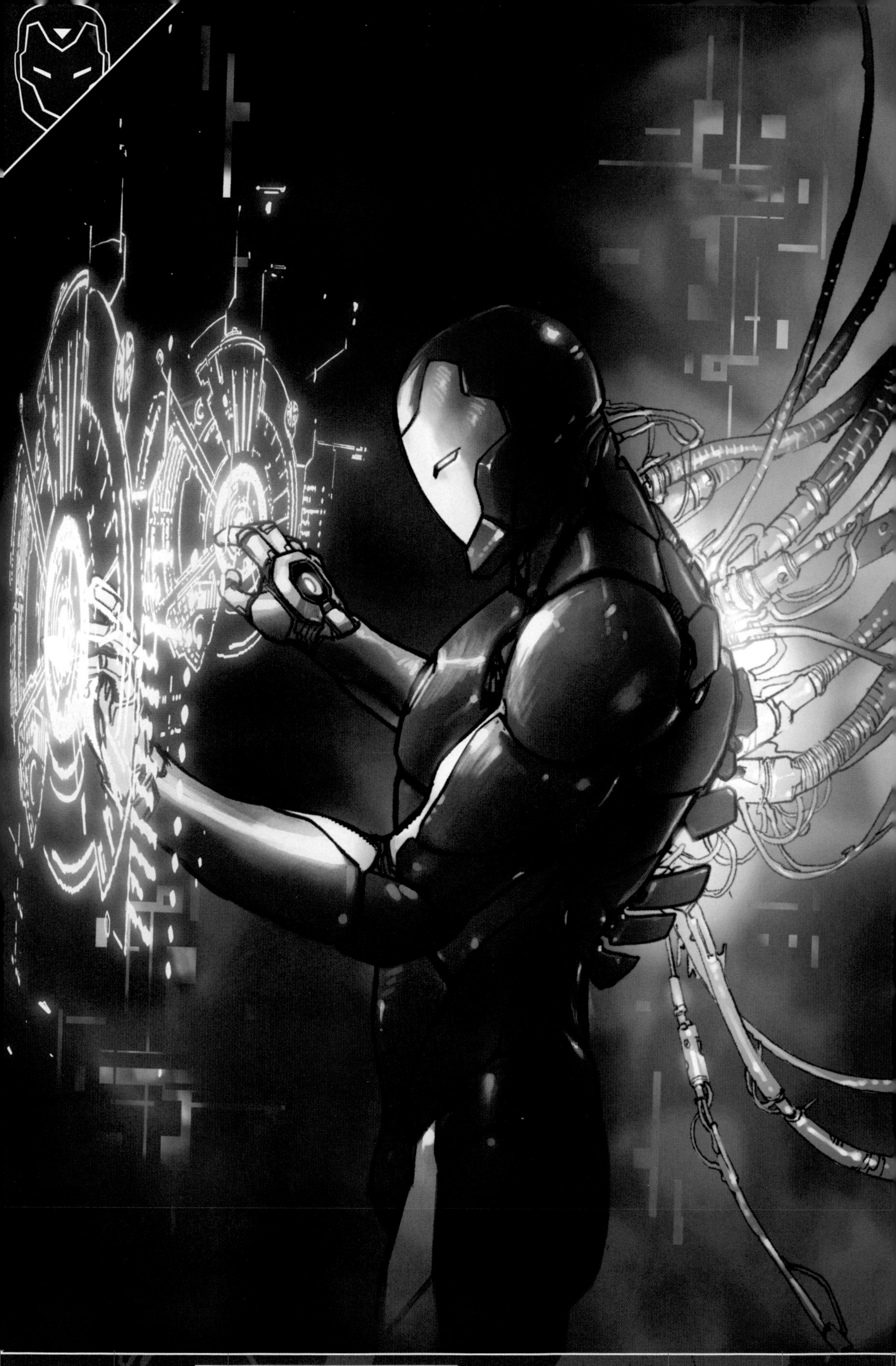

#1 YOUNG GUNS VARIANT BY SA

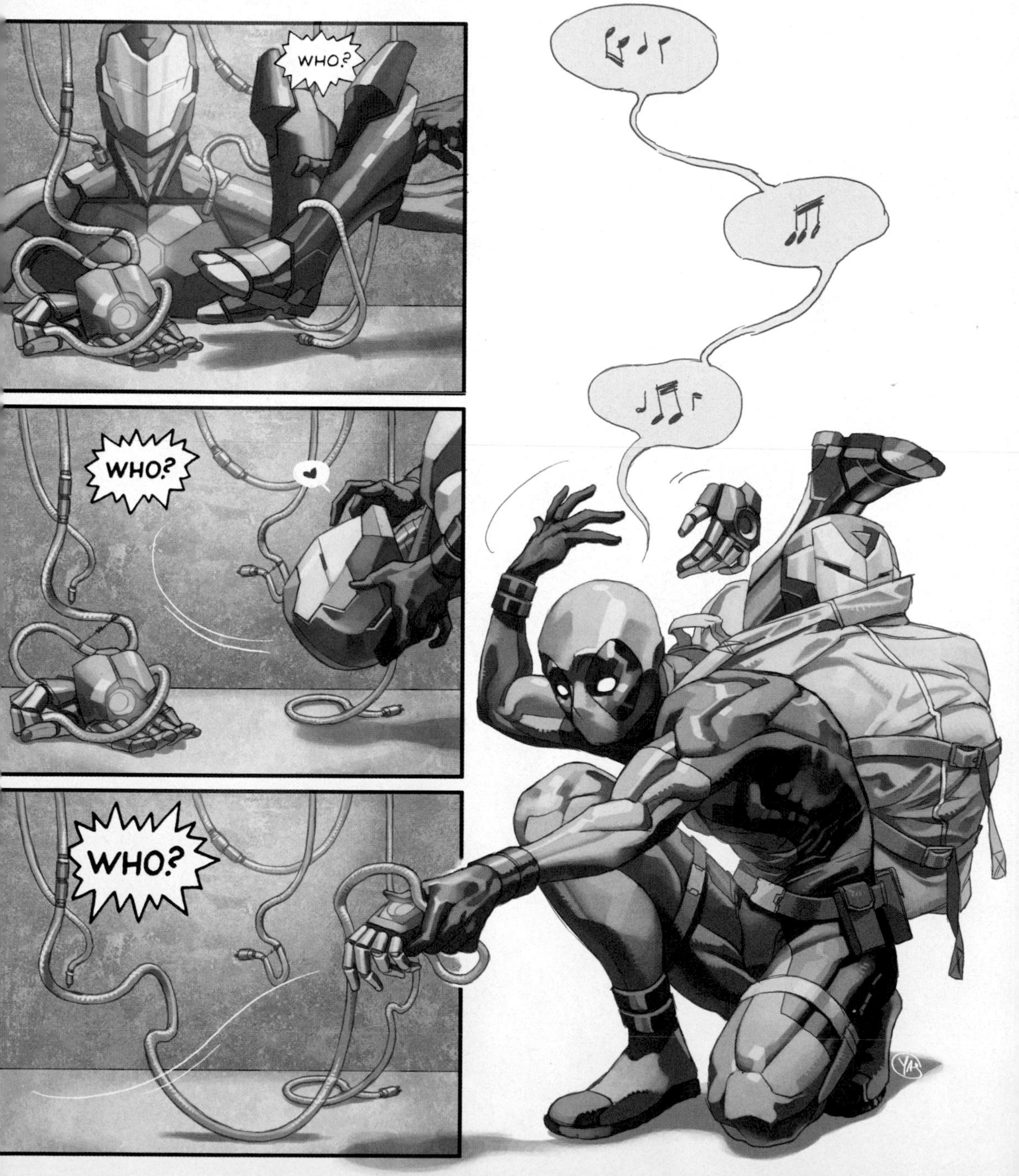
WHO?
WHO?
WHO?

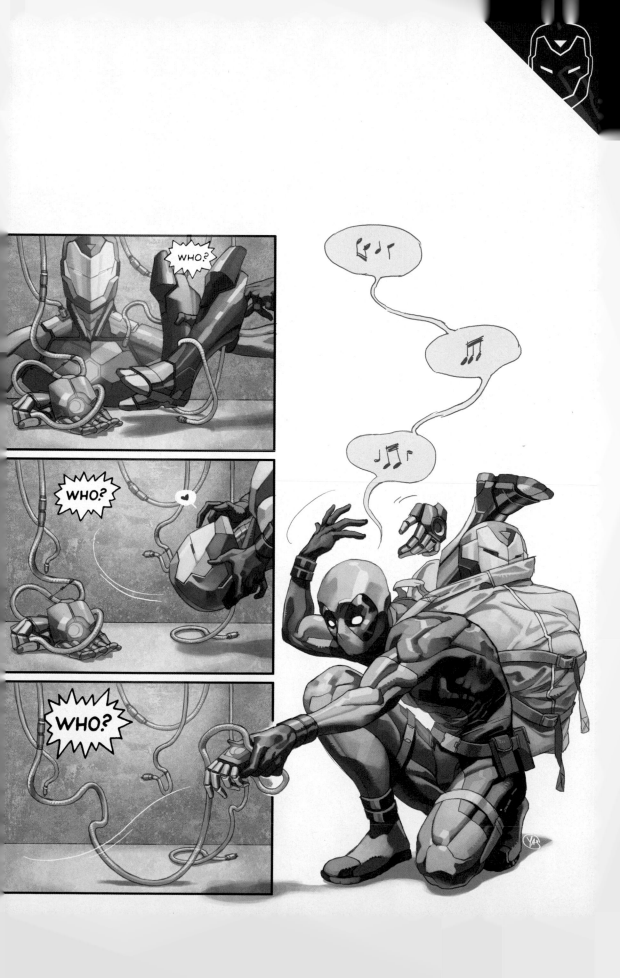

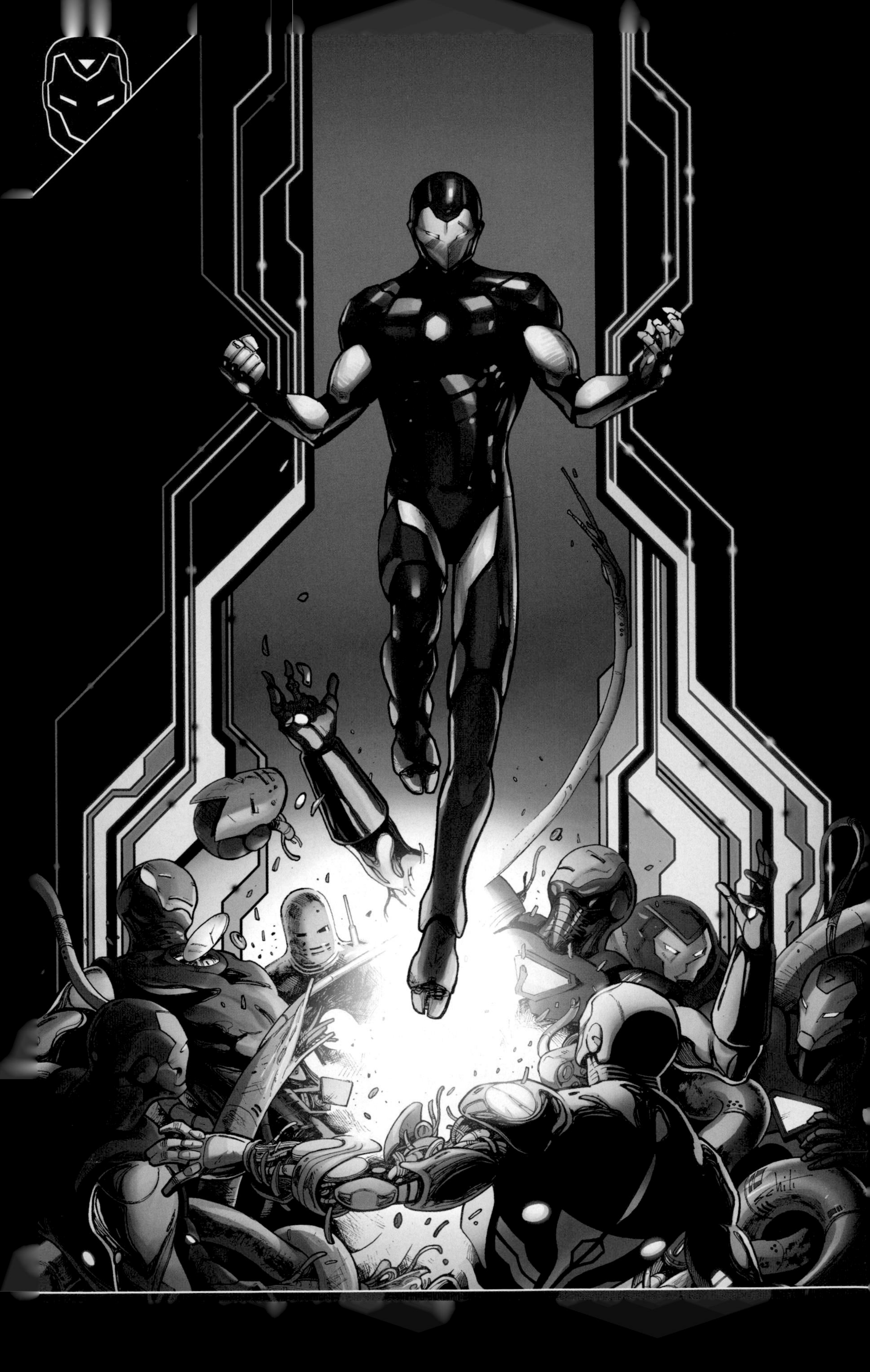

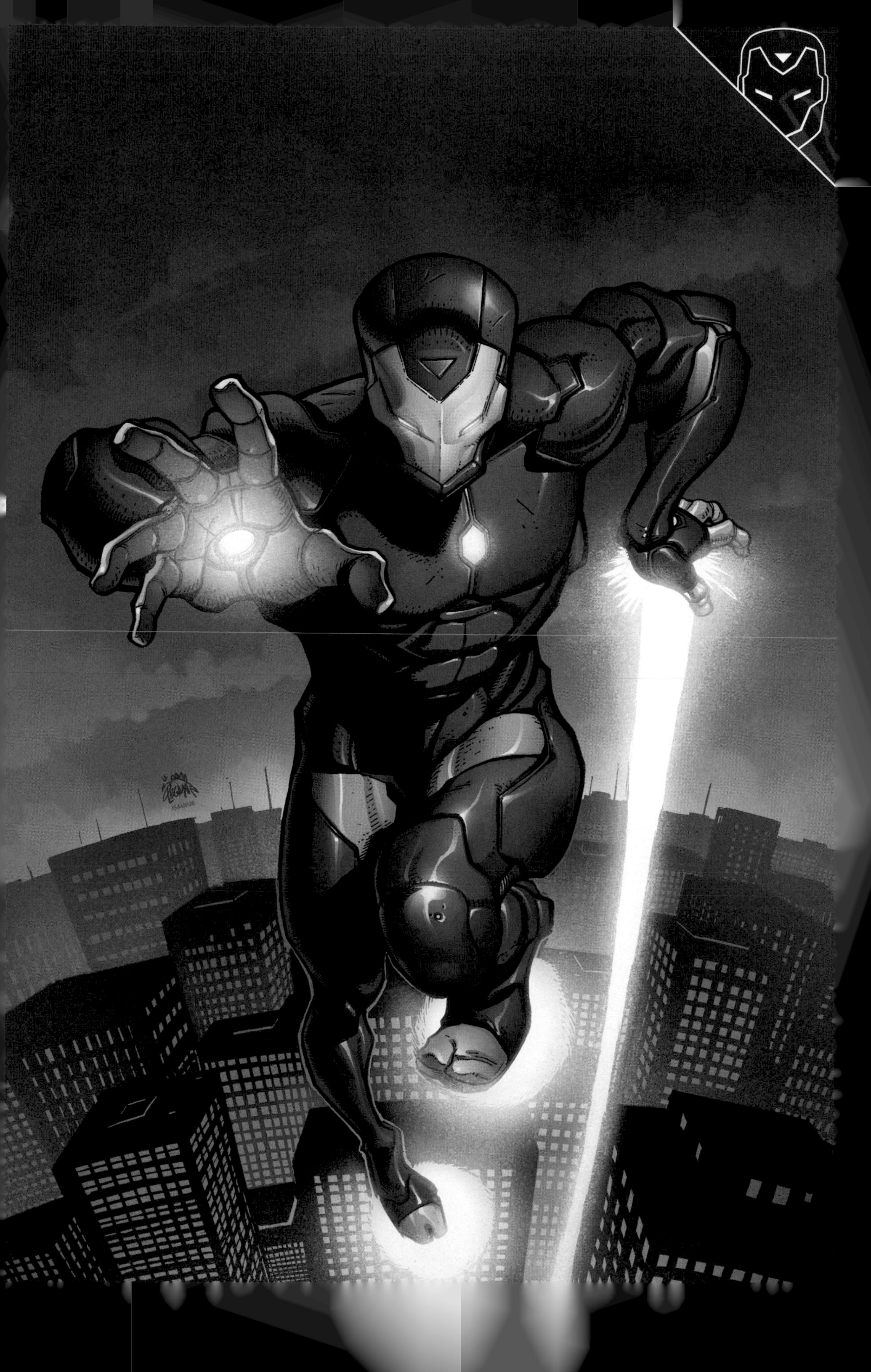

#1 CLASSIC VARIANT BY BRUCE TIMM

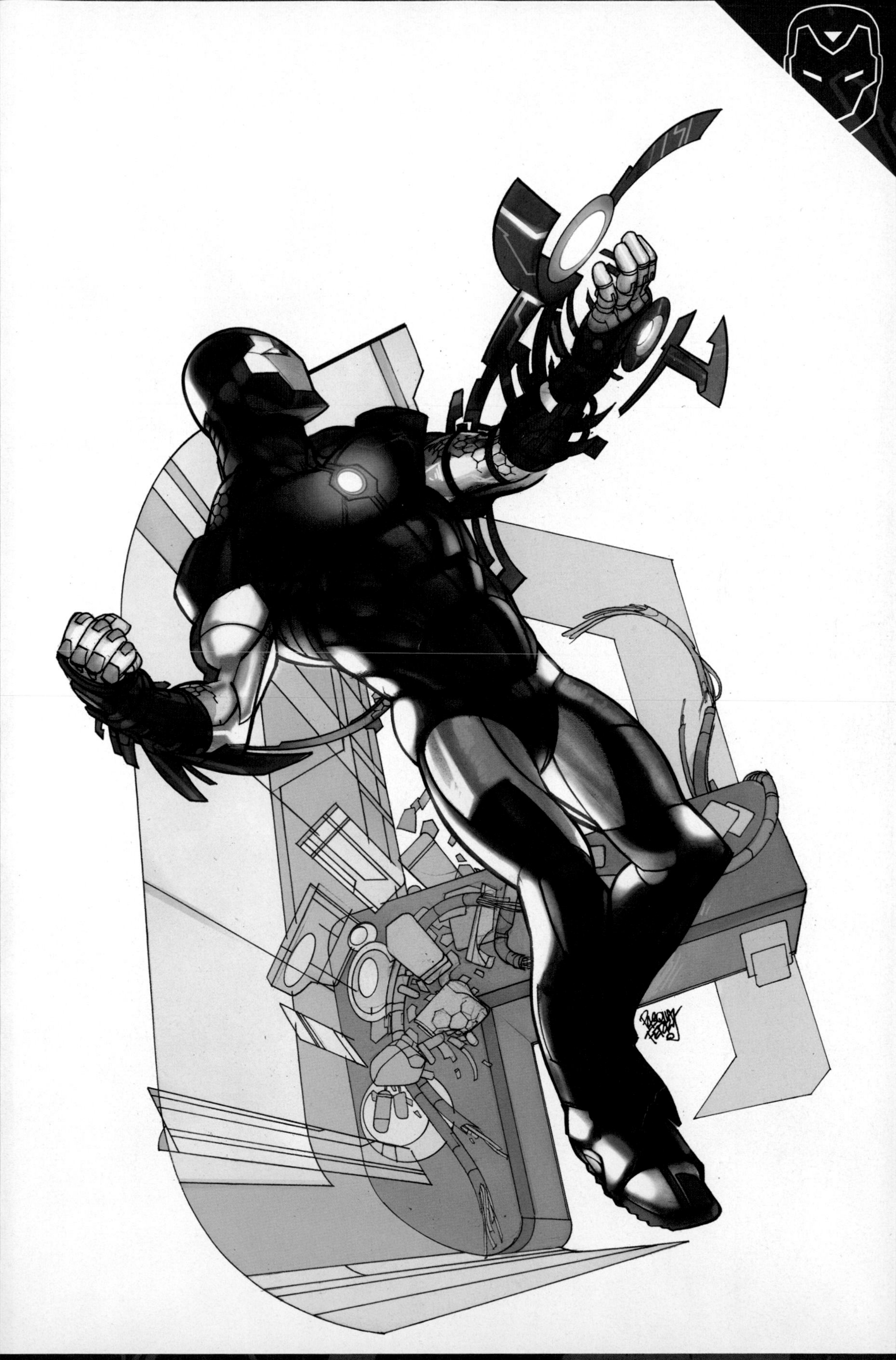

#1 VARIANT BY **PASQUAL FERRY**

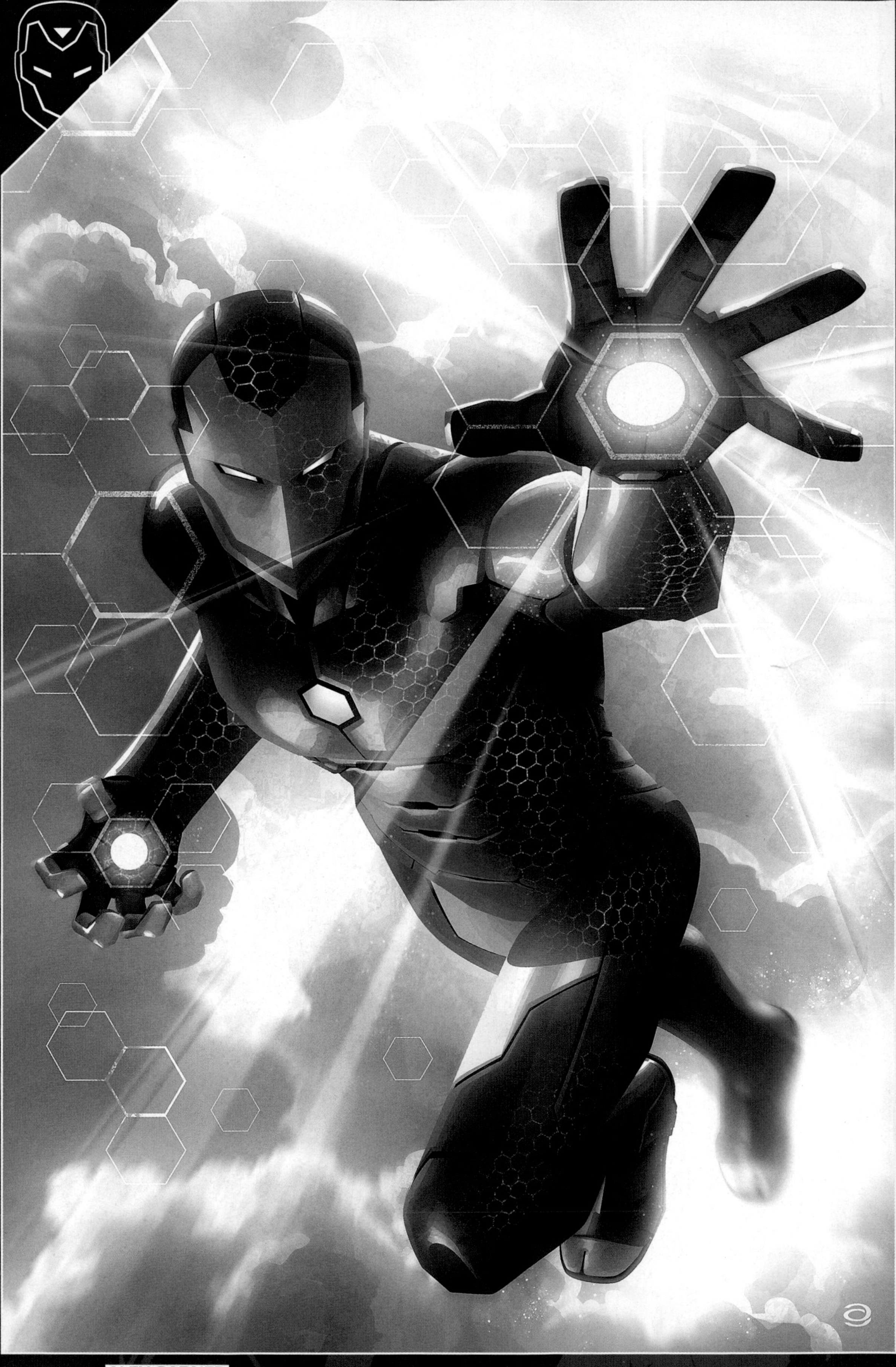

#2 VARIANT BY ALEX GARNER

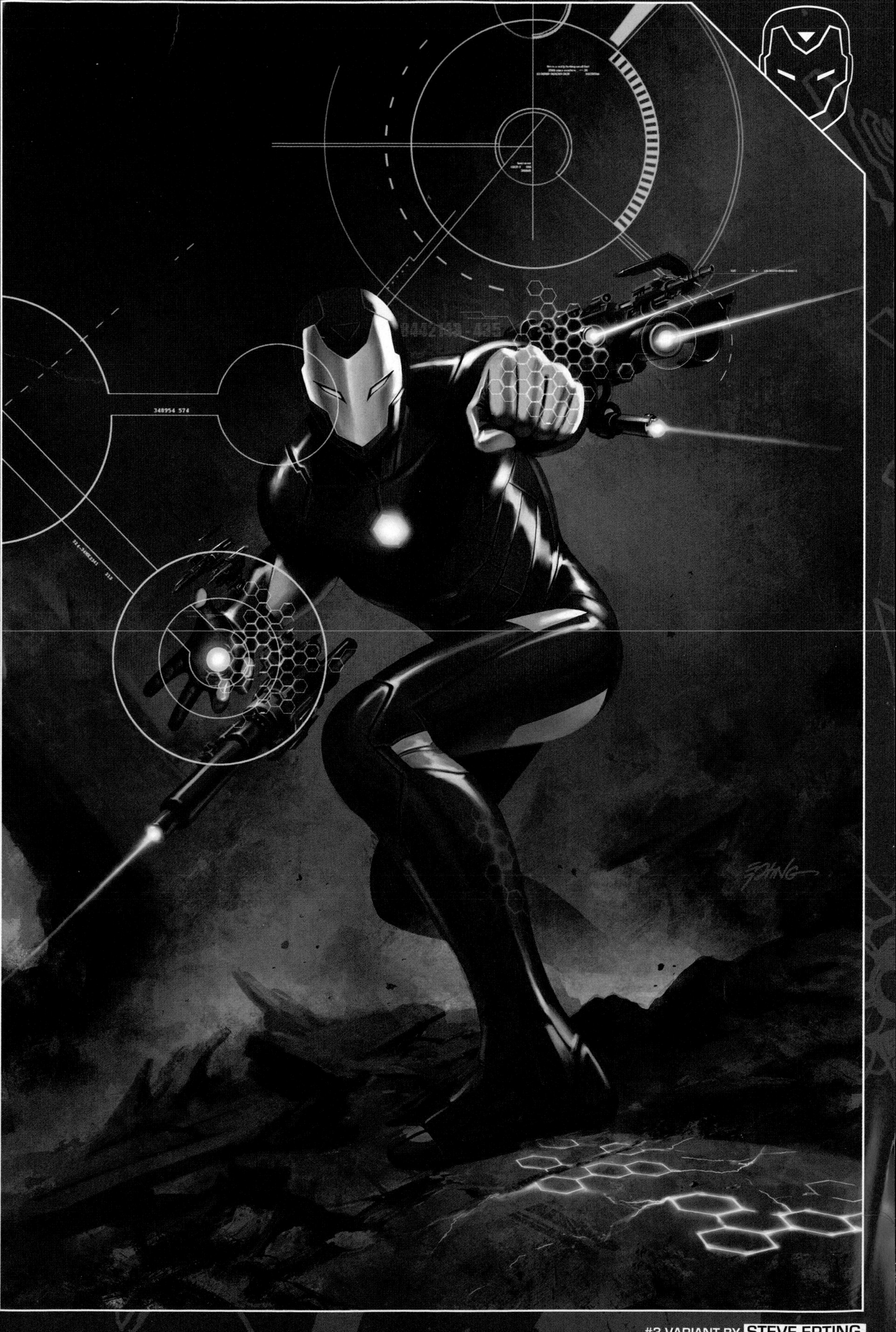
348954 574

#3 VARIANT BY STEVE EPTING

FREE
DIGITAL COPY

TO REDEEM YOUR CODE FOR A FREE DIGITAL COPY:

1 GO TO MARVEL.COM/REDEEM. OFFER EXPIRES ON 5/6/18.

2 FOLLOW THE ON-SCREEN INSTRUCTIONS TO REDEEM YOUR DIGITAL COPY.

3 LAUNCH THE MARVEL COMICS APP TO READ YOUR COMIC NOW.

4 YOUR DIGITAL COPY WILL BE FOUND UNDER THE 'MY COMICS' TAB.

5 READ AND ENJOY.

YOUR FREE DIGITAL COPY WILL BE AVAILABLE ON:

MARVEL COMICS APP FOR APPLE IOS® DEVICES

MARVEL COMICS APP FOR ANDROID™ DEVICES